D1328511

The Road to Damascus

Books by John A. O'Brien

THE ROAD TO DAMASCUS

TRUTHS MEN LIVE BY

THE FAITH OF MILLIONS

EVOLUTION AND RELIGION

THE PRIESTHOOD IN A CHANGING WORLD

PATHWAYS TO HAPPINESS

COURTSHIP AND MARRIAGE

A HAPPY MARRIAGE

THUNDER FROM THE LEFT

DISCOVERING MEXICO

The Road to Damascus

The Spiritual Pilgrimage
of Fifteen Converts to Catholicism

EDITED BY

John A. O'Brien

Garden City, N.Y.

Doubleday & Company, Inc.

1951

Nihil Obstat:

   Thomas E. Dillon,
      Censor Librorum

Imprimatur:

   ✠John Francis Noll, D.D.
      Bishop of Fort Wayne

And as he went on his journey, it came to pass that he drew nigh to Damascus; and suddenly a light from heaven shined round about him. And falling on the ground, he heard a voice saying to him: Saul, Saul, why persecutest thou me?

ACTS 9: 3–5

Acknowledgments

The editor and the publishers wish to thank the many authors, agents, and publishers for their kind permission to reprint quotations from the titles listed below. All possible care has been taken to trace the ownership of every quotation included and to make full acknowledgment for its use. If any errors have accidentally occurred, they will be corrected in subsequent editions.

We acknowledge likewise our deep indebtedness to the contributors to this symposium. Busy men and women, engrossed with many and varied tasks, lecturing, teaching, and writing, they responded with zeal and generosity to our invitation to tell why they embraced the Catholic faith. All had achieved recognition in the intellectual world, chiefly as creative writers whose works attracted widespread attention.

Some are the authors of best sellers; others are the producers of scholarly volumes; all have a message of profound significance to every man and woman concerned with the meaning of life and the drama of the human soul in its quest for God and religious peace, security, and happiness. Without exception, they tell the story of their religious pilgrimage with sprightliness, with sympathy and understanding for wayfarers traveling along other highways, and with engaging candor.

It has been a labor of love for all participating in this

co-operative undertaking. This expression of our gratitude to them is, we're confident, but a faint reflection of the reward that will be bestowed upon them by the Giver of every good and perfect gift—the Father of light and truth.

JOHN A. O'BRIEN
Notre Dame, Indiana
March 10, 1949

Contents

The Road to Damascus

INTRODUCTION: THE ROAD TO DAMASCUS

John A. O'Brien

THERE is an ancient road that runs from Jerusalem to Damascus. On that road Saul of Tarsus was traveling, bent on his mission of arresting Christians and taking them bound to Jerusalem. When nearing Damascus he was suddenly stricken from his horse; a blinding light shone upon him, while he heard a voice saying: "Saul, Saul, why persecutest thou me?"

Dazzled and amazed, Saul asked: "Who art thou, Lord?" And He: "I am Jesus whom thou persecutest."

Trembling and astonished, Saul inquired: "Lord, what wilt thou have me to do?"

And the Lord said to him: "Arise and go into the city, and there it shall be told thee what thou must do." Now the men who went in company with him stood amazed, hearing indeed a voice but seeing no man.

Accordingly Saul, still blind, was led by his companions to the home of Judas, on the street that is called Straight, in Damascus. Thither God sent Ananias and directed him to receive Saul into the Christian fold. Astonished, Ananias recalled Saul's fierce persecution of the Christians.

Whereupon the Lord said to him: "Go thy way; for this man is to me a vessel of election, to carry my name before the Gentiles, and kings, and the children of Israel."

Accordingly Ananias went to the home where Saul was remaining in prayer and in fasting. Laying his hands upon Saul, he said: "Brother Saul, the Lord Jesus hath sent me, He that appeared to thee in the way as thou camest; that thou mayest receive thy sight, and be filled with the Holy Ghost." And immediately there fell from his eyes as it were scales, and he received his sight; and rising up, he was baptized. . . . And immediately he preached Jesus in the synagogues, that He is the Son of God.[1]

During the nineteen hundred years which have intervened since that dramatic event, the road to Damascus has become the symbol and the synonym of the road traveled by the long army of pilgrims from the dark domain of doubt into the white light of God's truth. It is the road worn smooth by the feet of countless hosts of converts to Christ and to His Church. That is the road traveled by the fifteen men and women who tell the story of their journey in this book.

The greatest and the most stirring dramas in human life are those which occur in the inner theater of the soul and hence escape the eyes of men. When those stirring scenes can be externalized and something of their pathos, travail, and splendor be caught in words, the story never fails to hold the reader in rapt and enthralling interest. Fortunately the travelers who describe their spiritual Odysseys in this book are all artists in the use of words; thus they are able with unusual clarity to lay bare before our eyes the drama of the human soul in its quest for God.

Their experiences, their gropings, their confusions and uncertainties, and the means by which they dispelled them as they journeyed along the ancient highway to Damascus have an interest, a meaning, and a message for all thoughtful people today.

Now, as perhaps never before, is there an imperative need for light to guide the groping footsteps of millions to the citadel of religious truth, peace, and happiness. The unparalleled destruction and carnage of two world wars and the ominous forebodings of another vastly worse have shaken man loose of his old illusions of progress, automatic and inevitable, and have brought him perilously close to the brink of annihilation. He is

[1]Acts 9.

14

restless, unsettled, and fearful. He is searching desperately for an anchor of security, a foundation that will stand unshaken even though the heavens fall. A spiritual distemper, born of these disturbing doubts and dreadful uncertainties, is the prevailing malaise of our day.

The experiences of the men and women who have made their pilgrimage over the road to Damascus to find the answer to their restless questing constitute a much needed antidote for the uncertainty and confusion of today. They have found that inward peace which the truths of Christ have always generated in the hearts of men. "You shall know the truth and the truth shall set you free." Uttered by Christ centuries ago, these words sound the keynote of the hymn of joy and triumph sung by all these pilgrims. May the stories of their spiritual Aeneids cast some rays of light that will help guide the faltering footsteps of other pilgrims in their quest for truth, peace, and happiness—the goal of so many millions today.

COME INSIDE

Evelyn Waugh

Evelyn Waugh comes of a literary family, his father, Arthur, being a critic and publisher and his brother, Alec, a novelist. At the age of seven Evelyn wrote a 500-word novel in nine chapters; it was entitled *The Curse of the Horse Race*.

Born in 1903 in London, and educated at Lancing School and Oxford, he was successively a student of painting, a schoolmaster, and a journalist before beginning his literary career. In 1928 he published his first book, a life of Rossetti, and in the same year published his first novel, *Decline and Fall*. This was followed in rapid succession by *Vile Bodies*, *Black Mischief*, *A Handful of Dust*, and *Scoop*. The latter, a satire, ranging from the savage to the lighthearted, came out of his experience as a war correspondent in Ethiopia.

In 1930, when Waugh was but 26, he embraced the Catholic faith; so most of his writing has been done since his conversion to Catholicism. In *Vile Bodies* he gives a horrifying account of the smart upper-class English set just after World War I. While he describes the antics of his bright young people in a sprightly manner, he is not unaware of the underlying tragedy of these lives and that is the picture which he presents in *A Handful of Dust*. Alexander Woollcott characterized the author of this novel as "the nearest thing to genius among the young writers who have arisen in post-war England."

The versatility of Waugh's literary ability is reflected in the wide range of his writings. His *Black Mischief* is a fantasia on an Abyssinian theme. Then again he has turned his hand to works which are near to being travel books, such as: *Labels, A Mediterranean Journal* (published in America as *A Bachelor Abroad*); *Remote People* (relabeled here *They Were Still Dancing*); and *Ninety-two Days*.

Just before the onset of World War II he published *Mexico: An Object Lesson*. All these works are characterized by a sprightly style and many contain humorous passages that stretch into the hilarious.

There is a serious side to Waugh which the reader can discover in his book on *Edmund Campion,* a Jesuit martyr of Elizabeth's time. Therein the reader will find an explicit statement of Waugh's religious beliefs. The volume depicts the heroic Campion in sharper and brighter lines than previous portrayals; and a strong, supple, noble prose so distinguishes the work as to place it among the half-dozen best biographies of our time. The work was deservedly crowned with the Hawthornden Prize. It is significant, too, that the volume is dedicated to Father Martin D'Arcy, S.J., then a professor of philosophy at Oxford University and later Provincial of the Society of Jesus in England, who had received Waugh into the Catholic Church.

During the war Waugh served with the Commandos, narrowly escaped death, and rose to the rank of major. *Put Out More Flags* (1942) was the March choice of the Book Society in England. But the work which won him acclaim on both sides of the Atlantic and gained for him a secure position as a novelist of penetration and power is *Brideshead Revisited*. In 1947 Loyola College, Baltimore, awarded an honorary degree to Waugh for his distinguished contributions to English literature.

The *Tablet* of London acclaims *Brideshead Revisited* as "the finest of all his works, a book for which it is safe to prophesy a lasting place among the major works of fiction." Waugh himself regards this as his best work. His previous favorite had been *A Handful of Dust,* which deals entirely with behavior. "It was humanist," remarked Waugh, "and contained all I had to say about humanism."

Brideshead Revisited is the story of a great British Catholic family through the decades between World War I and World War II. In this novel the author introduced God and thus brought upon himself the criticism of Mr. Edmund Wilson. Commenting upon this criticism, Waugh writes in *Life* for April 8, 1946: "He was outraged (quite legitimately by his standards) at finding God introduced into my story. I believe that you can only leave God out by making your characters pure abstractions. . . . They [modern novelists] try to represent the whole human mind and soul and yet omit its determining character—that of being God's creature with a defined purpose. So in my future books there will be two things to make them unpopular: a preoccupation with style and the attempt to represent man more fully, which to me means only one thing, man in his relation to God."

In its review of *Brideshead Revisited, Time* characterized Waugh as a stylist unexcelled among the contemporary writers of fiction. *Brideshead Revisited* was a best seller on both sides of the Atlantic and has been widely acclaimed by critics as destined for a permanent place in English literature.

His recent novel, *The Loved One,* is now achieving the rank of a best seller and bids fair to rival *Brideshead Revisited* in popularity. It is noteworthy that two other British novelists, Graham Greene and Bruce Marshall, who rival Waugh in popularity and prestige, are likewise converts to the Catholic faith.

In 1937 Waugh was united in marriage to Laura Herbert. At this writing they have four children and reside in a Gloucestershire manor named Piers Court in England.

I WAS born in England in 1903 with a strong hereditary predisposition toward the Established Church. My family tree burgeons on every twig with Anglican clergymen. My father was what was called a "sound churchman"; that is to say, he attended church regularly and led an exemplary life. He had no interest in theology. He had no interest in politics but always voted Tory as his father and grandfather had done. In the same spirit he was punctilious in his religious duties.

At the age of ten I composed a long and tedious poem about Purgatory in the meter of *Hiawatha* and to the dismay of my parents, who held a just estimate of my character, expressed my intention of becoming a clergyman. The enthusiasm which my little school-fellows devoted to birds' eggs and model trains I turned on church affairs and spoke glibly of chasubles and Erastianism. I was accordingly sent to the school which was reputed to have the strongest ecclesiastical bent. At the age of sixteen I formally notified the school chaplain that there was no God. At the age of twenty-six I was received into the Catholic Church to which all subsequent experience has served to confirm my loyalty.

I am now invited to explain these vagaries to American readers.

First, of my early religiosity. I am reluctant to deny all reality to that precocious enthusiasm, but it was in the main a hobby like the birds' eggs and model trains of my schoolfellows. The appeal was part hereditary and part aesthetic. Many are drawn in this way throughout their lives. In my case it was a concomitant of puberty. But those who do not know my country should understand that the aesthetic appeal of the Church of England is unique and peculiar to those islands. Elsewhere a first interest in the Catholic Church is often kindled in the convert's imagination by the splendors of her worship in contrast with the bleakness and meanness of the Protestant sects. In England the pull is all the other way. The medieval cathedrals and churches, the rich ceremonies that surround the monarchy, the historic titles of Canterbury and York, the social organization of the country parishes, the traditional culture of Oxford and Cambridge, the liturgy composed in the heyday of English prose style—all these are the property of the Church of England, while Catholics meet in modern buildings, often of deplorable design, and are usually served by simple Irish missionaries.

The shallowness of my early piety is shown by the ease with which I abandoned it. There are, of course, countless Catholics who, for a part of their lives at least, lose their faith, but it is always after a bitter struggle—usually a moral struggle. I shed my inherited faith as lightheartedly as though it had been an out-grown coat. The circumstances were these: During the first World War many university dons patriotically volunteered to release young schoolmasters to serve in the army. Among these there came to my school a leading Oxford theologian, now a bishop. This learned and devout man inadvertently made me an atheist. He explained to his divinity class that none of the books of the Bible were by their supposed authors; he invited us to speculate, in the manner of the fourth century, on the nature of Christ. When he had removed the in-herited axioms of my faith I found myself quite unable to follow him in the higher flights of logic by which he reconciled his own skepticism with his position as a clergyman.

At the same time I read Pope's *Essay on Man;* the notes led me to Leibnitz and I began an unguided and half-comprehended study of metaphysics. I advanced far enough to be thoroughly muddled about the nature of cognition. It seemed simplest to abandon the quest and assume that man was incapable of knowing any-thing. I have no doubt I was a prig and a bore but I think that if I had been a Catholic boy at a Catholic school I should have found among its teaching orders someone patient enough to examine with me my cal-low presumption. Also, if I had been fortified by the sacraments, I should have valued my faith too highly to abandon it so capriciously. At my school I was quite correctly regarded as "going through a phase" normal to all clever boys, and left to find my own way home.

The next ten years of my life are material more suitable to the novelist than the essayist. Those who have read my works will perhaps understand the character of the world into which I exuberantly launched myself. Ten years of that world sufficed to show me that life there, or anywhere, was unintelligible and unendurable without God. The conclusion was obvious; the question now arises: Why Rome? A Catholic who loses his faith and rediscovers the need of it returns inevitably to the church he left. Why did not I?

Here, I think, the European has some slight advantage over the American. It is possible, I conceive, for a man to grow up in parts of the United States without ever being really aware of the Church's unique position. He sees Catholics as one out of a number of admirable societies, each claiming his allegiance. That is not possible for a European. England was Catholic for nine hundred years, then Protestant for three hundred, then agnostic for a century. The Catholic structure still lies lightly buried beneath every phase of English life; history, topography, law, archaeology everywhere reveal Catholic origins. Foreign travel anywhere reveals the local, temporary character of the heresies and schisms and the universal, eternal character of the Church. It was self-evident to me that no heresy or schism could be right and the Church wrong. It was possible that all were wrong, that the whole Christian revelation was an imposture or a misconception. But if the Christian revelation was true, then the Church was the society founded by Christ and all other bodies were only good so far as they had salvaged something from the wrecks of the Great Schism and the Reformation. This proposition seemed so plain to me that it admitted of no discussion. It only remained to examine the historical and philosophic grounds for supposing the Christian revelation to be genuine. I was fortunate enough to be introduced to a brilliant and holy priest who undertook to prove this to me, and so on firm intellectual conviction but with little emotion I was admitted into the Church.

My life since then has been an endless delighted tour of discovery in the huge territory of which I was made free. I have heard it said that some converts in later life look back rather wistfully to the fervor of their first months of faith. With me it is quite the opposite. I look back aghast at the presumption with which I thought myself suitable for reception and with wonder at the trust of the priest who saw the possibility of growth in such a dry soul.

From time to time friends outside the Church consult me. They are attracted by certain features, repelled or puzzled by others. To them I can only say, from my own experience: "Come inside. You cannot know what the Church is like from outside. However learned you are in theology, nothing you know amounts to anything in comparison with the knowledge of the simplest actual member of the Communion of Saints."

THE GREATEST THING IN MY LIFE

Fulton Oursler

Author, playwright, editor, lecturer, and supervisor of the popular radio program, *The Greatest Story Ever Told,* Fulton Oursler is nothing if not versatile. Born in Baltimore, he started out as a news reporter on the Baltimore *American,* became music and dramatic critic, wrote short stories for magazines, and in 1923 became editor in chief of *Metropolitan Magazine.* He has written for almost every popular magazine and for religious journals of all faiths as well for the past thirty-five years.

He served from 1931 to 1942 as editor in chief of the Macfadden Publications, which included *Liberty* and ten other monthly magazines with a circulation of sixteen million a month. In 1944 he became senior editor of the *Reader's Digest,* where his feature articles have made his name familiar to millions. His plays, *Behold This Dreamer, The Spider, All the King's Men,* and *The Walking Gentleman,* stamp him as a dramatist of imagination and power.

He is the author of eight novels, and of many detective stories written under the name of Anthony Abbot. Mr. Oursler is one of the few detective novelists who have assisted the police in solving actual crimes. He has lectured on methods of criminal deduction before the National Academy of the F.B.I. His detective stories include: *About the Murder of Geraldine Foster; About the Murder of the Choir Singer; About the Murder of the Night Club Lady; About the Murder of the Circus Queen; About the Murder of a Startled Lady; About the Murder of a Man Afraid of Women; The Creeps;* and *The Shudders.*

His recent book, *The Greatest Story Ever Told,* a life of Christ, bids fair to become one of his most successful works, rivaling the phenomenal success of his radio presentation of the same mighty theme. This program enjoys one of the largest radio audiences in America and has received eleven national awards. It is sponsored without any commercial advertising, and the scripts are read in advance by representatives of the Catholic, Protestant, and Jewish faiths, assuring it a universal appeal.

Father Flanagan of Boys' Town, written in collaboration with his son, Will Oursler, and scheduled for publication in the fall of 1949, brings to the American public a close-up of one of the most colorful figures of today. His *The Precious Secret* shows the wisdom and the fruitfulness of lives characterized by unfailing love and unselfish service.

On September 7, 1925, Mr. Oursler married Grace Perkins, an author and former actress. He embraced the Faith in 1943, and his son and daughter have since done likewise, while Mrs. Oursler was born in the Catholic faith. Mr. Oursler is a regular speaker on the Catholic Hour radio program, carried by the National Broadcasting Company from coast to coast. His favorite hobbies are ventriloquism and sleight of hand.

FOR THE first fifty years of my life I belonged to the eminently respectable majority. Being a white man, I was also native-born American and Protestant. On both sides my family descended from the earliest settlers of Maryland. My ancestors fought in all the American wars. I was a member of the Sons of the American Revolution. As a Protestant, I was named after the Rev. Dr. Charles Fulton, who had performed the wedding service for my mother and father. From my earliest years I attended Sunday school and at the age of ten I was baptized in the pool of the pulpit of First Baptist Church in Baltimore.

In spite of this religious upbringing, in the middle of my teens I announced to my friends that I was an agnostic. In that dry and unsatisfied state of mind I continued until 1943 when, by the grace of Almighty God, I became a member of the Roman Catholic Church.

By my conversion I lost my standing in the eminently respectable majority. Now I was identified with a minority, and I soon discovered the difference. My experience since becoming a Catholic has been constantly exciting, and I can say with conviction that there is not treasure enough in the earth to tempt a convert away from the constantly increasing spiritual satisfaction of his new estate. This satisfaction deepens even though some old friends—not all, by any means—are puzzled and pained by his act; even though he finds that the faith which is so beautiful and so exalting to him is the object at times of suspicion and cynical contempt.

"Whatever made you become a Catholic?"

How many times those words have been addressed to me! Often they are spoken in kindly interest. But now and again the tone in which they are uttered is withering, or meant to be. The questioner manages to suggest, by a nuance of voice, deft and distant but unmistakable, that he had always regarded me as a person of intelligence and liberalism and finds it impossible to reconcile that estimate with what he considers an embrace of superstition and conspiracy.

Some of my friends now regard me as an intellectual serf. At least one advocate of religious freedom tried to organize a boycott against me, just after I was nominated for a place on the board of directors of a welfare organization. This liberal lady took time out to call up members of the organization, urging them to vote against me because, she declared, I had no will of my

23

own and on every question was bound to vote as Rome commanded. That I was, nevertheless, elected was gratifying, not to my vanity so much, but because my confidence in the common sense of average people was thereby reinforced. In that confidence I have yet to be disappointed. I tell this experience, not because it has been common, but because it has been rare. Most people accept my conversion with a kind of wistfulness, as if they, too, could do with faith, if they only knew how to overcome their own skepticism. Suspicion, and even active dislike, come from a restless few who seem to take satisfaction in finding something to suspect, something to fear.

My only regret is that for so many years of my life I did not know that such an adjustment to the universe was possible within the soul of man.

The approach to such an adjustment is naturally an intensely personal matter, difficult to relate. I do not feel that I can tell all of that, here or elsewhere. There is too much of it that belongs in the secret places of the heart. Everyone who faces the blinding light of the Damascus road sees things in himself that he will never tell. On the other hand, I do believe that every man blessed with the gift of faith owes it to his fellow man to tell what he can of his conversion, in the hope that someone else may get from the story a glimpse, a little bit of help, and find for himself the same release.

At no time, I thank God, did I ever lose the sense of the wonder and mystery of life. More, I can say truthfully that in dusty years of doubt I was always, unconsciously or otherwise, looking for the water of life. How else can I explain a long preoccupation with the study of many religions? With a shudder now I think of the time I wasted, plodding through holy books of Asiatic religion, together with magniloquent tomes of charlatans and pretended seers and mystics of many lands. But of course I found only reflected light in that darkness. Soon I was convinced that only science held the truth; the only true priesthood must be the white-coated army of research scientists. No one could reveal truth. Man was to dig it out of the rocks, steam it out of test tubes, calculate it in the mathematics of relativity. Even this opinion faltered as I began to meet and talk with physicists and mathematicians, for very soon I discerned that, while expert in their own fields, they had no head for synthesis, no heart for seeking a meaning in life. They played with the pebbles of fact they had picked up on the shores of knowledge.

In the year 1935 I had come to agree with Goethe when he said: "I see that nothing can be known." It was at this point in my life that I made a vacation trip to the Middle East and spent a week in Palestine. And almost literally on the road to Damascus I began to turn back to Christ.

Many converts have told the story of their mental and spiritual struggles, patterns of philosophical inquiry that they have followed, their intellectual struggles and victories. Much of what they went through I would repeat here, if I felt able to tell the history of how I thought it out. But these intellectuals have rehearsed the history of such thinking much more explicitly than I have the skill and learning to do. Instead I shall tell a simpler history, concerned more with feeling and with action.

It began on the S.S. *Roma* one warm night when we were cruising from ancient Athens to the port of Haifa at the foot of Mount Carmel. On the upper deck I sat with my wife watching the ravishing spectacle of the stars over the Mediterranean. Idly we were talking of our plans for leaving the ship the next day. A car would meet us at the dock in the morning and after sight-seeing in the Zionistic settlements of the port city and a few hours on historic Carmel, we were to drive to Nazareth where Our Lord had lived with Mary and Joseph and then we would go on to the ancient city of Tiberias on the edge of the Sea of Galilee.

Suddenly I found my mind stirred with a strange nostalgia. All these names of Bible geography came trooping out of the attic of memory; names as familiar to my boyhood in Baltimore as Fort McHenry and Druid Hill Park—Nazareth! Capharnaum! Bethlehem of Judea! Jerusalem! Calvary! These old memories of yesterday were to be realities of tomorrow.

I think there is no travel experience comparable to a Christian's first visit to these hallowed places, even to one who felt he had put aside all religion, as had I. There was evocation wherever the eye would light. As the days passed, I was astonished to find how much of the four Gospels had remained in my memory and how many of the texts I could quote. The carpenter shop, the home of the Holy Family, touched my spirit with forgotten power. On the stony beach of the Galilean lake I looked around me, peopling the shore with Peter and James and John. By the ruins of the Synagogue at Capharnaum I stood wondering how the voice of the Master had sounded when it rang out here, commanding evil spirits to depart from a bedeviled young man, writhing on this very pavement. How could I guess that even then the devils of doubt and indifferentism which were in me were also being commanded?

From the stable in Bethlehem to the hill of Calvary I went with a strange awareness of deepening concern, a heartache like the throbbing of an old wound that had never healed. While I was still not a believer upon departing from Judea, I had reached a point where I was wishing that the story was true. On our homeward voyage I started work on a new book which I called *A Skeptic in the Holy Land.*

Looking back on it now, I see it as an ignorant and impious work. Yet in some of its anguished phrases there stirred the grief and loneliness and heartbreak that lie buried deep in every man whose faith has been lost. The last chapter of that book was far less skeptical than the first. Indeed, to read that book today is to discern between the lines the pale image of reviving faith coming through dark corridors of my thoughts like dawn creeping silently through the streets just before sunrise.

After the book was published I expected to forget the whole matter. But something had hold of me, would not let me go. I began to believe that the ethical statements of Christianity needed to be re-emphasized in a world that became less and less attractive as Nazism offered its hand, stained with the blood of the Jews, and received the clasp of Communistic Russia. No man with eyes to see and ears to hear could mistake the fact that one great and simple moral issue must sooner or later confront the world. Within our generation the people must make a choice between principle and expediency, between good and evil.

Every man, I felt, must contribute what he could to that struggle, and I began to consider one job that I could do which might help. That was to restate the ethics of Christianity in the simplest possible terms. More and more I was astonished to find a great illiteracy all around about the life and teachings of Christ.

One day I said to myself: "I will write an elevator boy's life of Jesus and try to make it as interesting as a serial story in a popular magazine. I will call it *The Greatest Story Ever Told.*

At this time I had not the slightest idea that I was already on the road to conversion. I began to read the New Testament and then various familiar biographies of Our Lord—Renan, Papini, even one by Charles Dickens. For two years I pursued this reading, making copious notes, until I began to feel that soon I might be ready to do the book. Then suddenly I found myself once more overwhelmed with doubt.

Did I really want to write that book? I am sure that I was so disturbed with inner conflict because I was reluctant to admit, or recognize, that I was being tempted to drop—or else accept—the whole thing. It came to a head when at a dinner party I met Father Ignatius J. Cox, a professor at Fordham University.

27

"How will you start," he asked me, "to go about designing your story?"

My plan, as I explained, was to reassemble in chronological form the history as it is told in the Gospels.

"And how long," Father Cox persisted, "do you think it will take to do that?"

I thought a few weeks. Father Cox smiled kindly. It had taken Père M. J. Lagrange a lot longer than that, he told me, and added: "I am going to make you a present of his *Harmony of the Four Gospels*."

After that conversation I had to face myself—did I intend to write the book or not? Wasn't I just a sentimental fellow who had been under some kind of poetic spell in Palestine? If I went back there again, wouldn't I look at it much more objectively? There was only one way to find out. That night I decided to make a second journey to the Holy Land.

The end of this second voyage was in Beirut, Syria, and that afternoon my wife and I rode through steep and snowy defiles of the Lebanon Mountains, actually and literally on the road to Damascus! And we slept that night in the city where St. Paul had been blinded by an access of the light. I like to think that night's dreams of strange and wonderful peace in the heart were a promise from my guardian angel.

This time I entered into the land of Our Lord through the northern frontier. I saw the snow on Hermon Hill, and how my heart pounded when across the shepherds' fields I beheld once again the waters of the Lake of Galilee. This time there was an immense difference in me. Since my last visit here I had read so much and meditated so much that the very air was rich with historic meaning, as if I breathed in the teachings of a blessed life. He had walked here and talked yonder, healing the sick, feeding the hungry, forgiving the sinners, and offering salvation freely and for all. I sat in an automobile but my soul was on its knees!

When at last I came home again I knew my job was

cut out for me. I was not ready to write; my ignorance was so vast, my eagerness so intense, that years of more study lay before me. The more I read, the more I thought, the easier it was for me to pray. The day came when I knew that I had come home. That was when I asked the late Father William J. McGarry, S.J., to begin my instruction. He died in the midst of my studies but Father Harold C. Gardiner of *America* and Father Martin Joseph Scott brought me safely into the fold.

Since then, my book, in advance of publication, first became a radio program, *The Greatest Story Ever Told.* Then it appeared as a finished volume. It may sound like false humility for me to say that I know how poor a thing it is compared with how fine I wanted it to be. But I mean it.

But that is only a beginning of the work I hope to do. Fifty years of neglect lie behind me. I must work fast to make up for that wasted time. So I ask all good Catholics, all good Christians, to pray for me. To all those who are attracted and yet frightened and reluctant, I say there is no way to peace on earth except in the footsteps of the Master.

ESCAPING FROM AN ATHEIST'S CELL

Gretta Palmer

Among the free-lance journalists of America, Gretta Palmer occupies a prominent place. Articles from her versatile pen have appeared in the *Reader's Digest, Cosmopolitan, Ladies' Home Journal, Look, Good Housekeeping, Collier's,* the *Saturday Evening Post,* and in other magazines. Her article, "Restricted . . . to Families *With* Children," in the *Reader's Digest,* appeared in all the *Digest's* foreign editions and attracted world-wide attention. The story featured the action of a St. Louis real estate man who went directly counter to the all too prevalent practice of restricting apartments to families without children by making his apartments available *only* to families with children.

Graduating from Vassar in 1925, Miss Palmer joined the editorial staff of the *New Yorker,* wrote a column for the Scripps-Howard syndicate, edited the New York *World-Telegram* Woman's Page, and served as war correspondent in Europe and Indo-China. She contributed the lead chapter to *Deadline Delayed,* consisting of war stories which correspondents could not previously publish because of censorship.

In collaboration with Father George, she wrote *God's Underground,* published in January 1949 by Appleton-Century-Crofts. This book narrates the experiences of Father George, a Croat priest, who, incognito, spent many months inside Russia and participated in the work of a vast network of secret Christians within the Soviet state. The volume was the selection of the Catholic Literary Foundation for January 1949.

Miss Palmer was born of a Presbyterian mother and of a father who was a lapsed Catholic. She attended a Unitarian Sunday school and spent two years in an Episcopal boarding school, but her religious education, as far as effectiveness was concerned, she reports, was near the zero mark. She resides at the Waldorf-Astoria in New York City, and finds herself occupied in meeting the requests of magazines of national circulation for stories and articles from her gifted pen.

FIVE years ago I was a prisoner in a bright, bleak, narrow cell which I called the universe. Things were very tidy there—it is easy for the poor to keep their possessions neat. Mine was a bare, modern, antiseptic universe with colorless, windowless walls and the strong, astringent smell of modern science. It had neon lights to read by, but it never admitted the sun. For forty years I had lived, with ups and downs, inside the cell called atheism.

There are virtues inside the modernist's narrow world, for no human being ever born could live entirely removed from grace. But we atheists were living on a subnormal plane; our virtues were devitalized, and they glowed with no superhuman glory. We had faith

—but faith in Freud and in a mystical, unproven principle of life called "progress." Since the brain does not thrive on prison fare, my believing mind was filled with a hundred contradictory fallacies, a thousand sloppily contrived assumptions. Because doctors had been able to wipe out smallpox, I thought it followed that they would shortly find a virus for man's hostility to man. Because the engineering sciences had been a great success, I expected *social* engineers to produce, within a hundred years, the principles on which a society of perfect men would operate as smoothly and with as little friction as a really good Diesel engine.

One of the most horrible things about the atheist's cell is that it is a fairly comfortable place in which to live. The inmates are not clamoring loudly for someone to free them; each of them is working very busily to exchange his present cell for another exactly the same, only a little larger and more enviably placed. The man in the five-thousand-dollar cell hopes, in a few years, to move into the twenty-five-thousand-dollar cell; then, he is sure, his troubles will be at an end.

I was not unhappy four years ago. I did not have pain or frustration or failure in my little cell with me, as goads to finding the way out. My life was a success according to the formula laid down by the psychiatrists. If anyone had suggested that I needed a God, I should probably have asked, "What for?"

Things were going well. My life was orderly. My thoughts were neatly ranged.

And then I became confused. Thank God, I became confused!

The war confused me. It showed, rather shockingly, that mankind was not getting along as well with its job of perfecting itself as I had hoped. The scientists were not delivering the goods. For while they had been frivolously measuring the stars and telling us how to increase the speed of aircraft, man himself had fallen prey to a deadly disease, the disease of human hostility. It was high time, it seemed, that someone should jog the scientists' nodding heads and point out their error in having let mankind get completely out of hand. I was quite testy with any scientists I was able to buttonhole.

"Look here," I'd say to them. "What Aristotle said about medicine is now known to be nonsense. Today's doctors have shown up his ignorance. But people still speak admiringly of Plato's *Republic*. That means that for thousands of years you haven't taken a *step* toward solving this question of how men can live amiably together. And now look! A world war!"

None of them, not one, pointed out the obvious fact that science has definite limits beyond which it can never go.

"Karl Marx," I said, "started with an obviously ridiculous idea: that man is moved solely by economic interests. But even so—even with so big a mistake as that at the bottom of his thinking—his one poor effort to understand society in social terms has changed the history of one sixth of the globe. When *real* scientists study history, things will begin to hum."

So I had a hazy notion that I'd skim over the fields of sociology and psychiatry and see what the boys knew. Then I'd get hold of some of the practical men—labor organizers, politicians, personnel experts—and see what *they* had found out. We'd hold a conference to pool all this knowledge and then we'd get a philanthropist to pay for research to fill the necessary gaps, and there we'd be. Society would be scientific, at last! It might take twenty-five years, but I probably had twenty-five years. And it would be great fun.

(I am afraid I also had a gratifying mental glimpse of myself graciously posing for the picture magazines as the liaison agent between these distinguished groups of scholars and statesmen. In fifteen years I'd probably have a cabinet post—Secretary of Social Evolution or something of the sort. There was plenty of "self-interest" at the bottom of the scheme, you may be sure.)

I began to read a *lot* of sociology. I began buttonholing learned men. I thought that I was being an intellectual pioneer, but I was really engaged in work much more important than that. For I was running my hands over the smooth, unbroken walls of my atheism, looking for a chink through which real sunlight might come in. I did not know it, but when I started seeking a new truth I began my search for God.

Being stubborn and utterly the child of my times, I spent five years thrashing around inside that cell, examining it in search of something which it could not possibly contain. For the only way that the atheist *can* arrive at fundamental truth is by smashing down the artificial walls inside which he has confined himself.

In five years I proposed what seemed the basic question to hundreds of the wise men of our times.

"The real trouble with society," I'd say to them, "is, obviously, man's hostility to other men. Now then, what do we know about that? How can we control it? How can we make everybody feel friendly toward society?"

One group of psychiatrists said hostilities ("aggressions") are stored in an invisible reservoir; drain them off, and that will be the end of them.

"Why, that's perfectly splendid," I said. "We'll get to work on it at once.

"You mean that if we give a man a hatchet and let him go to work smashing a tenement that is coming down anyway, he'll get along better with his family and friends?"

Some of them did mean just that. They even agreed that bullfights and prize fights "drain aggressions" and keep a population in a benign mood. (None of them ever lifted a finger to put this noble theory into execution, but they often read papers about it before learned societies. I suppose they still do.)

But just before I hopped the train for Washington to lobby for the admission of fighting bulls, another distinguished psychiatrist got hold of me.

"That's nonsense," he said. "Hostility is like a muscle: the more you exercise it, the stronger it grows. Bullfights make a population *crueler.*"

Then I met a third expert, who said that hostility is the same thing as love, only turned in the wrong direction. "Remove hostility from man," he said, "and you will paralyze him so that he cannot act at all."

My efforts to start at the very beginning—to found a science of society from scratch—were not getting along very well.

I tried other approaches, dozens of them. I read Jung and Freud and Adler, and then I read their middlemen, Menninger and Zilboorg and Alexander and Horney. I found a few kind words tossed toward God in some of Jung's writings and I noted the fact with surprise: odd that so medieval a notion should crop up in a scientific work! Then I read the social scientists: Sumner and Mead and Soule and Myrdal and Mumford and Burnham and Moreno and Burrow and Lewin and Mayo and Murphy and Dollard and Roethlisberger and Burgess and Cottrell and Lasswell and Sorokin and Pareto. I gave the semantics boys a whirl. I poked into "phylobiology" and "sociometry" and I even practiced, with some success, a curious psychological method of using prayer for the realization of one's desires, although both the author of the system and I denied the existence of any God on the receiving end.

It was all a very great waste of time, except for the fact that it taught me what shallow and unsatisfactory results arrive if materialist scholars ignore man's association with a personal God. For when atheist scientists attempt to study man, they undertake an intellectual absurdity. Man, studied as a creature separated from the God who is constantly communicating with him, can never be understood.

For years I failed to see this. I thought man was a bundle of "childhood conditionings." Recondition him, and all would be well. And so I studied the various methods by which commercial firms induce the public to buy their goods. I studied advertising. (If you could sell the public chewing gum, couldn't you sell it friendliness?) I studied the techniques of public-opinion polling. (What makes the public change its mind? Can we induce it to give loving-kindness a whirl?) I spent a lot of time on the moving picture as a medium of persuasion. (If you could make an audience "identify" with a kindly hero, wouldn't it become kindly too?)

It was in Hollywood that I began to get a faint inkling of where this search might lead. This was at the time when *The Song of Bernadette* had reached the screen. I wondered whether this idealization of saintliness would "affect the mores of the public." (For I used to talk in terms like that.) Among others who might be expected to know, I called a Catholic priest to ask him whether attendance and collections in the churches had shown any noticeable pickup in cities where the picture had been shown. (For I measured human conduct on such a scale of outward actions then.)

I forgot what his answer to *that* was. But when I pressed him for a more fundamental opinion, when I said, "Couldn't a series of such pictures make men pretty nearly perfect?" he said, "No." And when I asked why not, he gave me what I considered the most evasive, superstitious, and utterly ridiculous answer I had ever heard. He said, "Original sin."

In Hollywood again—on that trip or the next—I read about the Vedanta religion, which had engaged the passionate interest of such worldlings as Aldous Huxley, Gerald Heard, Somerset Maugham, and Christopher Isherwood. The swami who had influenced all of them was right there, in Beverly Hills. I went to see him in search of an article. And to him, too, I addressed the question with which I was now nagging the universe: "How can we change the heart of man, so that he longs for unity and peace?"

The swami was very kind. My brisk, practical, and Western viewpoint did not annoy him, although I made it clear that I valued religion only as one, possibly effective, instrument for the improvement of society, here and now.

"You of the West," he told me, "have good will and

a great desire to help each other. You are constantly taking up activities whose purpose is the accomplishment of good. What you do not know—what we of the Orient could teach you, is that one cannot perform a successful surgical operation with a dirty knife."

This did seem reasonable. Modern political leaders had enormously powerful instruments for swaying the minds of the public, but if they themselves were misguided men, their propaganda could only duplicate their own mistakes.

Who was to plan the planners in my new society? Who was sure enough of his own wisdom to dare use moving pictures, radio, billboards, and the rest to persuade all others to be like him? What man was so wise and good that a society composed of carbon copies of himself would be a happy one?

But I brushed this question aside as too difficult to answer. Instead of pursuing it, I went to Italy and North Africa in the summer of 1944. I did not go to see the war; I went to see Europe's exit toward peace. I thought that the earliest liberated towns of Sicily and Italy would be enlightening case studies: when men have passed through an experience of bitterness and hate, are their hearts purged, so that their native good will flows out freely? When everything has been leveled by bombing and destruction, do men build better from scratch?

The Brotherhood of Man was what I really hoped to find. And I found it. I did not find it where I had thought I would. There was very little love among the poor, half-starved, bewildered Italian civilians. But I learned in Italy that the combat soldier is the kind of man I had hoped science and propaganda might produce.

The selflessness of the soldier was the most beautiful thing I had ever seen. I do not mean the spruced-up soldier on leave in Rome, and certainly not the soldier-bureaucrat whom you met in Washington during the war. No, I mean the spent, exhausted, bitter, wholly dedicated soldier whom you met in cities that had been liberated a few hours before: there was my man. He had had burned out of him, by sorrow and suffering, any faint interest in "making character" with those who could advance him, or in "getting ahead in the world," or in any of the trashy ideals on which so many of our peacetime activities are spent. His immediate reaction to anyone who came along was a spontaneous, profane desire to "help the poor bastard."

"Take my cigarettes—I've got another pack." "Take my money, you'll need it more than I." "Let me go on that patrol, buddy. You've got a wife and nobody cares much if I get mine." . . .

When you have been privileged to meet such men you do not *think* much about what factors made them act like that. You are not in great sympathy with the slick psychiatric formula which says, "Having exhausted his aggressions against the enemy, the combat soldier has only libido left for his comrades." Nonsense! These men were gentle to the enemy, too, when he had fallen, and their violence was exhausted in only one direction: against themselves. They had "cleaned the knife."

But why were our soldiers so magnificent? Not, I promise you, because of any "indoctrination" as to the purposes for which the war was being fought. "What are we doing over here, anyhow?" was the commonest remark they made. For their girls? Their wives? No . . . for far too many of the men in combat had received those brutal little letters that began, "This is hard to write," and went on to tell of nearer, dearer men at home who had supplanted them. But the dough-boy never faltered when he got news like this. The world back home had become unreal to him. Only the men in his squadron seemed altogether alive; and for any one of them the combat soldier would and often did accept any torture that might come along.

These dedicated men were beyond the foolish little diagrams by which some social scientists hope to capture the human spirit. Even I saw that. The only possible attitude that one could take toward them was, humbly, to try to understand them and to give such infinitesimal assistance to a few of them as lay within the powers of a civilian intruder into their world. You could, at least, accept the discomforts which attended a trip to the front. You could, at least, brace yourself to behave under danger and not get in the way of men doing a difficult job. You could try, when you were tired and cold and hungry, to behave one hundredth as well as these men, who had been tired and cold and hungry for fourteen months and who were not free to leave at any whim.

If you have lived, for even a few days, with men like that, you find the questions that you ask are subtly altered. You no longer say, "What kind of committee shall I form to improve society?" You say, "How can I serve this extraordinary quality that men develop under conditions of unspeakable strain? How can I keep from getting in its way? Where do they get it? What is its source?"

For I found that nobility and unselfishness are catching; it is impossible, in the contagion of giving at the front, to hoard a bit of chocolate. But back in America, where nobody seemed to be outstandingly noble, hoarding again seemed the natural thing to do. Do you remember those under-the-counter dealings in butter and sugar and beef? Do you remember the five-dollar bills that enabled us to save our gas-ration cards? That was the world that I returned to in the winter of '44.

I hated that world. I went on hating it for a long time. But I did not know where to find its antithesis, where to look for the glory I had seen in Italy, except among the dirty, unshaved, tired men who were fighting America's war. So I went back to the war out of homesickness for heroism. I went to China in the summer of '45.

I saw the war end there and I visited a few of the little, heartbreaking wars of independence that were starting in the colonial areas (and are still being hopelessly waged today). I got to know revolutionaries and patient Chinese peasant-soldiers and I became proud

38

of the astonishing Americans who emerged into Shanghai, at the war's end, from twenty months or more of
lonely, dangerous living in disguise behind the enemy
lines.

In China, I think, I renounced that pretty vision of
myself as Madam Secretary in charge of Human Evolution. For here I ran up against men so lonely for a
woman from home that they had no shame in telling
you the things that were really bothering them. And
the conflicts that beset them are derived from such
endurance and selflessness, such a pitiless standard of
what the war demands of them that you wish you were
a combat soldier, too, so that you could talk in their
own terms.

Instead, I trotted out what had once passed for wisdom, when I had written it for the magazines. (For it
was all I had to give.) I said the pat little things
psychiatrists tell us in their slick little books. And I
discovered how hollow and how very silly these things
are.

But I really tried in China. I listened to the human
problems that were given me and I tried to keep up,
morally, with men who thought that it was perfectly
normal to live for four or five days without sleep on
benzedrine, if there was work to do, and then curl
up for three hours on the mud floor of a hangar with
their clothes on. I did the best I could—and after six
months I had accomplished absolutely nothing. I was
not wise enough to be any good at all to people like
this, and I had better abandon, I thought, any scheme
of wholesale social planning.

When I left Shanghai one of the officers at the air-
port had his arm in a plaster cast. While he checked
my travel order he groped for a match with his one
free hand. So I lit his cigarette and got onto the plane.

"And that," I said to myself as we took off, "is the
sum of my contribution to the China theater. They
can put it on my tombstone if we crash. 'She gave a
guy a light.'"

China should have taught the dullest heart that life

was too large to be contained inside my shiny cell. For I saw other sick and ragged men, with burning eyes, when they came down to Kunming from the prisoner-of-war camps where they had been held since the fall of Corregidor. I heard their stories and I knew, by then, that their stories would never be heard at home. The gap had become too wide. These men had refused to break under conditions incomprehensible to any of the rest of us. Torture, to you or me, is just a word, reminiscent of the dentist's drill. Waiting means, to us, that a train or a plane has changed our plans for a day. These men who came out, with grins on their gaunt faces, had sweated out years of waiting without any evidence except their own stout hearts to make them hope their imprisonment would have a happy ending. But not one of them—not one—had ever doubted that the war would finally be won.

New questions were clamoring for answers now.

"Consider," I asked myself, "that soldier who was tortured to give information and died without telling anything. There were a hundred of him—any of the men I see in Shanghai now can name him for me. Very well. Now suppose that a day after his death the enemy acquired the information he wouldn't give them, but from some other source.

"Was his death wasted, then? Doesn't it matter that he kept his secret?"

Judged by practical values, it did not matter at all. Not at all. The dead man was the victim of an accident as pointless as being run down by an automobile on Fifth Avenue. His sacrifice was a wasted sacrifice; it saved no other lives and it did not hasten victory by a single second.

But was his death really wasted? Didn't it matter, in any ultimate way at all, that he had died? Somehow it seemed to matter very much. That puzzled me. And there were other things adding to my confusion.

Everybody prays at a war; when grenades explode a yard away, and you are pressing your face into the earth, you do not plot or hope or hate: you pray. When

40

you see someone going off, quite wide-eyed and knowingly, on a mission from which he probably won't return, you can't give him the cheap and hearty good wishes of peacetime life. You pray for him. You come, gradually and mysteriously, to the conviction that almost the only useful thing that you can do for people in danger is to pray for them.

But what did *I* pray to? Something extremely vague and unformulated. Pressed, I should have shamefacedly come up with one of those wishy-washy phrases: "Higher Intelligence," "Order in the Universe."

But my cell was really cracking now. Against my stubborn will, and despite my arrogance, I had to admit that there were things in life which a Vassar education and a dabbling in psychiatry were insufficient to explain. The universe was becoming broader and stranger than I had supposed, and much more beautiful. No man-made work of art is as magnificent in its changeable and ever-fresh glory as the full moon. No man-limited philosophy can be anything but artificially narrowing. The real philosophy was beginning to come in.

Faith, I was now prepared to believe, might shed light on the question which still troubled me. Yes, it really might. Perhaps the Vedanta followers were right. Perhaps if we of the West accepted the religious knowledge of the Indians, and merged it with our own practical canniness, the problem could be cracked. Faith *plus* science might be needed.

I almost went to India to find out. I almost turned around and made for one of those colonies where students, under a *guru*, practice mysticism. The only thing that held me back, I think, was the fact that Hindu religion seemed an individualistic thing. And I was much less interested in an ineffable experience of union with God than I was in doing something, as soon as possible, to keep alive the glory in the soldiers' eyes. So I came home.

Emerson says, "When the half-gods go, the real gods

41

come." My half-gods are soldiers—good men under strain. But, superb as humanity can be when it must meet a crisis, humanity is always an uncertain altar at which to worship. No man, not even a martyred soldier, is noble enough to fill the vacuum in our hearts which is left vacant for God. The Brotherhood of Man is an intelligible ideal only if we look upon the brothers as having a Father. But that I had yet to learn.

So, "What is the source of the soldier's endurance?" I was asking. "Where does it start? I can sometimes catch the contagion of it, but I can't begin it by myself. Why not? This chain of human kindness must begin with *someone* who is so luminous a personality that everyone who comes along carries off some light. I must find such people and ask them how they do it. For they have the answer. All the scientists and statesmen need to do is to study them and tell the rest of us to be like them."

(I did not know it, or wildly guess it, but I had reached the first stage of a conversion then. For the earliest thing that priests say to those who wander, groping, in the darkness, is this: "Pray that you be allowed to see the Light, and that you will be given the strength to reach it.")

For as soon as we are humble enough to say, "I want to find the Truth, wherever it lies," we find it. But when we lay down our own demands for the shape that it must take, then it escapes us. When we say, "The truth must come to me certified by the Association of American Scientists," or "The truth is welcome only if *I* have discovered it for the first time," then we are lost indeed. We cut ourselves off from the Light whenever we cower in the cyclone cellars of our own narrow prejudices and insist that the sun find us there.

Yet . . . Light *will* penetrate into the narrowest opening. How grudgingly I widened the chinks for it! At home I ran away into a hundred futile activities, so that I should not have to pursue truth any more. I joined committees by the dozen; my mail is still heavy with the programs of groups who offer patent medicine

42

to the sick soul of modern man. I spent many hours with groups of veterans, hoping to recapture the spirit they had shown abroad; but now, back home, they had become civilians again, and civilians are not sublime enough to answer the questions I was forced to ask. I was blind to the evidence before me; I considered going out—in defiance of all reason—and attaching myself to the outskirts of another war: Palestine or China or Indonesia. For in the winter of 1946 it was still lamentably easy to shop around for a place where combat soldiers could be found. I still insisted that enlightenment must come *my* way. But I kept up the search.

It was an insistent, nagging search, and it reduced me to despair. Thank God, it reduced me to despair!

I do not know whether any convert is patient or wise enough to do the whole task of finding his way to Catholicism through the mind alone. I was not. I have been told that it is possible to prove, by unaided reason, the credibility of every doctrine of the Church. But it would take years of steady, scholarly plodding to arrive by *that* route. Mercifully, converts are given supernatural assistance to make the search for faith easier. Despair of reason led me toward the door.

It started out quite naturally enough. . . .

I was given several magazine assignments that made things easier. One of them (on censorship) forced me to examine, *au fond*, my fond belief that man, unaided, would always go like a homing pigeon for the best. Well, would he, really, now? If that was so certain a fact, why do we arrest the peddlers of obscene post cards, instead of letting them starve for lack of trade? Could it be that my belief in the perfectibility of man (granted a little better social system and education and a dab of propaganda) was founded on a real mistake? Must I face the utterly appalling possibility that man *might not be perfectible?* I must and did. I even decided that his intellect was untrustworthy.

The second assignment asked me to interview Monsignor Fulton Sheen of Washington, because his list of converts to Catholicism was an impressive one. This seemed a routine matter: I wrote him a polite little note asking for an interview. I got a very shocking letter in reply. With complete courtesy, Monsignor Sheen refused my offer. He did not, he said, like publicity. Moreover, his conversions were not of his doing, but were due to the Grace of God.

"What a fantastic and farfetched excuse," I thought. "Well, I'll try again."

So I wrote him another letter in which I pointed out several things: people were beginning to say that the Church was making converts of key people for political purposes. I'd help him to answer this charge. I dug up from one of his books a statement that he hoped its contents would lead some soul back to God: a magazine article might, I said, effect just this. It was a sales letter. It was designed to meet him on his own ground. As a final clincher, and to show him that I would not be prejudiced, I added the fact that I had been baptized a Catholic (although that had certainly been the end of the matter, so far as I or my family were concerned, for I had had no spiritual instruction in Catholicism and very little in anything else).

Monsignor wrote that he would be happy to discuss with me the possibility of my returning to the Church, provided I did not use anything he said for publication. Well!

"Now this," I said to myself, "is, of course, fantastic. I am as little a Catholic as a Moslem. But, after all, the Catholic Church is a successful institution, and Monsignor Sheen is one of its best-known priests. It is possible that he might shed some slight light on the question that is puzzling me."

So I wrote and said that I should be happy to talk to him, on his own terms.

A few weeks later he called on me and chatted quite casually about matters which had no relation at all to *me*. I was, I thought, completely unaffected by the visit. Nothing was said about instruction, except that if I ever wanted to reach him he would see me.

The weeks passed on and my confusion showed no sign of clearing up of itself. It became worse. It paralyzed action. For if you don't know what is worth doing, it is extremely difficult to do anything at all.

Well, this Monsignor Sheen had seemed kind, learned, and balanced. Maybe I should have a talk with him. Maybe I should seriously ask for instruction . . . carry my investigations into this strange world of faith. Sound, scientific procedure seemed to demand it. And, anyway, where had the *intellect* got me? Maybe a leap in the dark was the only way to peace.

And so I said to Monsignor Sheen, on our second meeting, "Let's not bother with the *rational* arguments for Catholicism. I'm prepared to admit now that the intellect is a blunt instrument incapable of dealing with the questions that disturb us most. For man has been reasoning since his existence began, and he has ended up in Hiroshima. Suppose you tell me about faith, all by itself, independent of the intellect."

Monsignor said, "You *can't* abandon your reason. That's the mistake the followers of Hitler made. That's the kind of thing that makes people believe that some man in Moscow, Idaho, is God, because he claims to be. Let me tell you what we Catholics believe, and if your reason rejects it, go away with my blessing. But I beg you, as a friend, don't throw in the sponge on using your intellect."

That was a surprise. And, later, when I found out a little of the richness and scope of Catholic scholarship, I laughed—wryly and sadly, but I still laughed—at my bumptious belief that Catholics have surrendered their power to think.

I said another thing in that first talk. I said, "I suppose that religions are all pretty much the same, and I have acquired considerable respect for the Hindus. Look at Gandhi and what he has accomplished through holiness alone! But I find it hard to believe, with them, that the proper end of every life is the attainment of a mystical experience. That doesn't jibe with the way we have been brought up to think. So we'll leave out mysticism, please."

Those two remarks show how far from Christianity I was that July. But by December I became a Catholic. I became a Catholic with no faint reservations, no intellectual holding back, no emotional desperation to drive me on.

I became a Catholic because I was looking for the truth, and I had found it. It is that simple. I had found the strange and very wonderful key to *all* the problems that had bewildered me. I had found that this key is, as G. K. Chesterton wrote in *The Everlasting Man,* a real key—it fits, and I believe that no other object in the world except that key will fit. It throws on the mysteries of human life the kind of enlightenment which you recognize at once as being true. You do not greet such truths with, "Let's check those proofs again." You say, with undoubting certainty, "Oh, I see!"

But such truths are not easily obtained by people like me; I examined every single Catholic premise, as it was shown to me, with a scrupulous and sometimes hostile refusal to have anything put over on me. I looked for a loophole at every stage. I was intellectually arrogant and self-assured. I began with the assumption that nothing so utterly unlikely as the divinity of Christ could possibly be true. I ended up, again with Chesterton, in saying, "It's too good to be true. But it *is* true."

I read far more exacting authors than Chesterton. I read anti-Catholics too. But, examined critically, their arguments always proved to have a catch. The reasons of Catholicism advanced by St. Thomas Aquinas had no catch. My conversion was a reluctant one; I knocked on every other door, making quite sure that there was nothing but a void within, before I was driven to the admission that this single door really opened on the secrets of the universe.

I discovered, in studying philosophy, that every difficulty and doubt which my atheism could contrive had been respectfully examined and disposed of hundreds of years before me. I found that there is no fact or

46

hypothesis of modern physics or astronomy which cannot be comfortably accommodated inside the ample arms of the Church. I discovered that, historically speaking, people seem to *leave* the Church because they want forbidden things, never because they want a deeper truth. I found that people *enter* the Church because they want the fulfillment of either heart or brain or soul. Many men have abandoned Rome because they wished to worship at the altar of man's self-sufficient intellect; nobody ever left the Church because the best in him could not find fulfillment there.

My most painful sacrifice, intellectually and emotionally, was the surrender of the belief in man's perfectibility. I did want to think that an extension of good will and a development of knowledge would enable all of us, here and now, to become happy and whole forever. It is the ideal of our century—the belief in unaided achievement of the Brotherhood of Man without a Father. It is the dearest fallacy of our times.

While I was studying and making things as hard as possible for myself, intellectually, other things were going on.

At one stage, a very early stage, Monsignor said to me, "Priests don't convert. We merely hoe the earth a little bit and make the growing easier." But he did not say, as psychiatrists say to you, "You will do the job yourself." He said, "God will come, if you watch for Him." He also said, "Read the Gospels. Very slowly."

I did that. It seemed to me that they were one long plea for faith. There is a pathos in these endless, overwhelming proofs of divinity performed before the eyes of a world which said, as our world says today, "There must be a catch somewhere. It's too unlikely to be true." The very evidence of their senses, supported by the prophecies of the religion which they believed, was not enough to make the Pharisees accept the fact of Christ's divinity. Today, two thousand years later, the evidence in favor of that truth is, I think, mountainous. And its living reality is an experience any of us can savor in a completely personal and unanswerable way.

47

Yet the modern world brushes it aside, preferring to put faith in a clever little Mechano-set universe which it has built for itself.

It would have been possible to follow Catholic reasoning as I did, and still refuse to believe: not many open-minded people have done this, but there are those who have taken instruction and still are not convinced. Perhaps they were afraid that such sublimity would make demands on them they could never meet. (If so, they were quite right—the demands are never met. But which of us is brash enough to say, "I will meet God only as an equal?") Or they may be so much attached to the old, materialistic philosophy that they cannot let it go, even when it has failed to stand up before a careful scrutiny. We are, all of us, inclined to cling to anything which represents a large emotional investiment, even if we know its worthlessness. And there *is* a sobering moment in conversion when we have to say, "The years I have wasted! The stupidities I have embraced! The wicked and incurable destruction I have caused!" It is a little like becoming naturalized; we must, for one bad moment, renounce the ruler and sovereign that once seemed dear to us.

But if you once open your mind to the *possibility* of a divine Man, you are out of the woods. Christ *could* have been a madman when He claimed to be God, but it is a curiously catching madness in which the world has believed for two thousand years. He *could* have been a cruel liar making gulls of the disciples by promising redemption. If so, it is odd that such a lie told to a group of fishermen in an obscure village of a backward colony, a kind of ancient Puerto Rico, should have toppled empires and led generations of men to martyrdom and monasteries and scholarly concentration on this lie. The only possible alternative answer is the truth of what He said: that He was truly God, and truly come to save the world. The "good man" theory, which would turn Christ into a Jewish Confucius, will not wash; good men do not delude friends into persecution with promises they cannot fulfill.

And if Christ is truly God, then everything else must follow.

And then it's over. Conversion has happened, all in a piece. There are things you still don't understand, but you know that they are all right and that they will be explained to your satisfaction when you ask. For the first time you approach your hours of instruction in order to learn, not to do battle. You find that you are surer that Catholicism is true than of anything else that you ever knew.

A conversion is like trying to open an old, heavy door that has been closed for many years. Dust and grime have glued its edges fast, and the oil in the hinges has long since dried away. The first heave doesn't budge it, nor the second. Sometimes it is so tightly sealed that we are tempted to say, "There isn't really a door here at all. It is just a pattern on the solid wall that looks like a door." And then we may stop pushing and relapse into despair. But something still assures us that there is a door and that it is worth while battering at it with our raw knuckles and straining with our tired shoulders in the hope that it will finally give way. When it does yield, we do not notice how or remember the sensation of the final shove. For by then we are staggering out, our half-blind eyes still blinking in the unfamiliar sunshine.

In such a way there was no moment when I could say, "Just now I began to believe." For belief is as much a matter of action as of thought. The man or woman who prays has performed an act of faith, although he may deny with his intellect that he believes his prayers are heard. He may try to explain away his prayer by saying, "It was a reflex from my childhood memories," or "It was a superstitious gesture, like throwing spilt salt over my shoulder." Nonetheless, he acted out a belief. He prayed.

There was a session, when I was still thrashing around in a sea of controversies—matching this philosophy against that, questioning whether Christianity, pragmatically viewed, had proved itself: doubting,

49

resisting—when I said, "Could one reason for the Incarnation be the fact that it is easier for us to love a human being than any other form a God could take?" I had surprised myself by the question; but as soon as I had stated it, I knew I believed in the divinity of Jesus Christ.

And that, I think, is the watershed of belief. Once a convert has embraced that truth, everything else is apt to follow. There are Protestants who would not agree with me. But I know that to me, at least, it follows that if you believe that Christ was truly God and that the Gospels are true accounts of what He said, then you must take His sayings seriously. And His sayings—written down when the Church had already spread to many lands—have implicit in them everything a modern Catholic believes. The knowledge has only been deepened and developed by new insights and by increased scholarship in the centuries since then.

There came a moment when I returned, for article purposes, to interviews with the kind of social scientists who had awed me a few years before. It was an immensely interesting experience. I now saw that these university dons, who express the liveliest contempt for philosophy in favor of what they call a "clinical approach" to human problems, were trying to build a science out of the poor, watered-down residue of scholastic thought. And they were unhappy men; they had thought themselves into a position which, even to them, was suspicious, uncomfortable.

"Truth," they said, "is never absolute. All we can do is to act as if something were true. If it works, it's true enough to satisfy us." But they looked dissatisfied. And "Truth," said another group of them, "is nothing but mathematical formulas, which have no reference whatsoever to the actual life we lead. Cause and effect do not exist in nature, but to live we have to pretend that they do."

"These are raving madmen," I told myself. But they were not. They were distinguished scholars in one of

America's foremost universities. And when I said to them, "It cannot be that silly a universe," they assured me that it was.

Had I become so bright that I was suddenly able to pick the holes in the logic of men who have far better trained minds than mine? Not by any means. But I had had a flashing glimpse of the kind of universe it is; I had spent a few months in the company of philosophers who see things right side up, and the old, pragmatic tests no longer satisfied me.

That sense of having obtained a north on your compass is one of the great gifts the convert enjoys. He knows, now, how to meet and test an unfamiliar statement. His universe has direction at last.

But the strangest effect of a conversion to Catholicism is the sense of liberation. At once we are freed from the cruel demands made on ourselves to save humanity, singlehanded and without God's help. The "social conscience" of the modern atheist is a driving thing: see how it forces him to join committees, to thrash about the country lecturing and heckling, to read five newspapers and fifteen magazines. They are so many Marthas, these modern, scrupulous reformers. "And only one thing needful."

That one thing, of course, is love. St. Augustine said it all: "Love God and do as you will." Loving God and being intellectually convinced that He is in the Church, the heart leaps forward gladly to perform the small, ritualistic services asked of the good Catholic. It attempts to avoid the things displeasing to Him. But it does not dwell too morbidly on its own imperfections—the good Lord did not make a beautiful world crammed full of friendship, love, art, and poetry in order that we might turn our backs on it and worry about our own uglinesses.

The Catholic is not hag-ridden by a sense of urgency to find the formula that will cure the ills of the modern world; he is humbler in his expectations of himself. He knows that the one thing needful may lead to prayer, to small sacrifices, to charities, or to trying to do perfectly whatever is in hand. The next three minutes are always the crucial ones; the future is God's business, not ours.

So there is a wry amusement for the convert in hearing, from his kindly and agnostic friends, that it is fine that he has found "comfort" in his religion. Comfort, indeed! Catholicism is adventure, growth, excitement, suspense, and it is as far removed from a slippers-and-hearth conception of comfort as human experience can take us.

But because we are still Christians, ours is a universe with a heaven and a hell. We believe that the attempt to understand the world by viewing it as suspended with no top or bottom is as provincial as if we studied the fiftieth story of a skyscraper, while pretending that it had no supports to bear it up and no roof to cover it. You could measure that story very carefully. You might calculate its floor space and make hypotheses about its position vis-à-vis the other office buildings. But so long as you did not know that there were forty-nine floors under it and a roof on top of it, your theories as to how it got there and what kept it in position would err.

The Catholic's universe is thus a universe that makes sense, and the only one that does. It is also a universe that has a happy ending. It is a moral universe in which, as our human intuitions tell us, virtue is never wasted. It is a universe in which, as our hearts ask us to hope, we can always do immensely helpful things for those we love, even when they are distant, even though they have died. It is, as the best in us tells us, a universe in which all humanity is bound together by a deep, unspoken bond. Even the atheist admits this common destiny where he works for the future of humanity; he knows, as we know, that life was not meant to be spent on his own advancement in riches and prestige.

But the atheist has no explanation of *why* he ever turns a finger for the future of mankind. He would be more logical if he asked, as one consistent skeptic did,

"What has posterity ever done for me?" His vague notion that we want a better world for the sake of possible great-great-great-grandchildren, who may never be born, is as mystical as anything in religion and a good deal less logical. Why should you, a complete man or woman, sacrifice yourself today for the fate of a single one of your genes in the year 2269? It is like cutting off your head to save a finger.

No, the best is in all of us; and the part, that we cherish most and know is the best, can find no support and no fulfillment in a world from which the supernatural has been cut off. Our reason knocks itself out with foolish contradictions when it pretends that the universe is a mechanical one, coldly twirling in space without rhyme or reason. Our healthy desire to help our neighbor leads us to such distorted and hurtful errors as Fascism or Communism, if it is allowed to operate without regulation.

That is the wryest tragedy of the modern world today; that most of our good works and the things our "social conscience" asks us to do are futile. Men busy themselves with programs for the betterment of the world—and the world becomes worse. They read or write "inspirational" books and feel a thousand times less inspired than the men who built the cathedrals. They attend improving lectures—and are rarely improved. They try to be kind to everyone around them —and find that their kindness breaks down when it is most needed and that man, unaided, is a cruel, unsympathetic, and unreliable friend.

Men find that their hearts are stirred by some heroism performed during the war or after. In the rationalist world where they live they brand this response "sentimental twaddle," yet the response stays with them and is realer than the rationalist mind.

The moderns try to build a little philosophy for living out of something from Confucius, from Dale Carnegie, and something that they remember from Sunday school and find that it is impossible to follow these rules without a stronger motivation than they are apt to get by musing on them, now and then. And sometimes they try it and find that this motivation can be found only in one mood: the mood of prayer. In only one attitude: upon their knees. From only one Source: a God whom they worship.

Man cannot get real, personal help from the god of the modern pantheists—the god who set the universe whirling and then retired. Nor from the other god who is evasively described as "higher order" or "basic intelligence." No modern man who controls electricity by turning the switch that sets on his radio is going to worship "incomprehensible force"; force is his servant. No intelligent human being can worship a God whom he imagines as being rather like electricity, for he is bigger than such a God. Man can worship only a God who was and is his Maker; a God who sends into his mind and heart the best things that he finds there— and finds them with surprise, for he knows (none better) that they never came from him or from his subconscious. Man knows this because he is well aware (none better) of the poor and shoddy contents of his subconscious, which is stored with the events and memories of his own imperfect past.

And so all converts find, in time, that the patent medicines for the soul have failed as they will always fail. The short cut to perfection I was looking for was never found. The "science of society" turned out to be a ridiculous contradiction in terms, for science measures things, and man, having a soul, is immeasurable. My effort to engineer mankind, to turn human events into a kind of superengineering turned out to be a will-o'-the-wisp. Every man has free will, and it is hedged about with Godly safeguards through which no propaganda barrage can penetrate. Every man will always retain the God-given privilege of running amok or becoming a saint, no matter how you try to press him into a mold. Man will escape you, whenever you attempt to force him into any human arrangements, even if they are called "the good society."

But it is better this way. A future Utopia is a cold

and distant god to serve. But the God we worship is the God who is within us, and nothing can be closer than that. I know now the source that I was seeking when I asked, "Where does it come from, this light in the eyes of the combat soldiers?" It comes from God.

The Catholic's God is not two thousand years away in either Galilee or a future model state. He is as close as this second. Every act of the day can be sanctified and turned into a prayer in the economy of supernatural belief.

The supernatural, that close at hand, is a boundless concept and it has, as a simple matter of historical fact, proved the most invigorating ideal man has ever known. The cathedrals were built as love offerings by men of faith, and the greatest paintings of the Renaissance sprang from the exuberance of the painters' love of God. Most of the true and beautiful things we have today are a watered-down inheritance from men who knew how to believe. Even our sense of man's dignity before the law and our belief that children must be treated with kindness, even our "social conscience," spring from Christianity; the pagan world knew nothing of these. The best things in our heritage have all come from the same gesture of humility; it is only by bowing their heads and saying, "Let it be done unto me," that men rise to the heights. That is the religious paradox.

It is easier for the humble to acknowledge the Light than it was for me, for they have never misused their minds and wills to build defenses against it. The crushed and desolate, too, find it less difficult to reach the sun than the modern atheist-Pharisees who are too proud to admit their need of God. The man or woman whose world is lighted by the cold and sterile neon bulb of "scientific determinism" is, I suppose, the least apt of all to discover that true sunlight can exist.

So I have been miraculously fortunate in escaping from that atheist's cell in which only fungus thoughts can grow. I have also discovered, *Deo gratias,* that there is a simple, quite accurate name for the cramped and narrow universe in which I lived my life until a year ago. The name of it is Hell.

The new world into which I have entered is flooded with the sunshine of God's love. His divine artistry is mirrored in the running brook, the smiling meadow, and the tall trees which lift verdant fingers in prayer and praise to their Creator. I glimpse His artistry as He paints the wayside flowers and lights the evening star. All nature, tremulous with His presence, is articulate in His homage. Books, people, the experiences of every day also echo Him, so that I can best describe the new world into which I have come as at least the foothills of Heaven.

AN INVITATION HEEDED

Frances Parkinson Keyes

Frances Parkinson Keyes, the author of many best sellers and one of the most popular novelists of our day, was born in 1885 in the Monroe House at the University of Virginia, where her father, John Henry Wheeler, was professor of Greek. She received her education in private schools here and abroad. Her formal education was interrupted in 1904, when, at the age of eighteen, she married Henry Wilder Keyes. In 1921 George Washington University conferred the degree of Litt.D. upon her and in 1934 Bates College (Lewiston, Maine) gave her the same honor.

Instead of living in an ivory tower wherein many writers pass their days, Mrs. Keyes has lived in the busy center of social and political life. As the wife of the governor of New Hampshire and later as a Washington hostess during her husband's term of office in the United States Senate, 1919–37, she had a prominent official and social position. She has traveled around the world, made many trips to Europe, and has visited Iran, South America, and Mexico. She has woven scenes from her travels into her novels, thus giving them a rich historical background.

Mrs. Keyes has been for many years a contributor to *Good Housekeeping* and an occasional contributor to other periodicals. From 1937 to 1939 she was the editor of the *National Historical Magazine,* published by the D.A.R., but because of differences in policy and aims she resigned from membership in the society in 1939. She holds membership in a number of patriotic societies and is in frequent demand as a lecturer.

For years Mrs. Keyes has been a prolific writer. Beginning in 1919, she wrote *The Old Gray Homestead. The Career of David Noble* in 1921, and her *Letters from a Senator's Wife* in 1924 found her with a large reading public. In 1930 came *Queen Anne's Lace* and the following year *Silver Seas and Golden Cities.* From then on, almost yearly a book came from her pen, and in 1940 the story of Bernadette of Lourdes, *The Sublime Shepherdess.* In the same year she wrote the story of her conversion, which she calls *Along a Little Way. The Grace of Guadalupe,* published in 1941, tells the touching story of Juan Diego and the apparition of Our Lady of Guadalupe, patroness of Mexico. Her book, *All That Glitters,* is a novel of Washington. *Crescent Carnival* is a story of New Orleans. Her book, *Also the Hills,* is a novel of wartime Washington. *The River Road* (1945) is a novel of the Louisiana sugar plantations. Her recent *Came a Cavalier* is another best seller and has further enhanced her reputation as a novelist of charm and distinction.

Mrs. Keyes received the Siena Medal for 1946, an award conferred annually by the Theta Phi Alpha sorority to a woman who has made an outstanding contribution to the spiritual life of our country.

In October 1939 she traveled to Lisieux and in the Chapel of the Benedictines, where Thérèse Martin made her First Communion, Mrs. Keyes was received into the Church by the Bishop of Bayeux and Lisieux. By a happy coincidence she had been present in the Basilica of St. Peter fourteen years earlier when the saintly child of Lisieux had been raised to the altar as St. Thérèse, "The Little Flower of Jesus." Two years before her conversion she wrote *Written in Heaven,* the story of this little saint of our own time. Mrs. Keyes was widowed in 1938. She has three sons, two grandsons, and a granddaughter. Her hobbies, she confesses, are collecting dolls, fans, costumes, and crucifixes.

I HAVE recently taken a step that seems to me momentous. I have not taken it hastily. Indeed, I have been considering it for nearly twenty years, and for ten I have known that someday I should do so. It is momentous to me personally, both because it represents one of the most significant decisions of my life and because it is inconsistent, in a way, with my background, traditions, and training. And it may seem momentous within the sphere of my personal influence because, as a writer, I reach out to thousands of persons whom I never see, and whose own mental image of me may be suddenly shattered. These persons have a right to understand what I am doing, whether they approve of it or not. Many of them have honored me with their confidence. The time has come when I feel that I should try to honor them with mine. I do not want them to feel bewildered when they read an announcement which I know is bound to amaze them. I do not want them to say to themselves and to each other, "So Frances Parkinson Keyes has become a Catholic! But why?"

Here is the answer, in so far as I can express it:

Perhaps it may seem a simple, even an inconsequential one. I was not drawn toward Catholicism, in the beginning, by any turmoil of spirit or any dogmatic dissension. I am one of those fortunate human beings who was born with religious faith, and who, with the passage of years, has found this faith increasingly strong and sustaining. I use the word "fortunate" advisedly, for it has always seemed to me that a person who does not possess it should elicit sympathy; it is not easy to acquire and maintain when it is not indigenous. And I use the word "religious" in its general sense, which may be wholly undenominational, or connected with any denomination, as the case may be. In other words, I have always found prayer a refuge, a solace, and a power; many of my prayers have been answered, and in most cases where they have not, I have lived to be thankful that this was so. I have always found worship a privilege and an inspiration, and it has been possible for me to test the truth of this

58

under all sorts of conditions, in many parts of the world. I have always possessed, for a lay woman, a fair knowledge of the Scriptures. At the age of four I was taught to read out of the Bible by my paternal grandmother, who was one of the most learned, courageous, and devout women whom I have ever known. Since then I have taught all my own sons to read in the same way, and I myself have read portions of Holy Writ in five languages besides English. Biblical allusion comes naturally to me, and I can quote countless passages from memory. I would no more think of traveling without a Bible than without a toothbrush, and after fifty years of close acquaintance with it I constantly find new meaning and new values in it.

With so generally soul-satisfying a basis, it is natural to ask why I should have striven to change its form in any way. If I may be permitted to say so, without seeming to cast the slightest reflection on any kind of faith, so long as this is sincere, it has not been so much a question of strife as of growth. My paternal grandfather was a Congregational clergyman and all the members of my family, on both sides, were members of the Congregational Church. Eventually I married into another Congregational family. I went to church as a matter of course, to Sunday School, and to Christian Endeavor meetings. I went willingly and contentedly. But by the time I was nine years old, when the question first arose as to whether I myself should "join the church," I did not want to do so. I was conscious of a lack of completeness, for me, in the services I was attending and the doctrine I heard expounded. I did not know just what was lacking, but I felt that there was something.

I recently heard a story which illustrates my own frame of mind at that time, as far as I can interpret this. In Washington a large Presbyterian church and a large Catholic church stand almost side by side, and the little girls who attend a parochial school directly behind them are encouraged to undertake frequent devotion. Two of them, becoming slightly confused as to direction, wandered into the Presbyterian Church by mistake and, upon looking up to the place where they expected to see the altar, beheld only a formidable array of organ pipes. They immediately arose from their knees and hastened to the door, where they met the pastor to whom I am indebted for this story and who happened to be going through the vestibule. Observing their manifest distress, he asked if there were anything he could do to help them. "Oh, sir," one of them exclaimed, "we wanted to talk to God, but we don't find Him!"

I believe that this little girl's bewilderment was akin to my own childish perplexity. I have said before that I am a great believer in prayer. As time went on, I found it urgent, for various reasons, to pray with increasing frequency. I was not wholly satisfied, or sufficiently sustained, when I did so only at stated hours, on certain days. I earnestly desired and desperately needed to find a way of praying at any hour, on any day; and very often, when I attempted to enter the church of which I was a member, I found it locked. The result was that I sought out one that was open, and this was a Catholic church.

The times when I sought out a church for purposes of prayer were not all moments of anxiety, though there were many of these. I shall never forget a silent hour which I spent enfolded in the gloom and grandeur of the Toledo Cathedral. The old verger, seeing me sitting there, approached me deferentially and asked me if I would not like to see the treasure. I told him that I had been sight-seeing all day, that I was too tired to see anything more. As a matter of fact, I could not kneel or even formulate any coherent sentences. I merely sat. He looked at me for a moment and then he said quietly, "*Bueno!* A church is a good place in which to rest, señora." And after that he went away. I have never seen him again. And I have never forgotten what he said, either.

Then there was the day when I heard that, for the first time, a story of mine had been accepted for a serial. It was in the middle of a morning, a weekday. My husband was at his office, my sons all at school. But I was so bursting with joy and pride that I had to tell someone at once. And I had to give thanks, because of this wonderful thing that had finally happened, after years of discouragement and defeat in the field of fiction. Ten minutes after receiving the editor's letter I was in church.

There have been many middays when, after excited shopping along the Faubourg St. Honoré, I have dropped in at the Madeleine to give thanks because I had been able to earn the money to pay for the pretty dresses and chic hats I had bought. There have been many midnights—in Manila, in Santiago, in Freiburg, in Washington itself—when I have gone to one beautiful candlelighted church after another to give thanks for God's Greatest of all Gifts to men. In Manila it is customary—or at least it used to be—to leave the fashionable ball at Tiro el Blanco, add a mantilla and an all-enveloping cloak to one's evening dress, and go to Christmas Mass, returning, after this was over, to the ball again. In nobody's mind was there any idea that it was unsuitable to mingle secular and sacred joy in this way.

I was profoundly impressed by this fact. The more I traveled about, the more it was borne home to me that no Catholic with whom I came in contact seemed to consider that any reasonable pleasure was in itself an evil thing. It could be converted into evil, of course. But that was entirely different. Enjoyment of life, in all its normal phases, was regarded as natural and desirable.

I heard this viewpoint embodied in a charming old Spanish legend. St. Peter, so the story ran, was accustomed to ask suppliants at the gates of heaven whether they had taken advantage of all the earthly joys made available to them through the goodness of God. If they admitted that they had not, he shook his head sadly. "Alas, my child," he then said in a somber tone, "how can you expect to be ready for celestial joys if you have not prepared yourself for them through the medium of terrestrial joys? I shall be obliged to send you away unless and until you learn better." Recognizing that St. Peter would probably have many other peccadilloes with which to reproach me, I decided that he should never do so on this particular score!

The change in my own viewpoint, of which I had hardly been conscious, was brought home to me in full force for the first time when I was spending a week end in Boston. One of my sons was then at the Harvard Law School, another at Harvard College, and the third at Milton Academy. I suggested that after church, to which we all went together, each bring a boy who was far from home to a midday dinner at the quiet hotel where I was staying with my secretary; after dinner we would make up two tables of bridge. I recall that one of the boys invited was a member of the Soong family, a brother of two charming women, each of whom has been the wife of a president of China. With the flair for cards typical of his race, he won almost every rubber; his pleasure was apparent and gratifying. The other guests were also loud in their thanks for a day that had "seemed like home."

They lingered so long that I was late for a supper engagement with an aunt. By way of explanation I laughingly said that I had been playing bridge all the afternoon with a group of youngsters, who had had such a good time that they did not know when to stop. I shall never forget the chilly silence with which this announcement was greeted. I was conscious of reproving eyes all around the family board. For an instant I could not imagine what was the matter. Then I realized that in the opinion of my relatives I had not been creating a harmonious and helpful atmosphere for my sons and their friends; instead I had been breaking the Sabbath Day and encouraging the young in bad habits. In my own turn, I was frozen with horror that such a construction could be put on "a source of innocent merriment." I felt then that I was nearing a parting of the ways.

I felt still more certain of this parting after a gloomy Sunday which I spent alone in London. At four in the afternoon I went through the pouring rain to vespers at Westminster Abbey. After the service was over I wandered down the nave to look at the tomb of the Unknown Soldier, which I really wanted to see. But almost instantly a severe verger appeared at my side and in a somber tone ordered me to pass on out, as the abbey was about to be closed. "But surely you keep it open for prayer and meditation," I protested. "Not on Sunday, madam," he informed me in a voice of finality, and I went forth into the rain again.

At the same time that I was absorbing the essential joyousness of Catholicism as contrasted to the essential austerity of Puritanism, I was also observing the unswerving policy of the Catholic Church in regard to what, for lack of a better expression, might be called basic decency. With this, so I discovered, it never compromised. In the midst of a confused and chaotic world it remained steadfast in its attitude not only toward the famous Seven Deadly Sins, but toward degeneracy and depravity in any form. It declined to countenance lewd literature or debased dramatics. It stood unswervingly for the permanence and sanctity of family life. It encouraged and upheld its children's groping efforts to achieve and maintain a state of grace, guiding and forgiving, but never condoning.

All this roused my admiration and challenged my courage. I had been brought up to set stern standards for myself, but all around me I saw these standards slipping; I had begun to wonder whether they really mattered so much after all. At that stage I had never written a best seller, and it is the natural desire of every author to achieve one; I felt that perhaps if I wrote a different type of book I should be more successful. All around me I saw disrupted families which were apparently getting along very well; I thought it was perhaps not worth while to insist on the maintenance of an unsevered circle.

It was the attitude of the Catholic Church, with which by this time I had become thoroughly familiar, that made me realize, more than any other one thing, that the old standards were not all gone, that they did still matter, that they were vital and essential, and that they always would be. It did not seem strange to me, as an author, when I achieved a place on a national best-seller list and on the White List at the same time. I knew that this was the way, for me at least, that things would have to be. It did not seem strange to me, as a woman, when the clouds that threatened my personal peace evaporated. I knew that this also was bound to happen.

As I continued to go, with increasing frequency, into Catholic churches, I did this with a mounting sense of naturalness and of joy. In the beginning I had gone primarily to pray, when I could find no other churches open; in course of time I went also for correlative reasons, because, in the remote places where I was, there was actually no other church of any kind and because churchgoing is as essential to me as breathing. I learned, not as a precept but as a practice, the universality of the Catholic Church; I knew that in this respect at least it met one of my most overwhelming needs. I learned that while it was the open door of the church which gave the first sense of welcome, it was the Real Presence which transfigured and sublimated this. Previously I had often wondered, when I entered a church which had once been Catholic but had been shorne of its altar during the Reformation, why it seemed so sterile to me. Now I thought I knew.

I went to church in Portugal, in Spain, in Italy, in France, in the Azores, the Canaries, Cuba, and Puerto Rico; to small chapels and great cathedrals, to the cloisters where nuns knelt in seclusion behind the grille, and to the sanctuaries where the scum of the pavements found refuge. I went to church in all the major and many of the minor cities of South America, including Magellanes, which is the southernmost city in the world. And finally, one snowy silent afternoon in midwinter, I went to the shrine of St. Anne de Beaupré, in Canada.

It was not a time of pilgrimage. There was not a soul in the church besides the friend who was with me, and myself. I dipped my fingers in holy water as I entered, knelt down, and crossed myself, in the same way that I had done hundreds of times already, first merely because it seemed courteous to follow prevalent custom in the house of God, as one would in the house of a friend, and later because this had become instinctive. I had the rapturous feeling of one intimately united with God. I seemed to hear a divine voice whispering in my inner ear, "Come in, my child, come in." I surrendered to the divine will and I feel that God bestowed upon me the priceless grace of faith. That deeply moving experience marked the climax in my soul's quest for God and the fullness of divine revelation. I discovered then and there the joy of believing, the rapture of faith in God, the ecstasy of heeding His divine invitation and clasping His outstretched hand.

Returning to my hotel room, I sat down to write a sonnet addressed to St. Anne, or rather to permit my fingers to form the words of one that flowed without effort from my mind.

Anyone who has ever written verse at all knows that the sonnet is one of the most difficult types to achieve, and I have often spent days in trying to perfect one; yet on this occasion the words were all on paper within twenty minutes. Just as I finished writing, the friend who had been with me at the shrine came into my room. I read the sonnet aloud to her, and when I finished I saw that her eyes were full of tears. "I am glad I was with you when this happened," she said, and nothing more. When I reached my own home it came about that my eldest son, who has always been exceptionally close to me in spirit, was the first person I saw. He had hardly looked at me when he said, "So it has happened at last! I have known that someday it inevitably would!"

For a long time no one besides these two persons had

certain knowledge of what had taken place. But there were some who had begun to guess that I had "Catholic leanings," and the forms which the opposition to these assumed ranged all the way from the sublime to the ridiculous and back again. The most laughable objection raised was that they would "injure my social position"; the most serious that "no woman of my intelligence could possibly subscribe to blind beliefs."

Personally I have always felt that a social position so insecure that it could be shaken because one lived or did not live on the "right" street, because one was seen or not seen with the "right" people, was somewhat precarious to begin with; and I have never known anyone whose standing was unassailable to worry about it or even to give it undue thought. The kings and queens, the presidents and potentates whom I have known have all been very approachable and pleasant; the only persons I have ever met who tried "to put me in my place," or to impress me with theirs, have been what are called in New England "small potatoes." In the situation under discussion the acquaintances concerned frequented cathedrals abroad and were gratified beyond measure if their visiting list included members of the continental nobility; but shuddered at the thought of any Catholic contact in the United States. Therefore they had never taken pains to find out what its character might be. "Convents are the most terrible places!" I was told repeatedly. "You've no idea!" . . . "Well, have you?" I always inquired in return. "How much time have you spent in one?" The answer was invariably a blank stare. And I could not refrain from smiling, as I remembered the long periods of peace with which my life had been beatified at the Abbaye des Bénédictines in Lisieux, France, and other intervals, scarcely less significant, which I have spent in various similar places.

As to the charge that no woman of my intelligence could believe blindly, I have never laid claim to remarkable intelligence, but still I found that my usual reply did not bring back a convincing counterretort. "There are two miracles which I am sure you do accept," I ventured to say; "one is the miracle of birth and the other is the miracle of death. Both are universal and eternal. But as far as I know, they have never been logically explained. Can you do so?" There would be a moment's silence and then I would go on. "Well, in that case, why should it be hard to accept other occurrences which seem phenomenal? I do not see how it can be, consistently!"

My work took me, to an increasing degree, into Catholic countries, and finally the way opened, through no initiative of my own, for me to write the life of St. Thérèse of Lisieux. While I did so, I lived at Notre Dame du Pré, the Abbaye des Bénédictines where she was educated; and I was also in close and constant communication with Carmel of Lisieux, where she spent her cloistered life, where one of her sisters is still prioress and two others members of the Community. There I had an opportunity to see at close range the cheerful, radiant, and saintly life of the nuns, who exemplified for me day by day the beauty of holiness and the holiness of beauty. I likewise came in contact with many high prelates, as well as priests and nuns at other convents, and I was deeply impressed by their spirituality and sanctity.

Long before, when I had been on the point of starting on a journey which took me to remote places, a great statesman had said to me: "Remember that no matter where you go, you will always find two gentlemen: the British vice-consul and the Catholic priest. If you get into any kind of a jam, go to one or the other. He will be able and glad to help you." I have never got into any kind of a jam, but on the other hand I have had many occasions to observe the astuteness of the great statesman's estimate. My mind reverted to it frequently, during my first sojourn at Lisieux, and eventually I decided to have a talk with the bishop. I knew that, as a gentleman, he would give me every consideration, even though he might feel it his duty, as a churchman, to discourage me. I told him everything that I have put down here on paper, and much besides.

When I had finished, without asking a single question, he told me that he would be glad to arrange for my reception into the Church at any time. Then he blessed me. It was as natural and as simple as that.

There is a beautiful story of a mother who took her child with her when she was received in private audience with the Pope—Pius X, I think it was, though I am not sure. As she was leaving, the Holy Father said to her, "Bring your little boy back with you tomorrow. I will confirm him." Somewhat startled, she asked, "But isn't he too young to know what that means?" The Pope placed his hand gently under the child's chin and looked into his eyes. "Do you know what God is, my son?" he asked. "Yes," the child answered, "God is love." . . . "You see," remarked the Holy Father to the child's mother.

I thought of this story after my first talk with the bishop, not once but many times. It was two years before I talked with him privately again. In the meantime I had twice thought that the moment was at hand when I might make a public declaration of faith, and twice I had been thwarted, or so it seemed to me. But I received constant encouragement from the Mère Hôtelière at the Abbaye des Bénédictines at Lisieux where I had returned annually. I had confided my hope to her also, and we frequently discussed every phase of it. "You must not be so disheartened," she kept saying. "There are no stone walls between you and your soul's sincere desire. There are only curtains. Several of these you have drawn away already. I do not think many remain for you to part."

It was with these words ringing in my ears that I went to see the bishop a second time. "Monseigneur," I said, "I hoped that last year I might come and ask you to fulfill your promise of receiving me into the Church and I could not do so. Now in a sense I am free. And yet in another sense I feel that I am not." I told him what I meant by this and his answer came unhesitatingly.

"I think that you are right, my daughter," he said. "If

this week had ended on a note of war instead of on a note of peace, I might not advise you in this way.[1] I might tell you that in spite of what you had said, I believed it would be best for you to enter the Church now, since you wish to perform this act in Lisieux and since it might not be possible for you to return to France next year. But under the circumstances I think it best that you should go home now and return to us later. I shall have one more talk with you, when you come back, to finally examine the state of your soul. But I am not disturbed about this, and I beseech you not to let anyone else trouble your peace of mind. I know that in the interval before I see you again you will pray a great deal. I assume that you will also ponder, read, and study. But not, I hope, to the point where you will become anxious about details or worried by non-essentials. God has given you great faith. Rejoice in it. Do not ever permit it to seem like a burden and never doubt that you will return to us. And now, my daughter, let me bless you again before you go."

I departed in peace. And through the turmoil of the following winter I tried to follow the good bishop's instructions. I never let my faith become a burden. I never grew anxious about details or worried over non-essentials. And I never doubted that I would return to Lisieux for the "fête"—as they always called it—for which the good Bénédictines of Lisieux had watched and waited so long. I knew that I was at the very threshold of the Church that was waiting to welcome me. The way I had taken to reach it, as I describe this, seems even simpler than it did before, perhaps hardly worth a description at all. Yet was it not St. Thérèse herself, in whose sanctuary I had learned so much, who taught us not to despise the "little way" but to tread it thankfully? I was secure in the consciousness that it was, and that she had helped me to find the road which, great or small, was after all the only one for me.

I tried to put my house in order, both figuratively

[1]This was immediately after the Munich Conference.

and literally. I did my work, which was heavy, for I wrote a long novel outside editorial office hours, and went on several long lecture tours. I was always terribly tired when I went to bed, and often I did not sleep very well. This was nothing new, but I found a new way of passing the wakeful hours; I spent them in a state of reflective prayer, which supplemented, without supplanting, my more formal devotions. The process proved infinitely restful; I can commend it to anyone who wishes to rise refreshed, even if other benefits of such reflection are disregarded altogether. And "when spring rolled round again next year," I began my preparations to return to Lisieux.

I am not using a figure of speech when I say that a royal welcome awaited me there. The nuns never neglected an opportunity to impress me with the spiritual aspects of the experience that awaited me. At long last I had the great joy of being received into the fold by the bishop, in the chapel at Notre Dame du Pré where St. Thérèse made her first Holy Communion. I was startled when I was suddenly asked to recite the Apostles' Creed and the Lord's Prayer, as I had never said them in French.

"May I recite them in English?" I stammered, under my breath. It was the first hard moment, and it was the bishop who made it easy for me, as simply and naturally as he had assuaged many others.

"Of course," he told me in an answering whisper, "God understands every language as well as every heart." I believe it was this statement which sounded the keynote of that day, and of all the days which have followed, for that matter. It was a day in which my heart was filled with joy and happiness. I knew past all shadow of doubt that in this consecrated chapel I had come home. That was why nothing seemed unnatural. I belonged. I was not a stranger within the gates, or a guest courteously received. I was in my Father's House at last and He had made it mine.

Soon presents were pouring in, and telegrams. The Holy Father had sent his apostolic benediction. The

70

nuns showered me with their hearty congratulations. The bishop bestowed upon me fatherly advice which sank deep in my mind and heart and which I shall carry with me to the journey's end. He spoke so simply and so serenely. He reminded me that God understands all languages even as He understands all hearts. He counseled me to make good use of whatever gifts the Lord had bestowed upon me. I know that everything the bishop said was wise and kind, no less than challenging, and I have tried in a humble way to put it into practice. Oftentimes I have occasion to recall to mind the words he spoke with such fatherly kindness, words which have never failed to bring peace and strength to me.

"Simplify your life," said the bishop, "do not keep on taxing your strength and your spirit to the breaking point. When you learn to distinguish better between essentials and non-essentials, you will gain in repose what you lose in excitement, and life is always bound to be a thrilling adventure for you. There is no need that you yourself should strive to make it so. You have a pleasing penchant for laughter. Share it with those to whom it comes less easily. The good God is not a harsh master but a gentle Father. He rejoices in the happiness of His children. Go often to Communion. It will not only uplift you, it will assuage you. There is no better method of praying than the one which comes so naturally to you. Take constant refuge in it. The more you pray, the more you will be able to work. And your work is important. Do not minimize it in your own eyes. The printed page reaches thousands who can be reached in no other way. The spoken word reaches thousands more. Testify to the faith that is in you. Let your light so shine before men . . ."

Perhaps the bishop had more confidence in me than I deserve. Perhaps the ends he outlined are too great for me to meet. Perhaps my "way" will always be a little one, though it may widen and lengthen after all. It is too soon to tell. I can tread it only a step at a time, and those steps are slow. But often, in the past, I have thought—materially speaking—that my path was not only rough but obscure, that it led nowhere. Then suddenly, without warning, I found that it had taken me by a devious route to a broad and beautiful highway. I learned that whatever else I had to face, life held no blind alleys for me; there was always a way out. I think that—spiritually speaking—a similar experience may be in store for me, that this time the obscure path will lead upward as well as onward. I have no reason to doubt that this is so. I have every reason to believe it, and so in closing, I say:

I must go forth upon a pilgrim's journey;
Along a strange and dimly hidden road;
I cannot see what joy or care
Is waiting for me there,
Nor can I tell its length or test my load.
But this I know,
That faith will light my journey,
And mercy share the burden I must bring;
That love divine will ever tread the road with me,
And lead the pilgrim to the palace of the King.

The road I'll take upon my pilgrim's journey
May tread its way through sunny valleys fair;
May lie in gloom, may even lead
Where danger waits for me,
And I may find both joy and sorrow there.
But this I know,
That faith will light my journey,
And mercy share the burden I must bring;
That love divine will ever tread the road with me,
And lead the pilgrim to the palace of the King.

THE VERDICT OF HISTORY

Ross J. S. Hoffman

Research in history was the path that led Ross J. S. Hoffman into the Catholic Church. The main theme of his writings is the psychological and spiritual interpretation of history. He has embodied the results of profound historical research in *Great Britain and the German Trade Rivalry, 1875–1914,* which won him the George Louis Beer Prize of the American Historical Association in 1934. *Tradition and Progress* further enhanced his reputation as a penetrating thinker and accurate scholar.

He was born in 1902 of Protestant parentage, in Harrisburg, Pennsylvania. He was educated at Lafayette College, receiving his A.B. in 1923. He continued his studies at the University of Pennsylvania, where he served as assistant instructor in history from 1924 to 1926, receiving his M.A. in 1926 and his Ph.D. in 1932.

In 1926 he married Hannah McCruden, and that same year was appointed instructor in history at New York University, and in 1935 was made assistant professor. In 1938 he joined the faculty of Fordham University and in 1944 was designated professor of European history.

Though Dr. Hoffman had been an agnostic, his research in history turned his mind more and more to the Catholic religion and in 1931 he was received into the Church by Father John P. Monaghan, S.J., of Fordham. To explain this step to his friends, who considered it "rather strange behavior," he wrote his book *Restoration,* which might be characterized as a study in the philosophy of history, and which will repay careful reading.

Dr. Hoffman further embodies fruits of his historical research in *The Great Republic,* a study of international community, which aims at the revival of the values that underlie constitutional democracy, freedom, authority in the state, and an international order based on Christianity. In 1944 he published *Durable Peace,* a volume dealing with the outstanding problem of our day.

Besides writing historical works, Dr. Hoffman is a frequent contributor to periodicals. In recognition of his contributions to historical scholarship he was awarded an honorary Litt.D. by Villanova College in 1936 and an honorary LL.D. by Marquette University in 1937. In the following year he was elected president of the American Catholic Historical Association. Among his favorite recreations are golf, gardening, and reading light fiction, especially that of P. G. Wodehouse and Hilaire Belloc.

IT WOULD be difficult to say with certainty just what experience was the beginning of my march toward Catholicism. The whole early background of my life was essentially Protestant, although during my lifetime neither of my parents was an active member of any Protestant communion. No systematic religious instruction was given me in childhood, although my mother often told me stories from the Bible. She was not apathetic toward religion, as my father gave appearance of being, but was then and still is a quite religious woman. So far as I can put her faith into words, she seems to believe in Christ as a divine authority, but she is intensely individualistic, opposed to dogma and all ecclesiasticism, and very subjective in her conception of religious truth. It is religion of the inner spirit without cult of any kind, a somewhat inarticulate conviction hard to formulate into a creed.

Considering the nature of it, there can be nothing surprising in the fact that a number of years ago she was much interested in Christian Science. Several of my aunts became members of that sect, and although my mother did not follow their example, she did permit her children to attend the Christian Science Sunday school. That was all resembling formal religious instruction to which I was subjected during childhood. I do not think it left a very deep mark on me, and I was never actually received into Mrs. Eddy's select communion, nor for that matter into any other save the Holy Catholic Church. The first year in college happily extinguished forever what belief I had acquired in Christian Science. I could not square its curious doctrines with the world about me, and when I found that it actually denied the reality of the material universe I discarded it as an untrue philosophy. That rejection was a conscious intellectual act and no mere lapse into indifference fading at length into unbelief.

The ensuing college years had no positive significance in my religious life. Immersing myself in secular studies, especially history and the social sciences, I gave little time to thinking about religion. Life was busy and happy; I had no serious troubles and success came with startling ease. To be sure, the college honored religion by requiring all students to take courses given by a kindly Presbyterian chaplain, but like most of my friends I did not take these courses very seriously. Nobody, in fact, seemed to take them seriously, save the earnest lads planning for the Protestant pulpit, and I moved mostly in circles which were not theirs. One could pass the courses very easily and I invariably got A's apparently for a mere manifestation of interest, which, I fear I must confess, was not much more than a wish to divert the hour by starting an argument. That created the impression that one was a thinker, and the chaplain was such a charitable fellow that he gave high marks to us self-confessed agnostics and seemed to think that we were wrestling earnestly with God. This man showed a very warm and cordial interest in me, and although he did not seem to be very popular with the students generally, I heartily liked him and often visited him in his study. But I would have nothing of his religion, which was a simple Bible Christianity that he was trying somewhat frantically to "reconcile with modern science."

The more he sought to persuade me, the more incredible his beliefs came to appear, and I left college hardly doubting that supernatural religion was a thing suitable only for quite feeble and unemancipated minds. The whole atmosphere at college, I think, was really unfavorable to religion. No one could put his finger on any part of Christianity and declare that part to be an absolute certainty. What flourished on the campus was a rather denatured, modernized, elusive Protestantism. Those who taught it seemed vague and uncertain, and the ablest teachers not only did not teach it but almost studiously avoided even referring to it. They were cautious in expressing their own religious views and one found it hard to resist the suspicion that they did not really believe much in Christianity. Some whose confidence I gained certainly did not, and because I admired them most I formed the opinion that intelligent modern men did not regard Christianity as anything more than a pious fable tied up with some rather commendable morality. My first contact with Protestantism ended therefore in total rejection of it.

I do not believe that rejection can be rightly ascribed to a mere deadness of the spirit. I was really quite a zealous fellow for starting movements to improve the moral level of the campus. Like so much of modern Protestantism, I found a substitute for religion in uplift activity. Moreover, I became immersed in socialist literature and imbibed all the conventional radicalism of the age. In reading history I felt a burning sympathy for all the great rebels who had fought tyranny (especially ecclesiastical tyranny) and advanced what seemed plainly to have been the great cause of liberty. Such men as Luther and Voltaire were heroic giants whom I virtually idolized, and the whole roster of champions of national and popular freedom since the French Revolution was for me a veritable gallery of saints. I had a host of heroes in the ranks of contemporary radicals, and I longed to join the war upon the Church and capitalism, which I felt very sure were one and the same. I had an unerring instinct for minority movements, and was forever annoying "right-thinking" people with unpopular opinions on religion, politics, and economics. The disposition I describe almost led me (the fact is not strange) into the Protestant ministry.

Toward the close of my senior year I played with the notion of entering a liberal seminary to do graduate work and fit myself for the pulpit. My idea was not very clear, and doubtless it would never have worked out, but it seemed to me that many eminent churchmen did not accept any part of Christianity save the social gospel of helping the downtrodden. I thought that, like the Mohammedans, I could honor Christ as a prophet, the prophet of a renovated social order. It seemed possible to slide over the supernatural and use the pulpit for preaching socialism, pacifism, cosmopolitan-

76

ism, and other branches of the latest enlightenment. I would be a kind of John Haynes Holmes clergyman, have a church in New York, write for the advanced reviews, travel in Europe, meet famous liberals and radicals, and pontificate on all the questions worthy of my interest. Even though I did not go into clerical life, there was the attractive seminary offer of a few years' graduate study at almost no cost, and I was without funds. Something like that was in the back of my head although I may here fail to do it justice. But the plan did not materialize and I believe even the mood passed rather quickly. I decided instead to go to graduate school to study history, which, after a swing around Europe and teaching a term in a secondary school, I did.

The first trip to Europe had an important influence upon my religious viewpoint. I went off alone, a very young man, and it seemed a tremendous adventure. It gave me a long-awaited opportunity to be alone with myself and to think leisurely. The time was shortly after the close of World War I, in which I was deeply interested, and I gave my attention rather to learning contemporary conditions than to seeing and reflecting upon the Old World. Nevertheless, it was on this trip that I first came to know something of and to acquire a feeling for the great memorials of medieval religious life. I visited wonderingly many old Catholic places and even heard many masses. But of course I looked as one who did not see, and in my monumental ignorance of the Catholic faith all this made little impression at the time. For me the Church remained what I presumed it had ever been: a great organized superstition standing against all that I hoped for in the world. Doubtless long ago it had done important work for civilization (of which I was but dimly aware), but in the twentieth century it was so obviously an obstacle to enlightened progress. Was it not a compound of priestcraft and belief in miracles, which the march of civilization was leaving stranded in the rear? Nevertheless, from this experience dates the beginning of a gradual realization that the Christianity which I had rejected in college was very different from that of the historic Mother Church. I began from that time onward slowly to realize that historic Christianity was far richer, far more profound, fascinating, wonderful, and lovely than the Calvinistic dish which had previously been served up to me.

Returning to America, I put in several months teaching in a small high school. The work was very easy and consisted simply in guiding young students over an elementary survey of European history. In those days I studied little but talked much, and I read the fashionable current literature as I never had before. I fell in heartily with that Dreiser-Mencken *Zeitgeist,* and I could not get enough of such writers as Wells, Shaw, and Bertrand Russell. My drift then was in the current of real atheism and I was carried very far down the stream. A conviction was hardening that all religion, even of the most attenuated kind, was false, and the seeking after it a pathetic emotional weakness.

I am sure it is very true that when I entered graduate school I had a quite pleasing opinion of myself as a daring and advanced thinker. And therefore it was not at all pleasant when I presently fell to suspecting that not only were my mental powers quite ordinary but that I had taken up advanced study with a preparation rather below average. The intellectual competition was much stiffer than any I had previously known and it was not long before a certain loss of confidence and doubt of my abilities overtook me. The need for a great deal of serious and careful study came home with considerable force, and I hope that I slipped a little from my altitude of intellectual conceit.

History, so Napoleon once said, is the only true philosophy. That observation, if not entirely true, at least suggests a great truth. The study of history does not always make men wiser, but it can and most certainly should do so. A philosophy based on history, if that history be true, is one based on experience, which is a very trustworthy guide. Historical study punctures very disconcerting holes in many of the political, moral, and social theories developed by the shallow speculations and rationalizations of every age, but especially of an age that is contemptuous of the past, such as our own times. It shows us how very often our new truths are nothing but old lies, and it breaks down that assumption of continuous upward progress which confuses so much of our thinking. Historical study should develop a deep respect for the past; it should enable one to stop looking down upon his ancestors, to become the contemporary of Augustine or Francis, to live and walk with them, to realize that they, too, ran the gamut of human experience and that their experience is as valid as ours. Thus are we freed from what Mr. Chesterton somewhere has called the degrading slavery of being mere children of our age.

Now the point of all this is that progress in sound historical knowledge began gradually to liberate me from a number of lightly and superficially gained secondhand convictions. Once I had been quite sure that history taught us a number of definite and special lessons, that it was the great arsenal of proofs for such contentions as, for example, that mankind is steadily ascending through ever higher stages of progress toward some unseen but nevertheless highly desirable goal, that the human mind is growing wiser all the time, that justice grows ever more triumphant. But I slowly came to the conclusion that this was very largely nonsense, and I was able to perceive that a great deal of what I had called "progress" was only movement toward certain discernible (for those with eyes to see) ends which are anything but desirable. This altered point of view came very slowly and I shall not try to trace it now.

Preoccupation with historical studies for some time did not weaken my atheistic point of view. I was, of course, learning how socially useful religion might be, but feeling at the same time no personal need for it myself. I know that I came in time to the morally indefensible position that religion was a necessary instrument of social control but quite unnecessary for the enlightened individual—an opinion which led at length to a sense of the miserable tragedy that men, in order to go on living, must believe in some figment of their imagination. The chief reason for this religious stagnation while engrossed in history was, I realize now, that I had plunged into a fairly intensive study of the nineteenth century before getting an adequate grasp on the larger history of Christendom and Western culture.

I was studying closely the growth of liberalism, democracy, socialism, industry, capitalism, tariffs, imperialism, diplomacy, constitutions, etc.; but the spiritual heritage of more Christian times got almost no attention; and my study touched the churches only in reading with approval of the successive disestablishments, and of the devastating attack by science and the higher criticism upon what I still presumed to be essentially Christian orthodoxy. In brief, it was only the strictly secular and secularizing aspects of modern history with which I was concerned. The papacy seemed for long an exotic plant in my garden of liberalism and revolution—a relic of the Dark Ages which would pass with the onward march of progress, and which was not quite irrelevant to the really significant movements in modern civilization. It and the whole thing for which it spoke seemed the unwearied opponents of a higher level of culture and therefore doomed to go down. I did not even admire the venerable monarchy, for I was reading such books as Thayer's *Dawn of Italian Independence,* which paints an almost wicked picture of the popes a century ago. The Church and its head seemed the implacable and unreformable enemies of a freer and more humane world, the allies of Metternich, the Ferdinands, and all the despotic crowned conspirators against the rights of man. I was almost instinctively on the side of the Carbonari, the Free Masons, and all the anti-clerical revolutionaries, and remained there even long after I had formed more critical judgments upon their behavior.

The second year in graduate school brought my first systematic and really fruitful inquiry into medieval civilization. A course in the institutions of the Middle Ages gave me an insight into the constitutional growth of the Church, Roman and barbarian law, and early monarchical institutions. The course was an advanced one, presupposing on the part of the students a considerable fund of knowledge about the general character of medieval culture, and I found it necessary to read widely in order to understand what the professor was talking about. Up to that time there can be no doubt whatever that my ignorance of the Middle Ages was nothing short of scandalous: for me it was all a kind of black chasm bounded on the one side by Merovingian barbarity and on the other by Petrarch's sonnets and the brilliance of the Renaissance.

All that my undergraduate survey had left with me were hazy notions of monkery, baronial lawlessness, barbaric crusades—an age when the ablest minds are said to have eschewed all interest in this world and pondered the problem of how many angels could dance on the head of a pin. Some of the emperors who warred upon the popes, Henry IV and the great Fredericks for example, had made a favorable and lasting impression on me, as had giants like Hildebrand and Innocent III. I remember liking very much Peter Abelard and Arnold of Brescia, for if a man got into trouble with the Church I felt vaguely that he must have been contending rightly. St. Bernard left me cold, and so did Dominic; the only saint I think I really liked was the immortal Francis, although that was not because I knew anything about him but because I had got the impression he was something of a "liberal." As for the multitude of heretics in that age I thought of them as unfortunate martyrs to the cause of religious liberty. This confession of abysmal ignorance should not be taken as a reflection upon my professor, for the truth is I never gave his course the attention it undoubtedly deserved. I have now taught long enough myself to know how possible it is, especially in the study of medieval history, for students to come out from a course with a passing mark but with minds immaculately unspotted by any sound information and genuine understanding.

But to get along with this, the point is that coming to grips with the mighty twelfth and thirteenth centuries was a profoundly important intellectual experience for me. I discovered that fresh world of myriad variety and richness of color which has ever since seemed to me as beautiful as dawn. This is no sentimental nostalgia for things Gothic, no mere romanticist fancy. There were vigor and health in that world, and passion, heroism, and hard thinking. Fists and brains then were perhaps more splendidly active than in any other time since the great age of the Greek city-states, and my temper is such that I like that kind of activity. I became and I remain convinced that life has never been more thrillingly worth living than it was when Francis, Thomas, Innocent III, and Dante stalked this earth. The secret of it all was that men had timeless and priceless values to defend, and that upon the whole of European society was stamped the conception of a wise and beneficent spiritual power to which men in every walk of life owed a supreme obligation.

Writers on the later so-called Renaissance period have exulted over the birth of individualism—the coming of a new man emancipated from the restraints of asceticism and the limitations imposed by the corporative, hierarchic structure of thirteenth-century society, the man with high confidence in himself, bold, self-reliant, autonomous. But far richer in individuality was the civilization of St. Thomas' time. The colors of medieval life were like the glass of a cathedral window. Despite the uniformity of religious allegiance and the concept of a universal thing called Christendom there was the most astonishing cultural variety. Popular speech, dress, manners, art, have never been less conventionalized. The Middle Ages were the classic age of queer people, of freakish individuals, and I do not see how one can make the acquaintance of medieval saints, or even visit a museum of medieval antiquities, without being impressed by the fact.

Men were never more defiant of pattern; the common spirit which animated them seems to have made a different dance of every life. In that unified, corporative, spiritually directed civilization men were very free, very objective, very little self-conscious; and this, I fancy, goes far to explain the richness of medieval individuality. Every flower in that fresh and lovely garden of life, in which Francis sang his verses of thankful joy for God's goodness and love, I came to see had sprung from the soil of Catholic Christianity. The Church was the mother of the new learning, the founder of the great universities, the inspiration of the great new architecture, the patron of towns and guilds, the defender of popular liberty, the very citadel and source of European culture and unity, fabulously rich in the capacity for galvanizing new life in a thousand directions. The truth came home to me that this "organized superstition" had presided over, nay, created, the most attractive and inspiring civilization of which I knew anything at all. I was not then and I am not now foolish enough to think it possible or even desirable to attempt the restoration of outmoded institutions. It never occurred to me that we could or should go back to the Middle Ages; but it did occur to me that the spirit that animated them was immeasurably fertile and timeless, capable of penetrating the body of any civilization and restoring it to life and health.

So it was that my discovery of Catholic civilization led me on to a tireless investigation of the Church. Her history became my favorite field of reading, some of her saints my favorite historical characters. I became a strong admirer and a defender of the Church, and was always delighted when opportunities came to reveal the enthusiasm to others. More and more the Church assumed for me the pivot position in the whole history of Western civilization since the disintegration of the ancient Roman Empire. Thus I became a friend of the Church (which sounds somewhat silly, I think), and my friendly interest did not flag. I fell to visiting Catholic churches with considerable frequency because of this interest aroused by history. I did not always like what I saw there, but the fascination did not relax and I took considerable delight in learning something of sacraments, liturgical forms, the precious meaning of the mass, etc. It became something of a hobby of mine to acquire as much information as I could about the Faith, and I read a good deal of popular apologetic literature. I was deeply moved by Mr. Chesterton's splendid books and read all of them I could lay my hands on. I began, in short, almost to love the Church before it had occurred to me that one might love God or even have an intelligible and rational belief in Him.

Meanwhile, there passed a few years which I spent teaching in a university, lecturing on medieval and modern European history, and giving my whole time to studies in those fields. My undergraduate radicalism sobered down slowly, although uneasiness over some of the outstanding currents of modern history kept steadily mounting in me. And not only did my respect for the Church as the central force in our civilization go on growing, but again and again I was able to discover in the Faith a revolutionary and blasting criticism of those currents and a solution to the problems they have created. I have a somewhat political and sociological temper of mind, and the great forces of capitalism, nationalism, liberalism, democracy, and socialism have engaged much of my thought.

My early position on the extreme left I abandoned for a kind of centrist position, but as I grew distrustful of socialism I became even more hostile to the excesses of capitalism, nationalism, and the failing liberalism of the nineteenth century. Behind most of the critics of the present social and economic system I saw only more of the same materialistic philosophy that characterizes its defenders, and I was coming to know dimly that society, if it was to live on, needed some creed or ideal transcending bare material values. The socialist Utopia of peace and material prosperity for all

84

fired me with no enthusiasm. I reached the dilemma of our bankrupt liberals and could see no solution at all for the stupendous problems that face our civilization. Although I had missed participation in the late war I knew fairly well what that war was and why it came about. I did not want to see any repetition of such fratricide, but yet the ideal of permanent peace which we are trying to realize did not appear so much better. It seemed to be only the ideal of a banker's peace for the security of business. If it was to be realized, then I suspected we should simply be in for another age of the Antonines and I knew what would then follow.

Yet some banner against the tribalistic nationalism of our time had to be raised, and here was one of the places that the Church came in to offer a solution of the problem. The national state was not evil in its very nature, and it was un-Catholic only in its selfish egoism; taught to respect the rights of others, there was a place for it in a moral order whose ultimate aims were universal and spiritual. A Christian peace seemed a peace with purpose and justification. Without admitting the claims of the Church, I saw that it possessed the only adequate and morally defensible peace program that could be put before the world. The Church alone was able to point beyond peace, to give a reason for it, and, therefore, to excite a lasting will for it.

I have indicated that the evolution of our social-economic system and its attendant enormities have commanded much of my thought and study. Perhaps no ideal has been more constantly before me than the ideal of social justice. I stood with the socialists until I came to regard their thinking as unrealistic and to see that they had no cure for material greed, which is the cancer of our society. Their anti-religious bias fortifies that same immoderate concern for material things which has given us the capitalistic order they seek to overthrow. They will not slay the monster with their program for a secular Utopia of fraternal equalitarianism. Socialism has, of course, in the last generation

85

been crumbling into mere opportunist reform (which is often very good social engineering), and Bolshevism, which contains all that was ever bad in socialism plus an increased and more bitter hatred of Christianity (for it knows its only real enemy). I shifted with the socialists of the right into pure opportunism without losing an ounce of my passion for social justice, but I could see no victory ahead for us. I quite lost faith in the progressive and ultimate triumph of critical social intelligence and human liberty over the gathering forces of capitalistic feudalism and neo-pagan tyranny. It seemed to me that we did not care enough for victory. There were no timeless and priceless values that we were willing to defend against the price of a little more immediate comfort. The liberals, I think, will give way inch by inch; indeed, it is plain that is exactly what they are doing all over the Western world; like the Stoics, they mean well but have not heart enough for a real revolution. They recognize nothing actually worth dying for.

Now here again the Church came in to offer a set of principles and a program, realistic and just, penetrated with the spirit of charity. I read again and again the great *Rerum Novarum* of Leo XIII, and each time my mind seemed washed by a clean, bracing wind. There is no more searching analysis of the evils in modern economic society, and it seems to me to be a much more revolutionary document than the *Communist Manifesto;* for it strikes the root causes of social disorder and, if applied, its principles would universally pluck them out. Let any man who foolishly thinks the Church to be the conservative ally of things as they are, no matter how bad they are, read Leo's doctrine or the recent *Quadrigesimo Anno* of Pius XI, and then let him measure the gulf between the world as it is and the world as the Pope would have it. I think he will agree that our world is much nearer Moscow than Rome, and that Pius XI, not Stalin, is the real revolutionist.

Gradually the conviction grew upon me that the

Church was a great kingdom at war with all the enemies against whom I had ranged myself. It proposed peace that men might fight all the harder in a genuinely worthwhile cause. It was the only cure for nationalism that was not worse than the disease, and it raised up moral economic principles with which to fight the greed of both right and left. It went to the root of all social injustice: absence of charity. It sought to deliver men from industrial slavery and defended liberty against its major enemy, the modern absolutist state. It beckoned man to the perennial crusade, the permanent revolution, the most radical and blasting of all revolutions: "I bring not peace but a sword." For long the challenge would have been quite irresistible had I been able to believe. When a realization of the immense political, economic, social, and moral potentialities in Catholic Christianity came home to me, I felt that it was the greatest disappointment in the world. For it was the answer to everything; only the answer was false.

I have dwelt at considerable length upon my preoccupation with secular problems because most of my intellectual experience had concerned them. For half a dozen years the major part of my life had been given to these matters. They were "shop" for me, my stock in trade, and they explain why it was that the sociological and political aspects of Catholicism were the aspects of the Faith that first presented themselves forcibly to me.

But in the course of time real spiritual hunger began also to grow in me, and it was contributed to in large measure by the collapse of secular loyalties which had commanded me for so long. A certain paralyzing indecisiveness crept over me as they dropped away one by one; capacity for decision of mind and action was diminished, and some of the zest of living began to go. I found myself joining the panic rush for escapes. As life lost more and more of what meaning it had held I felt a general debilitation threatening me, and my whole point of view was resolving into one of pure negation. There was no pearl of great price, nothing of stable worth and permanent validity. I had no yard-stick with which to measure the world, no flag under which to fight it. I felt myself growing "sick," and old, so to speak, like a man of the later Roman Empire.

Whatever inclination there may have been toward making a general landslide of life, the circumstance of having become a husband and father acted as a strong brake upon it. My wife is a daughter of the Church and a very sane, wise, perceptive woman. I had a great deal of respect for her opinions, and a quite fathomless respect for her character. I learned to detect in her some of the influences of the Faith upon character, for I think that it nourished in her the really great virtues of charity, honor, and courage, and beautified her life in countless ways. It seemed to have given her a balance, a serenity, and a mysterious wisdom which are evidently the rewards of virtue. Yet I must acknowledge in all honesty that for long she acted as a check upon whatever disposition I had to become a Catholic. I suppose it was nothing but absurd masculine pride; certainly when I called it by that name it ran out like a devil. That she prayed God to perform again the miracle of bringing sight to the blind and converting me to the Faith I now know, but she never even hinted to me of any such desire. In fact she used to say jestingly that her prayers were enough for both of us, and that if I were ever converted to the Faith I should probably become a single-minded fanatic.

I had the usual measure of troubles and worries that visit men who marry and found families, but I shall not relate them. They were not serious, but they had a maturing effect on me, I think, and served to reveal my spiritual poverty and the shallowness of agnosticism. They left their marks and broke down some of that self-confident autonomy of spirit which I had cultivated in more irresponsible years. They did not convert me, but they did chasten me a little and give me a view of my interior bankruptcy. One's utter loneliness in a meaningless world enveloped in darkness came home with greater force, and I was slowly taught that if God actually existed and cared about men, then I had need of Him.

These experiences contributed each their measure to my ultimate decision to seek religion seriously again, or shall I say for the first time? And all the while a thousand other small, fleeting experiences made for the same end. It would be quite impossible to set them down, for often they were so elusive as to escape me almost immediately after they occurred. They came while reading, conversing, lecturing, loafing. A flash of perception would reveal some Christian truth wonderfully clear and convincing; some act of charity or heroism would open up a spacious vista of understanding; a Christian truth put to the test would be happened upon and it would ring true. If I possessed Mr. Chesterton's great gift for articulating this sort of thing I might profitably get these experiences before me on paper, but since I do not, any attempt would be very clumsy. Often the consideration of some great heresy, such as Manichaeism or Calvinism, brought sudden flashes of insight into free will, the Fall, grace, etc., and the testing of the heresies in their social consequences not only brought me to "feel" Catholic truth, but also to apprehend the basic importance of dogmatic structure in religion.

These flashes of insight were accompanied by a gradual expansion of my whole perceptive being. In spite of a developing pro-Catholic point of view, I had long remained in the intellectual bondage of materialistic rationalism, holding as credible only that which did not violate what I regarded as natural law. Miracles were simply nonsense, to be explained usually by the unreliability of witnesses. That there might be supernatural disturbance of the order of the universe was a preposterous notion; it did not happen, it had never happened, and any report of it was unworthy of belief. Christianity, I was prepared to admit, because of its long syncretistic history and the enormous span of the

Church's recorded experience, might symbolize in a mystic way some deep truths, but the account of its supernatural origins was a fable. To study the historical evidence attesting it was bootless since the documents damned themselves by their inherent incredibility. The universe was obedient to no laws but its own, received perhaps from a Creator, but nonetheless completely bound by them.

Now this view of the universe began to undergo modification. I came to see how narrow it was, how little it explained and how much it evaded. It skirted everything mysterious and closed the mind even to a recognition of mystery. It was silent on the question of what I am and why I am; it had nothing to say about birth or death; it skipped all the questions that really matter. It confined one's whole being in a tiny fortress of feeling without a single window for light from without. If this was freedom of thought it was, as Mr. Chesterton has remarked, like the freedom of a jail from the outside world. It came to appear a profoundly unphilosophic way of looking at the world, and it brought to me a kind of intellectual shame for having been so long content to live in a very little universe. I used to speak of myself as a "rationalist" the while I was shutting my mind to a realm of transcendental truth outside the fortress of my being, and also hidden within me, toward which right reason pointed imperiously.

An absolute confidence that God exists awakened in me as these implications of reason became more demanding upon my mind. Deafened ears came at last to hear the truth which the whole universe shouts. The argument from order and design was irrefutable, and those who dismissed it as a stale or exploded contention had never met it rationally. It is an old and timeless truth. The Author of the universe is a Creative Personality, separate from His creation as an artist is separate from his work, and every stroke on the cosmic canvas is from His brush. As we contemplate that, every road of our thought leads out into the mysterious region of truth beyond the limits of our world of sense and reason. But could man penetrate this mystery, or even feel his way into it darkly? Plainly not without a special light of revelation. Had that been given?

That was the question which I came at long last to raise in deadly earnest. Had a light been lighted? I knew enough about the religions of the world and the history of Christianity to feel an overpowering certainty as to where it was if it was anywhere. A tree is known by its fruits. I had wandered through a forest of trees, and if there was one special tree whose fruits were life and light I was sure I knew how to find it.

I decided that I would test this light, that I would strive to determine whether there might really be a spiritual home for me (and for all men), or whether all really was void. The position from which I moved forward was substantially this: God exists and He made the universe and man; since He created man He must care for man (unless man is no more than a kind of whim of God, which surely does not satisfy the mind); since all things must be possible to God supernatural revelation was not by its very nature incredible. Also I felt very sure that the eye with which to recognize a revelation could not be the eye of the intellect alone, since that would make of God a secret to which only the learned could be privy. Although divine revelation, granting for the moment its possibility, would certainly not violate right reason and sane intellect, yet I felt it must be recognizable also through other and deeper channels of understanding common to all men. Every man cannot be learned, but he can have love, good will, and purity of heart. It seemed to me, therefore, that the chief test of the truth of revelation must lie in its successful recognition by men of simplicity and humility, and in the nature of its transforming influence upon their lives. And yet another conviction was this: I was very sure I could not love God without apprehending His Personality in the Incarnation. Without that He could be only an abstraction, difficult to grasp as a genuine reality; and moreover, the keystone of the whole arch of Christianity was not there if Christ were nothing more than a philosopher. I had come to see clearly what, it seems to me, so many persons fail to grasp, namely, that *Catholicism is an organic whole springing from the germinal seed of the Incarnation.* So that my last question was just the old question and the most deeply important one that has ever been asked: "What think ye of Christ?"

I acted upon my decision by seeking help from one who was wonderfully equipped to give it. He set me a simple exercise. "Divest yourself," he advised, "as completely as possible of all previous ideas of Christ that you have ever entertained. Take the Gospels as historical documents throwing light upon a strange and unknown personality and approach them as a rationally-minded man hearing for the first time of Christ. See then what you think of Him afresh. Your mind has reached a measure of maturity, you have seen something of men and speculated upon their nature. You have encountered various philosophies and, through reason and experience, learned to assess them. Your experience has a certain validity. Now check the personality and the philosophy of this Man with the experience you have had in the world of men and ideas."

I followed the general direction of these suggestions and took up the Gospels anew with quite the same attitude I would take toward any other historical documents. I sought to study a man and not a God, for I was deliberately proceeding upon the theory that no man had ever been or ever could be God. Let there be no mistake about this: the idea of the Incarnation was purposely excluded from the exercise. It proved a very interesting and quite surprising inquiry, for although I believe that in the past I had read, at intervals and in broken sections, every word of all four documents, I had never before attempted to draw a full-length portrait of Christ. Not the least part of my surprise now was the discovery that I had never really known much about Christ. I had known somewhat vaguely the Christ of the Sermon on the Mount, the preceptor of humility, brotherly love, and self-effacement. I had known the meek Christ, but I had not known the *terribly* meek Christ, nor the angry Christ of authority and violent words. Here, I saw, was no mere benevolent philosopher urging the gentler virtues, but an imperious and demanding figure who taught "as one having authority and not as the scribes."

But the greatest amazement was finding myself becoming a partisan of His enemies. For the first time in my life I began to have some understanding of the mad rage which this presumptuous and irritating Person must have aroused. I began to wonder what we would think of a man who, after violating one of our most precious institutions (as He broke the Jewish Sabbath), coolly remarked that he was superior to it. I thought we should have rather a serious case against him as an outrager of our laws. My reaction to Jesus at Nazareth when He entered the synagogue, read from the Scriptures, and announced their fulfillment that day, was exactly the same. I murmured with the people who heard Him, "Is not this the son of Joseph?" And when He rebuked them I was strongly tempted to join with those that "rose up and thrust him out of the city."

Again and again I was scandalized by His acts and words. When He presumed to forgive sins I said with the scribes and Pharisees, "Who is this who speaketh blasphemies? Who can forgive sins but God alone?" He exhibited a most arrogant and offending egotism: "Behold a greater than Jonas is here . . . behold a greater than Solomon is here." I also discovered in this preacher of the Sermon on the Mount a quivering and terrible anger which found expression in such words as "hypocrites, whited sepulchres," and "generation of vipers," and in such awful threats as the one for the city which should not receive His disciples: "It shall be more tolerable for the land of Sodom and Gomorrah in the day of judgment than for that city." This Man's tongue could sting like a whiplash laid upon an open wound. And I found in Him, too, a demand for personal allegiance reaching the very limits of effrontery. His disciples are to keep His commandments and not to be scandalized by Him. "He that loveth father or mother more than me is not worthy of me"—so does He ask that loyalty to Himself be the first of all loyalties, making bold to promise His disciples that if they would take up the cross and follow Him they should have a crown of life. What kind of man was this who could ask for Himself all that men could conceivably owe to God? "All things are delivered unto me by my father . . . I and my father are one . . . He that hath seen me hath seen the father . . . I am the way, the truth and the life"—what preposterous sayings are these from a mere man! I understood for the first time the passion of the high priest when he rent his robes and said, "What need we any further witnesses? You have heard the blasphemy." I was both puzzled and scandalized by His vaunted sinlessness: His most violent words of denunciation were reserved for hypocrites, and yet He could ask, "Which of ye convinceth me of sin?" Such words from one who is no more than human are downright revolting. The more I speculated upon the character and personality of the man Jesus the more offended I became, the more monstrous His imposture appeared. His fellow countrymen "wondered and said: How came this man by this wisdom and miracles? Is not this the carpenter's son? . . . Whence therefore hath he all these things? And they were scandalized in his regard." And so was I.

It seemed to me, indeed, that if this Man were just a man, like any other man, it would be charitable to write Him down as a lunatic; else the Pharisees were right and He met a deserved end. But as mere man He was not credible at all, for He was a defiance of the common nature of man. No man putting forward the preposterous claims He made for Himself could have also inspired that perfect love which we find His disciples paying to Him, for He scandalized even them on several occasions. Nor is it even imaginable that any man could unite so perfectly in himself the qualities of meekness and terrible anger, and although with knowledge of his own stainless perfection could yet weep with compassion for all men. How indeed could it have been that this imperious egotist lived and taught a timeless philosophy of life, yet surrendered willingly His own perfect life in the passion and ignominy of the cross? His absolute sincerity stands proved on Calvary, yet He declared Himself to be God! A man who would set out to be God (as blasphemous an imposture as can be imagined) must, it seemed to me, end in moral ruin. But Calvary was surely not that. It became very plain to me that Jesus was not to be explained in terms of humanity alone, not even humanity touched with lunacy. The latter theory is unworthy of discussion. The Sermon on the Mount and the parable teachings are sanity and we all know it. The mind of Christ had a flashing, rapierlike gift for going to the heart of things in swift simplicity. The theory that he was insane cannot survive a thoughtful reading of the Gospels.

I could not conceive of more than four possible interpretations of Christ. He was (1) a philosopher and prophet, only human but sane; or (2) He was a lunatic; or (3) His character as we know it in the Gospels is wholly or largely fictitious; or (4) He was the Incarnate Son, true man and true God. Now the first two theories failed to solve the riddle of this strange personality. As a mere man I found it impossible to believe in His real existence, and when I subjected Him to the lunacy test I found Him superlatively sane. But what of the theory that the whole Gospel story is fiction or just a legend grown up around some man of forceful personality, some impressive Eastern prophet?

With the exception of a few writers who have never been taken seriously, no historical student questions the historicity of Jesus; many, however, have striven laboriously to show the Man of the Gospels as one very much obscured by decorative legend. Was this not the most probable explanation of Christ? The East has always been prolific in cults and prophets, and the Roman Empire swarmed with them in early Christian times; so that it seemed rather plausible that the Christ we know from apostolic writings was the creature of fertile religious imagination or even conscious fraud. This is the theory of most persons who find themselves unable to give credence to the doctrines of the Incarnation and Redemption.

Now I was no expert in the so-called higher criticism, but I was not so innocent of a knowledge of antiquity and the history of the New Testament as to be unable to see the weakness of the legend theory. Indeed, I am now disposed to think that this is the weakest of all the theories. It cannot be squared with the ascertainable facts of early Church history. I know the early days of the Church are commonly regarded as having a rather dim historical visibility, but actually that is not the truth at all. I began to see that this visibility was not so low if one was able to grasp the nature of the Church and to estimate rationally the value of tradition as historical evidence. Even the documentary evidence is much more formidable than most persons appear to realize, the New Testament alone containing four sketches of the life of Christ, a history of the early Apostolic Church, and twenty-one letters from the hands of Paul, Peter, James, John, and Jude. I am not aware that any other phase of first-century history is so copiously documented.

But the great question was how far this New Testament portrait of Christ departed from a likeness of the Man as He actually was. There seemed no conceivable way of resolving that problem save by speculation, but all such speculation has been governed too much by personal philosophy. Now I tackled the problem in this fashion: I considered the nature of the Catholic Church and her history, contrasting what she taught in one age with what she taught in another. That is to say, I sought to discover deviations in doctrine from one age to another in order to determine whether, in the clear light of unimpeachable historical record, it was in the nature of the Church to make departures from the original deposit of alleged revelation.

I went back to the Council of Trent, from there to Constance, from there to Innocent III and the Fourth Lateran, then back to Nicaea, and from Nicaea to the apostolic documents. Instead of discovering doctrinal deviations and improvisations I found that one of the most conspicuous characteristics of the Church was a constant, purposeful conservation of doctrine, a careful guardianship of the whole treasure of revelation. The Church, of course, grew in function, in definition, in assimilation, but it did not innovate any teaching foreign to or inconsistent with the faith of apostolic times. The history of the Church from the age in which the New Testament books were written down to the present day revealed a constant and unchanging nature, and it was in that nature to maintain with jealous care a certain body of doctrine. Now if the New Testament portrait of Christ disfigures and obscures the original Man, the nature of the Church during the first few decades after Calvary and Pentecost must have been in striking contrast with the nature of the Church at the time, say, that Paul wrote his earliest epistles and Mark composed his gospel. This amounts to saying that those who knew Jesus personally—that is, in the flesh—made a legendary figure of Him, while all the generations that came afterward disfigured the concept of His personality not at all. The more I thought about this, the more absurd it appeared. From what I could learn of Peter, Paul, and the other Apostles it seemed quite unbelievable that they were perpetrators of a great fraud. If they sincerely believed in what they taught to the world (and their sincerity is proved by their martyrdom), surely they must have regarded their knowledge of Him as the most precious of all knowledge and therefore not to be tampered with. Moreover, they were mostly simple men, close to reality, and such men are not so easily deceived by things they see, touch, and experience. The more I strove to build up, through historical imagination, a picture of apostolic times the more firmly I became convinced of the honesty and trustworthiness of the first witnesses.

So there was left only one possible explanation of the riddle of Christ: He was what He claimed to be —the Incarnation of God, the Divine Word made flesh. When I added His divinity to His humanity the pieces of the puzzle fell into shape. I could find no escape from that conclusion and I felt that I must either banish it all from my mind as an insoluble enigma or accept this only possible solution. But that solution no longer warred with my philosophic outlook upon the universe; it no longer violated my experience of myself and of my fellow men. Moreover, I found myself coming under the imperious spell of this mighty and towering Personality, found myself capable of loving Him. God granted me the gift of faith, and I confessed with Peter: "Thou art the Christ, the son of the living God." He no longer seemed a remote figure out of the East two thousand years ago, but a timeless life as young and fresh today as ever. I had no sudden conversion. Faith came very slowly, and it was not easy to feel the reality of it after so many years of negation. As the new point of view was gradually gained I had alternating moments of lively conviction and sluggish doubt. But grace was not wanting and when I knew that I had found my Father, I also knew my Mother, the Mother of us all, and she deigned to adopt me as her own.

MY EASY ROAD TO ROME

Theodore Maynard

Born in 1890 in Madras, India, of English parents who were Protestant missionaries, Theodore Maynard studied for the Congregational ministry. His studies opened up a new vista and brought him in contact with the historical facts surrounding the establishment of a church by Christ.

The first priest to whom he spoke was the one to whom Maynard went for instruction, having already become convinced that the Catholic Church was the true Church. Thus as a young man he embraced the Catholic faith, and in 1915 entered the Dominican novitiate, where he remained seven months.

His first book was a collection of verse entitled *Laughs and Whiffs of Song,* to which G. K. Chesterton wrote an introduction. This was followed by *Drums of Defeat,* another book of poems, and *Carven from the Laurel Tree,* a collection of essays. These he soon followed with *A Tankard of Ale,* and a novel, *The Divine Adventure,* all written while he was working in the Ministry of Munitions during World War I.

Meanwhile, he had married Sarah Katherine Casey, an Irish girl born in South Africa, who was already the author of a novel and who was soon to write a play for the Abbey Theatre. Her literary career became somewhat hampered, however, by a family of seven children.

Theodore Maynard acknowledges the great influence of G. K. Chesterton upon his thought and writings and to a lesser extent that of Hilaire Belloc.

In 1920 Mr. Maynard came to the United States, where he has since made his home. He received his A.B. from Fordham, his M.A. from Georgetown, and his Ph.D. from the Catholic University of America. During all this time he continued his teaching and his writing. Dr. Maynard still thinks of himself chiefly as a poet, though since 1929 he has been devoting most of his time to the writing of biography and history.

His writings along these lines include *De Soto and the Conquistadores,* and this was followed by *The Odyssey of Francis Xavier* (1936); *The World I Saw,* autobiography (1938); *Apostle of Charity,* a life of St. Vincent de Paul (1939); *Queen Elizabeth* (1940); *The Reed and the Rock: Portrait of Simon Bruté* (1942); *Orestes Brownson: Yankee, Radical, Catholic* (1943); *Too Small a World: The Life of Francesca Cabrini* (1945); *Humanist as Hero: The Life of Sir Thomas More* (1947), and *Richest of the Poor,* a life of St. Francis of Assisi. His *Story of American Catholicism* (1941), which is perhaps his most important work, presents in a single volume the history of the Catholic Church in the United States from Leif Ericson to our own time.

He has written a book of literary criticism, *Our Best Poets* (1922) and has edited two anthologies, *The Book of Modern Catholic Verse* (1926) and *The Book of Modern Catholic Prose* (1927). In 1933 he published *Preface to Poetry*, a study of the meaning and technique of poetry. In addition to writing the numerous books already listed, Dr. Maynard has written many articles for periodicals on a great variety of subjects. On October 19, 1946, he married Kathleen Sheehan and resides at 44 Murray Avenue, Port Washington, New York.

M Y ACCEPTANCE of the truth of Catholicism thirty-six years ago, when I was a very young man, so far as it had a natural basis, reposed, it seems to me, on common sense. But to boast of so homespun a quality would be to prove its lack; one might almost as well be proud of being humble. I mention it only to indicate that my mode of approach should be possible to anyone.

As this disclaimer may seem too simple to be of much use as an explanation, I suppose I must say a little more about myself. Had I been inordinately clever, I might have discovered a number of reasons for not doing the common-sense thing, for that is often the way with clever people, as also with learned people. There may have been moments in my callow youth— I shudder to think of it now—when I plumed myself on my cleverness, but not for an instant have I imagined that I know very much. Though my work has been of an intellectual sort, as author and lecturer and (save the mark!) university professor, none of this was of my set design but came about by a series of accidents which I still cannot satisfactorily explain.

As a poet I had to do something for a living, and my poetry seems to have impressed people enough to make them invite me to write for them or lecture to them, something I did not find it very difficult to do. But as for knowing much, I have discovered with Bishop Stubbs that when I want to learn something about a subject the best way is to write a book about it. While my work has obliged me to learn a good deal, I am afraid that much of that knowledge has evaporated after the publication of the book in which it was embalmed. It is almost like the German I had to cram to meet the language qualifications I needed when I was working for a Ph.D. degree. By the way, it now occurs to me that I may also claim to be very industrious, but that was merely because I was compelled to be industrious to support a family of seven children. It was not hard work, however, that led me into the Church; that came later. It seems to me that I drifted into the Church quite painlessly and without effort.

In indicating the natural basis in the matter—which again I should say was hardly more than common sense —and in what will immediately follow about the predisposing circumstances, I do not forget that the essential factor in every conversion is the grace of God. It operated of course through my natural make-up and through the circumstances of my upbringing, but without the grace of God nothing would have served.

I started with the advantage that there was never a time I can remember when it was not impressed upon me that man's relation to God was immeasurably the most important fact in man's life. Logically there is no escape from the proposition that, if God exists at all, our business is a right adjustment to Him. I did not have to reach that basic point by logic; it was self-evident to me.

For this I have to thank my devout Protestant parents, who were missionaries in India. I also have to thank them for a Christian teaching which was, so far as it went, perfectly orthodox, except for an undue stress on this or that detail. Perhaps most of all I have to thank them for exhibiting their convictions in action, for an unfaltering devotion to God's cause. For me therefore Catholicism hardly meant more than a last step, though a long one, from the Protestantism of my upbringing.

Perhaps this is the reason why I have never liked to consider myself a convert. As I never see any of my Protestant relatives—all of whom are scattered at various places thousands of miles away—and as all my friends are either Catholics or nothing in particular, only very rarely am I reminded that I was ever anything except a Catholic. It may seem a confession to having lived in an ivory tower, but the secular world has never impinged a great deal on my consciousness, and when it does, it has even less reality to me than an all-but-forgotten Protestantism. I would prefer to say that whereas I was in my youth an incomplete Catholic I am now complete in my Catholicism.

Instead of writing a "convert article," I would prefer to give some account of why I remain in the Church. Sometime I may do this: at the moment it is perhaps enough to say that I stay where I am because there is nowhere else to go. I can now see how any one of a hundred chance happenings might have deflected me from the Church, even at the last minute. But it is beyond my power to imagine *not* being a Catholic, though I am aware that it would be possible for me to lose the Faith. Of one thing I am sure: if that should ever happen it would be all my own fault.

What I had was what very few people get nowadays, a great deal of Bible reading. For this, too, I am specially grateful, not the less so because the Scriptures came to me with the majestic roll of the King James version. Our religious exercises were, in fact, largely a matter of Bible reading, Bible study, Bible exposition. Its reading was looked upon as being virtually sacramental.

Though I profited by this, perhaps my main profit was the discovery, as soon as I left India and our circle of Plymouth Brethren, that there was really no such thing as the "simple Bible religion" I had heard so much about. For if the Bible was so clear a book, and an authority that needed no more than the illumination of the Holy Ghost, how was it that so many sects had come into being, with many varieties of opinion within each sect itself?

The Plymouth Brethren, as it happened, were much opposed to what they described as "sectarianism,"

102

and while managing to keep a uniformity of doctrine themselves, disclaimed being a sect or even the use of the name by which they were known. They believed themselves to have revived "primitive" Christianity and they operated upon the basis of an idea similar in some respects to the Catholic idea of the "soul of the Church." For while virtually denying the existence of a visible Church (though, if pressed, they would have said that they were that Church), they granted that all Christians, of whatever sect, who held to their own type of "fundamentalism" and who loved Our Lord and who (a very important point with them) had gone through the emotional experience of "conversion," were in fact, whether or not they were aware of it, Brethren, the elect of God. They would probably have admitted that even a Catholic here and there belonged to this category. At any rate I am sure that my father would have admitted that Father Faber, whose hymns he preferred to any other poetry, was one of the "Brethren."

I was not greatly interested at the time in this notion of unity—or any kind of Christian unity. What I saw was merely that no unity of belief had been achieved on the basis of the Bible, whose authority was postulated to be inerrable and unique; and I went on to draw the conclusion that it could not be achieved on this basis. What I did not realize as yet was that such an authority already existed. Indeed, so far as the Catholic Church was concerned, it was supposed that there were really two doctrines: an esotericism for the inner circle—the initiates—and something quite different for popular consumption, crammed with corruption and absurdity and superstition. Indeed, I fancy that the idea was that there were really *two* inner circles: one, which was very small consisting of people like Father Faber, and the other, somewhat larger, made up of the hierarchy, which knew better than the mass of Catholic people, but who took the cynical attitude that it was waste of good pearls to throw them before swine. All this seemed to me farfetched, and I could not but notice that no proofs were produced in substantiation.

So also with regard to the anti-Catholic prejudice which was in the air we breathed. Though I was given to understand that priests and nuns—especially priests and nuns—were very bad, their badness was not specified in the hearing of a small boy. But what did soak into my mind, after a reading of Foxe's *Book of Martyrs*, and from what I was continually hearing—I make allowance for a child's misunderstanding—was that Catholics were always plotting to get control of the government, after which of course they intended to send all "Christians" to the stake. Once when I saw a company of Sikh soldiers marching down the road in the direction of our house, I immediately took it for granted that they were on their way to arrest my father and mother and their associates. When nothing of that sort happened, I think a large part of my belief that Catholics were going to persecute Christians dropped from me.

When I grew older I was given the novels of Joseph Hocking to read. In several of them appeared a very suave, cultivated, and charming Jesuit of the name of Father Ritzoom. No ascetic, he did himself well in a gentlemanly way on port and cigars, but all this made him all the more sinister, as his main business seemed to be to get unsuspecting Protestant parents to send their lovely little daughters to Catholic convents to be educated, and, needless to say, proselytized. The convents themselves were largely kept going by the same Father Ritzoom, who was an adept in persuading young heiresses to take the veil and sign over all their possessions to the order. I am happy to report that these plots were always foiled in the last few chapters by the appearance of a fine upstanding young Protestant man (usually one who had seen through the pretensions of Rome and had left the Church), with whom the heiress fell in love and whom she married, the day before the one on which Father Ritzoom was to take her away to her incarceration.

The effect of this was quite different from the one intended. I was fascinated by the charming Father Ritzoom and thought it to the credit of Catholicism that it could produce a man so much more attractive than many of the grim "saints" I met in my own circle. I made a kind of mental note to look further in the matter.

At eighteen a still stronger dose was administered. My mother, then on one of her visits to England, took me to hear a lecture by an ex-nun named Edith O'Gorman. What she gave us was a highly spiced dish full of such things as being commanded, when she was in the convent, to eat a caterpillar and other improbable occurrences. And whatever effect the lecture had had upon my mind was further blunted by my reading of her autobiography, on sale at the door. Her lecture was hardly more than a condensation of this; and, as I read, my horror was changed into incredulity at the patent inconsistencies with which it was full.

A step in the Romeward direction, though I did not guess this at the time, was when I definitely disengaged myself from the Plymouth Brethrenism of my boyhood in India, but from which I had been partially released by my attendance at a nominally Baptist (but actually non-sectarian) school in England, and fell under the influence of the greatest preacher I have ever heard. This was Dr. Campbell Morgan, a man of whom my parents thoroughly approved, though they were disappointed that I had not come into formal association with their own religious group. From Dr. Morgan I derived an immense intellectual excitement and a further strong dose of the Scriptures and an ambition to become a minister myself. Though nothing came of this, it at once quickened my passionate interest in religion and started me upon what, I then supposed, was a broader path. This led me (much to Dr. Morgan's dismay) to what is called a more "liberal" theology and eventually, for a very brief time, to an association with Unitarianism. The respectable emptiness and desiccation and futile intellectualism I found there completed my disillusionment. I was by now ready to be a Catholic. In fact, it was only a few weeks after I had myself been preaching (supplying for ministers on vacation) in Unitarian pulpits—and mouthing God only knows what cloudy nonsense!—that I applied for admission to the Catholic Church.

Up to that moment I had never in my life spoken to a priest. While I was living in America when I was about twenty I did meet a few Catholics, but with none did I even mention religion except in the case of a high school boy who was preparing to enter Holy Cross College and who later became a priest. I undertook to coach him in mathematics, and religion hardly entered into that contact. But on my return to England I had taken to attending Benediction, maybe thinking that Benediction was Mass, at the Brompton Oratory and so heard a little Catholic preaching. This after Dr. Morgan's superb oratory seemed vapid and had nothing to do with my conversion. What did have an effect, however, was my consciousness that in a Catholic church there was a Presence, or at least a spiritual atmosphere unlike anything I had so far known.

When at last I did go to a priest, I simply called at the local presbytery at Chiswick, where I had just moved to new lodgings. And I had the good luck to be taken in charge by one of the curates, a very clever and amusing young Irishman, a product of St. Sulpice in Paris, whose theology was no doubt adequate but whose wide knowledge of modern literature was even better suited to my particular case. My instruction was of the most informal kind, consisting of almost nightly conversations about every possible subject (especially Sinn Fein), but in which I suppose the curate discovered that, hazy though I might be about many details of Catholic belief, I already had the Faith and was absolutely docile, eager to learn, and with no doubts or difficulties.

He gave me some Catholic books to read, and these I devoured with avidity. But I borrowed almost as many books on general subjects from his shelves and

(I think somewhat to his surprise) some of the volumes of Tanqueray's series on Moral and Dogmatic Theology. These I digested so far as my imperfect Latin would permit. But up to that time the only Catholic book that I had read, so far as I recall, was Newman's *Apologia*, and this had little bearing on my own case, as I had never had any association with the Church of England, let alone High Anglicanism.

There was, however, one book which deeply impressed me, which I read when it first appeared in 1909 and reread many times. This was Chesterton's *Orthodoxy*. It still seems to me a most extraordinary work and it sank deeply into my mind. On his last page the author did, indeed, run away from the question of authority by saying that he was quite ready to write another book on that subject under challenge. But whether or not such a challenge was ever made, Chesterton failed to write the promised book and did not himself enter the Church until thirteen years later. So far as I was concerned, this did not matter; long before that he had made a Catholic of me.

I was again fortunate. My parents were in India, so I was free to pursue my nefarious designs without their knowledge. Prior announcement would have served no purpose, as I had quite made up my mind. So when I had been received I presented them with a *fait accompli*.

As I might have known, they refused to take it as such. And when long argumentative letters about the errors of Rome proved unavailing, my father asked me to go to India, where he wished to show me what kind of thing "Romanism" in action was in that country. I could not but accept his invitation, and he thought my stipulation reasonable that I would examine whatever he liked to show me if I might be allowed to see at the same time whatever it was that the local Catholic clergy were able to produce in their justification. Only the outbreak of the war of 1914 prevented my going back to India. When in 1936 I published my life of St. Francis Xavier I had the pleasure of dedicating it to my father. This was also to his pleasure as he admired the saint very greatly, especially as he was working in Xavier's Tamil country.

One other thing I heard only after his death, though I had long surmised it. Speaking recently to a younger brother of mine, one who has given up all religious practice and probably Christian belief, I said, mainly to take a rise out of him, "I really believe that of all his children, I am the one who has most completely fulfilled our father"—this, though of the survivors two are actually members of the Plymouth Brethren. Somewhat to my surprise my brother said at once, "Yes, Father said so to me a little while before he died." It would have been expecting altogether too much that he should make any such admission to me. As for my mother, to the end she felt so strongly about my conversion that it was impossible for me so much as to mention religion to her. I was grateful that she so completely accepted my Catholic wife, though she must have looked upon her as another chain holding me in thralldom to Giant Pope, but in my wife's case she recognized extenuating circumstances; she had been born a Catholic, and so could not be held responsible.

My wife herself, however, like my children and some of my Catholic friends, have reminded me from time to time that I am, after all, "only a convert," whereas they are "born Catholics." To that I have my answer: "There is no such thing as a born Catholic." This I follow up by pointing out that their Catholicism is no credit to them, as they did not choose it. On the other hand I entered the Church of my own free choice.

There is, as I am well aware, a fallacy or two in this argument. Even those "born" into the Faith need to make continual acts of faith, not to mention other things, to remain in it. And though I was of course free to have refused the gift of faith when it was offered me, I could have done so only by making my damnation sure. I am not suggesting that damnation is prepared for the many people who come within an inch or two of the Church, and then stop there, or even

108

veer away; for I can understand that there may be many reasons for this. One of the most famous nuns in this country told me about one of its most famous professors—a leading Thomist who nevertheless has not become a Catholic and who perhaps never will—that when she ventured to question him on the point (for she knew him well) he answered, "Sister, you ought to understand better than anybody else why I have not become a Catholic." She did understand, and pressed him no further.

Yet even when faith is offered, there may be difficulties so personal as to be virtually insuperable. There may also be the kind of temperamental disinclination to make decisions that held Chesterton back so long. Canon O'Connor (the "Father Brown" of his detective stories) wrote to Belloc in despair that Chesterton would never become a Catholic unless his wife would take him down to the church and find the place in his prayer book for him; and she was not ready, at that time, to leave the Anglicanism to which she was so attached. It was astonishing to all who knew of this situation that at last he made the decision alone.

I can thank God that no such difficulties existed for me. All was plain sailing in my case; the worst I had to face was the disapproval of my family. So far as I know, I have lost nothing—nothing, that is, that I value very much. It is possible that certain doors have been closed to me socially; as I never wanted to enter them, that does not trouble me. It is also possible that I might have had more recognition as a writer had I not been a Catholic. I cannot, however, be sure about that. The idea has more than once occurred to me that secular reviewers are on the whole much more friendly to me than are some Catholic reviewers. And it may well be that had I not become a Catholic I would not have found anything in particular to write about. At any rate I know for a certainty that themes which at least bear in some way upon Catholicism are the only ones that deeply engage my interest.

As Catholic books seem to be the only ones I can

write, it is no special credit to me that these are the books I write. It therefore covers me with confusion to hear, as I often do, about "the apostolate of the pen," for though I hope my books do some good, I am merely doing, as best I can, the one job for which I am fitted. If the cast of my mind pointed from the start in the direction of the Church, my mind since then, because of my life in the Church, has been set in a Catholic mold from which I cannot escape. But of course I do not want to escape—either from that or from the unremitting toils of authorship. I might be tempted to say that these have been imposed to make up for the effortless manner in which I arrived at Rome, were it not that I enjoy my work so much. The main misgiving I have is whether heaven will be so easy to enter.

TO CHURCH AND CLOISTER

M. Raphael Simon, O.C.S.O.

Dr. Kenneth Simon was a Jewish psychiatrist who left a successful practice in New York to embrace the Catholic faith and to join the Cistercians of the Strict Observance, commonly known as the Trappists, who live a life of prayer, labor, and silence. His case is, therefore, one of unusual interest because it represents the approach taken by a searcher who was not only a Jew, steeped in the customs and traditions of Israel, but was also a scientist in mental pathology.

Born on August 6, 1909, in New York City, Kenneth Simon strangely enough was given the name of an Irish saint, Kenneth, who became a monk and a priest and was highly venerated in Scotland as the companion of St. Columban. The choice of the name was to prove more prophetic of the youngster's career and destiny than the parents could possibly have realized at the time.

After finishing public grade and high schools, he registered at the University of Michigan, where he spent two years. He then enrolled for a year of study at the University of Berlin and returned to the University of Michigan, where he received his A.B., M.A., and M.D. degrees. He served for a year as research assistant in history at the University of Chicago, and after graduating from the Medical School at the University of Michigan returned to serve as research associate in the department of internal medicine at the University of Chicago.

He served more than two years in internships and was the psychiatrist at Lincoln Hall, an institution for delinquent boys at Lincolndale, New York. His studies in philosophy under Robert Hutchins, Mortimer Adler, and Richard McKeon enabled him to secure a thorough understanding and deep appreciation of the philosophy of St. Thomas Aquinas.

More and more he felt drawn to a philosophy of religion and of life which answered the questions of his mind and ministered to the hunger in his heart. Two of his intimate friends, both Jewish, taking their own doctorates, found themselves thoroughly gripped by the well-reasoned philosophical system developed by St. Thomas and, like Dr. Simon, were drawn to embrace the Catholic faith.

Upon the completion of a thorough course of instruction by Father Joseph D. Connerton at St. Thomas the Apostle Church in Chicago, Dr. Simon was baptized and received into the Catholic Church on November 6, 1936. Feeling an irresistible call to the religious life, Dr. Simon, after investigating several religious communities, joined the Cistercians and made his solemn profession on November 6, 1946, and was ordained to the holy priesthood on May 30, 1947.

He is now a monk in the Abbey of Our Lady of the Valley, at Valley Falls, Rhode Island. His book, *The Glory of Thy People,* which tells the complete story of his conversion, was published by the Macmillan Company in 1948 and was immediately successful. In that book Dr. Simon, who now writes under his religious name, Father M. Raphael Simon, O.C.S.O., thus comments on his conversion: "Thus did I, a Jew, without becoming less a Jew, become a Catholic. This was thirteen years ago. Since then the expectation of my baptism has been fulfilled; the life into which I was born was continued, ever growing greater; this is the life of God."

In a brilliant preface to *The Glory of Thy People,* Monsignor Fulton J. Sheen thus sounds the keynote of Father

Simon's spiritual Odyssey: "Here is a man who went the whole way, who was content with no half-drawn swords, divided loyalties and compromising surrenders. Pascal once said in defense of the Evangelists' writing the truth in their Gospels: 'I will believe any man who has his throat cut for a cause.' And here, without saying it, the reader will be faced with one unanswerable argument: I will believe any man who leaves what Dr. Simon left to become a Monk of the Order of the Cistercians of the Strict Observance, and to live the rest of his days in the shades and shadows of the Cross where saints are made."

I AM grateful to the God of all goodness for the particular manner in which He led me into His great Church; I am grateful to Him for the family and race He chose for me.

Born of Jewish parents in New York City, I received religious education in the Reform Synagogue. I had the impression of biblical times as differing from the times in which I lived in this: God seemed to have lived in the midst of His people in the times of the patriarchs and prophets but He seemed strangely distant and silent in these times. There seemed to be an unaccountable gap.

Public high school and university study made the impression of a personal, living, loving God seem naïve and unreal. Instead, my attention was focused on the things of sense. Love of truth was directed to the ideal of accumulating facts, information. It seemed that knowledge ever advancing might be the guide to individual and social perfection.

Nonetheless, two years of a liberal university education assured me that something was wanting: something that would give order and unity and completion to factual knowledge. My third year, during which I studied at the University of Berlin, introduced me to philosophy and I realized that this was the science of sciences. As a practical profession I decided upon psychiatry, which required the study of medicine, upon which I embarked after completing the premedical courses during my fourth collegiate year.

Toward the end of these medical studies I had an opportunity to study philosophy. My friend Herbert Schwartz had just obtained his Ph.D. in philosophy at Columbia University, and was now at the University of Michigan, pursuing graduate work in mathematics.

Under his tutelage I entered upon that well-traversed road of philosophy which has led many to the Church of God. Of all the philosophers, the greatest were, as it seemed to me, Plato, Aristotle, St. Augustine, and St. Thomas Aquinas; and of their teachings, St. Thomas, following Aristotle particularly, had made a clear and objective synthesis. St. Thomas always refers to Aristotle by the designation *"the* philosopher."

Philosophy did me a great service. It corrected the errors of modern thought, showed me that the power of intelligence and reasoning is not exhausted by experimental investigation. In addition to the latter wonderful mode of discovery of truth, so splendidly fruitful in modern times, there is a complementary way to truth which completes, unifies, and orders the world of sense. This mode is the ascent from facts to principles and to the discovery of all the conclusions that can licitly be drawn from them. The instruments are not material but are the discipline of the intelligence in conformity with the laws of reasoning. The fruit is a certitude exceeding the certitude of observation and experiment, for these render an understanding of natural things only in so far as they imply and depend on the truths of philosophy, which the common sense of scientists contain imperfectly but often sufficiently.

There is room here only to give a brief list of the results of these philosophic studies. The chief pertain to the question of evolution and the history of the race, which in view of all the facts seemed to me to be better accounted for by two original human parents, created by God, rather than descended from lower animals; to the phenomena of mind which reflect an intelligence and will, immaterial powers having a root in an immaterial and immortal soul; to the possibility of the existence of complete incorporeal intelligent beings, "intelligences" in the language of Aristotle, i.e., angels; to the proofs of the existence of God, of a divine mind capable of fashioning the marvelously intricate universe, of a divine will capable of bringing this design into being from nothing, and of governing it through the natural laws which He instituted; to the possibility of revelation, by which He could communicate to men knowledge beyond the grasp of their reason, such as secrets of His own interior life; and of miracles, that is, the exercise of divine power over natural laws such as belongs properly to their Author.

In the realm of morality, philosophy assisted me again in my quest for truth. Here also I shall only briefly enumerate the conclusions to which it led me. Morality has an objective basis. Human reason recognizes those things which are morally good, those which are morally bad, and those which are indifferent. But false and contrary reasoning can render this knowledge void, in which case man is unable to attain his end. Every human being seeks what he believes to be good, and avoids what he considers evil, and ultimately what he desires and what he seeks is his happiness. But there is only one happiness for human nature, and for all men, and that is not to be found in those things which are a *means* but only in that which is the proper end of man. Thus food, shelter, and clothing are means to bodily health and comfort, and so is wealth, but not the end. So also the esteem of others, knowledge, and virtue are not man's end. In brief, not creatures, but the Creator is man's real good and end as He is also his beginning.

How vague and empty this at first seemed to me to be! Yet nonetheless I recognized here the solution to my quest. What I wanted was the explanation of life, the purpose of life, and the ultimate rock-bottom truth, absolute and certain. One word was the answer: He who always was, when nothing existed but Himself; He at Whose word (and according to the succession which He willed) the universe came to be; He, the Infinite,

Beauty itself, the Supreme Intelligence, our Own, our God.

External confirmation of my discovery was close by. For, having received my degree in medicine at the University of Michigan, I was now at the University of Chicago pursuing the study of philosophy. Dr. Robert Hutchins spoke of the intellectual love of God, and bade his honor students, if they would make sense of the Scriptures, to read them as if they were what they purport to be, a divine revelation—supernal truth. Dr. Mortimer Adler manifested the existence of God, using St. Thomas' five proofs; and declared that objective considerations of the different religions make it evident that the Catholic religion is the most complete. Dr. Herbert Schwartz recognized that his knowledge of God was itself a gift from God, a gift of grace, and in his gratitude he was determined to make a return of love for the love God has shown him.

The opinions of these non-Catholics were more weighty because of their intellectual competence and objectivity.

But one voice spoke to me more powerfully than theirs, more persuasively than my own reflections. One day, harassed and fatigued, I opened the New Testament at random, following an intuition that I would find solace. There I read:

No man can serve two masters. For either he will hate the one, and love the other; or he will sustain the one and despise the other. You cannot serve God and mammon. Therefore I say to you, be not solicitous for your life, what you shall eat, nor for your body, what you shall put on. Is not the life more than the meat; and the body more than the raiment? Behold the birds of the air, for they neither sow, nor do they reap, nor gather into barns; and your heavenly Father feedeth them. Are not you of much more value than they? And which of you by taking thought, can add to his stature one cubit? And for raiment why are you solicitous? Consider the lilies of the field, how they grow; they labour not, neither do they spin. But I say to you, that even Solomon in all his glory was not arrayed as one of these. And if the grass of the field which is today.

and tomorrow is cast into the oven, God doth so clothe: how much more you, O ye of little faith? Be not solicitous therefore, saying what shall we eat; or what shall we drink, or wherewith shall we be clothed? For after all these things do the heathens seek. For your Father knoweth that you have need of all these things. Seek ye therefore first the kingdom of God, and His justice, and all these things shall be added unto you. Be not solicitous therefore for to-morrow; for the morrow will be solicitous for itself. Sufficient for the day is the evil thereof. (Matthew 6:24–34.)

Seek ye therefore first the kingdom of God, and His justice, and all these things shall be added unto you. Here was a program for life, here was God's answer to my worries. Peace came and I determined soon after to find my end, not in myself, in my self-love, in my vanity, pride, ambition, but to find it in God.

To prevent self-deception, I determined to spend a portion of each day reading the New Testament, the Gospel of Jesus Christ. This was a name that stirred in me a spirit of rancor and resentment. Some said that He had never lived; others that His death was the work of Pontius Pilate solely, and this view pleased me. No doubt, I had thought, the Christians had placed the responsibility at the door of the Jews as an excuse to persecute them. Others, rabbis and leaders of modern Jewish opinion, claimed Jesus as a Jew, and the noblest example of Jewry.

Now, however, I was determined to allow the Gospels to speak for themselves. To obtain a fair and objective view, I suppressed those movements of antipathy and resentment which I perceived to arise from my prejudices.

The story was the story of the Messiah, of Him whom the prophets had foreseen and foreloved. Of Him, the dying patriarch, Jacob, had said:

The sceptre shall not be taken away from Juda, nor a ruler from his thigh, till he comes that is to be sent, and he shall be the expectation of nations. Tying his foal to the vineyard, and his ass, O my son, to the vine. He shall wash his robe in wine, and his garment in the blood of the grape.

His eyes are more beautiful than wine, and his teeth are whiter than milk. (Genesis 49:10–12.)

Now the story had as its setting that time when the sceptre was being taken away from Juda. A Roman governor was ruling in Jerusalem, the capital of Judea, the portion of the tribe of Juda. Still the Jewish high priest and the Sanhedrin retained a certain authority.

He whom the world since then has venerated as the greatest of the Jewish prophets, St. John the Baptist, was declaring that the kingdom of God was at hand. On the banks of the Jordan, Jesus, like many others of his Jewish compatriots and coreligionists, appeared. John exclaimed: "Behold the Lamb of God, behold Him who taketh away the sins of the world."

Several of John's disciples left him to follow Jesus, many others likewise followed Jesus, and soon Palestine was divided. The people loved and venerated Jesus, and the scribes and Pharisees, foreseeing the loss of their primacy, determined, as matters came to a head, to bring about His dishonor and death. They maintained an outward veneration for Him, for they feared Him, and in addition their plans were difficult to execute because of the love the Jewish people bore him. Finally one of His disciples betrayed Him to them. Led by Judas, a band seized Him during the night. Judged guilty of blasphemy ("for He made Himself the son of God"), at an illegal trial He was brought to the Roman governor and executed on the cross.

Such was the story which I read, bit by bit, quietly and gravely in the course of several weeks. I was deeply impressed by the words and actions ascribed to Jesus. Their wisdom, beauty, dignity exceeded anything literature, philosophy, or history presented. A special quality inhered in them, so transcendent that my intelligence asked in amazement: Who is this? Such was the question in the minds of the men of Palestine. This question allowed of no middle course. It was to be answered either by the answer of the scribes and Pharisees or by that of those selfless seekers of the truth who left all to follow Jesus. For myself, I soon determined to put aside all doubts and questions. Isaias, the great Jewish prophet who had lived before the time of the Babylonian captivity, had written:

"Lord, who hath believed our report?" (John 12:38; Isaias 53:1.) To which a disappointed God (to speak after a human fashion) has prophetically answered:

He hath blinded their eyes, and hardened their heart, that they should not see with their eyes, nor understand with their heart, and be converted, and I should heal them. (John 12:40; Isaias 6:10.)

But I willed to see with the eyes of my intelligence and to accept from my heart that truth which so gently solicited my assent and fidelity. When for the second time I had read of Christ's appearance to the disciples in the locked room of the Cenacle on the third day after His death, I realized that I believed, and that the loving Saviour had passed through the locked doors of my heart.

Now indeed my eyes opened and my heart melted, as I discovered the lovableness of Jesus. He was indeed the Son of God, the Second Person of the Blessed Trinity, come to earth through the medium of His Incarnation, by which He had assumed a human nature in the womb of the Blessed Virgin Mary in order to reconcile men to God and to make friends among men. These truths gradually unfolded in my mind and heart their glorious meaning, spreading a peace and unction therein which I had never before experienced.

One day, desiring to discover whether there was anything in Catholic doctrine which I could not hold, to which reason must dissent, I read the Apostles' Creed, which formulates the faith of the Church:

I believe in God the Father Almighty, Creator of heaven and earth. And in Jesus Christ, His only Son, our Lord, Who was conceived by the Holy Ghost, born of the Virgin Mary, suffered under Pontius Pilate, was crucified, died, and was buried; He descended into hell, the third day He arose again from the dead, He ascended into heaven, and sitteth at the right hand of God the Father Almighty, from thence He shall come to judge the living and the dead. I believe in the Holy Ghost, the Holy Catholic Church, the communion of Saints, the forgiveness of sins, the resurrection of the body, and life everlasting. Amen.

No, these assertions were above reason, but not contrary to reason. They were mysteries, but not superstitions. They were a light upon the hidden things of God; belief did not limit understanding, but extended it to those things which otherwise would remain unknown.

I was prepared by recent experience and reflection to see that the acceptance of the divinity of Jesus Christ and the revelation of divine things which He came upon earth to teach required the acceptance of the Catholic Church. If He had not appointed Simon Peter to be the Rock upon which His Church was founded, then His doctrine would not have had the safeguard which Peter's undisputed authority gave it.

And the Lord said: Simon, Simon, behold Satan hath desired to have you, that he may sift you as wheat. But I have prayed for you, that thy faith fail not; and thou, being once converted, confirm thy brethren. (Luke 22:31, 32.)

And if Peter's authority to confirm his brethren in the Faith had perished with him, the foundation laid by Christ would not have been for all generations. But with an unbroken succession of popes, Christ's doctrine is preserved and taught to all generations of men.

A convincing proof of the wisdom of Christ's building is the witness of Protestantism. Within four centuries, in the United States, statistics show that it has disintegrated into over four hundred different sects.

My Jewish origin was not an obstacle but an incentive to accept the Catholic Church as the true Church of God. Was not its founder, Jesus Christ, a Jew? His mother? His Apostles? The first Church, the Church of Jerusalem, was it not composed of Jews?

Had He not said, I have come not to destroy the Law and the Prophets, but to fulfill them; was not Catholicism, then, the religion for the Jew? That, unlike Judaism, it held out its arms to receive all men, only confirmed its divine origin in my estimation, for surely God must desire all men to be members of that Church which He founded for mankind. If my ancestors for two thousand years, heirs to the traditions of the scribes and Pharisees (a human and not divine tradition, as it seemed to me), had erred, ought I to approve their error by remaining a stranger to the true Church? As I looked to modern science for a knowledge of the details of the natural world, to philosophy for an understanding of ultimate principles knowable to reason, so I looked to Catholic theology for the true exposition of the truths which the Incarnate God had come to teach to the human race.

After my baptism on November 6, 1936, I found that all I had hoped for was abundantly fulfilled. In the Church I found that which had been lacking in modern Judaism. God was dwelling in the midst of His people, the spiritual Semites, in the phrase of the late Pope Pius XI. In assisting at Holy Mass, I felt the reverence which the Hebrews of old had experienced in the temple of Jerusalem, and as the Sanctus told of the entrance to the Canon of the Mass, I realized that solemn moment had arrived which in olden days came but once a year, when the high priest entered into the Holy of Holies, open to him alone, to offer the blood of the lamb for the sins of all the people. Here indeed upon the altar was that blessed Victim, the true Lamb of God, the crucified Jesus prefigured by the divinely appointed sacrifice of the Old Testament. Truly He is the Propitiation for the sins of all men, Who on Calvary offered for all His sacrifice, an abundant satisfaction for the sins of all men, including His enemies and executioners: "Forgive them, Father, for they know not what they do."

But now that I had found that rock-bottom truth of changeless certitude, which had been the object of my desire during student days, I was irresistibly drawn to live that truth. It seemed to me that the only sane, the only reasonable ideal was sanctity, union with God. Was not this the truth reason itself dimly foretold when it asserted that God alone was the true end of men, and that their happiness could not be found in themselves, nor in creatures, but in their Creator alone?

While I strove to live this life in the world, and in my professional life, I was nonetheless drawn to the religious life, that state of life approved by the Church wherein men live lives entirely consecrated to God. The three vows which constitute this state according to the counsels of Christ remove the three main obstacles to that union of friendship and love which is the true goal of the religious and especially, as I later learned, of the monk. These obstacles are the love of riches which the vow of poverty opposes, the love of pleasure which the vow of chastity resists, and the pride of life, the spirit of independence so prevalent in our day, which the vow of obedience, the most essential vow, attacks.

While my heart seemed to me entirely given to the Dominican Order, the Friars Preachers, whose motto is *contemplari et contemplata aliis tradere* (to contemplate and to give to others the fruits of one's contemplation—i.e., by the preaching and teaching of the Truth), yet in the course of the next four years I offered this desire to God, desirous only of entering that religious institute which His will should ordain, and to Mother Mary, His Mother and ours, I said, "I shall wear whatever habit you place upon me."

In all religious institutes which I visited, as the Discalced Carmelites, the Holy Ghost Fathers, the Cistercians of the Strict Observance, I saw the same peace and joy, the same fervor and modesty, the same charity. Here eyes were clear-sighted, calm, level, the countenances spoke of the instant acceptance of friendship, conduct was reasonable, sweet, and selfless.

Following my decision to be, by the will of God, a religious in the order of His choice for me, I was led by an irresistible and intelligent attraction to the Cistercian Monastery of Our Lady of the Valley. St. Bernard had desired that his monks should attain to the land of promise, the land overflowing with milk and honey, to the perfect life of contemplation wherein the soul is espoused to its Lord, and that, once having attained thereto by a life of solitude and prayer, it should never be separated from it. This, the ideal of St. Benedict, the Moses of monks, was embodied in his Rule. To the primitive and perfect observance of his wise rule, the founders of the Cistercian Order, themselves monks of St. Benedict, had sought to return by its literal observance. In 1892, under the auspices of Leo XIII, the congregations of Cistercians who wished to follow the primitive usages of these founders were united into the Order of the Cistercians of the Strict Observance, as they are officially designated today.

In the Cistercian life the ideal of all Christianity is pursued by prayer and penance; by prayer through which God in Jesus Christ is known and loved; by penance, through which the soul is freed from lesser loves. My life in the world and my observations as a psychiatrist made it plain to me that the greatest force for the freeing of men from all that disables and handicaps them and hinders their attaining to true happiness is the power of prayer and sacrifice, which obtains divine assistance for them. Hence I was disposed to adopt that life in which were united my own personal happiness and the greatest usefulness to others. I realized that my disorderly tendencies would always be with me; my pride would always seek to have its own way, hence I would always need the corrective of obedience to achieve true freedom; my vanity would always feed on the esteem of others, hence I needed the self-effacement of common life, where only those shine who are free from singularity and hidden from men and brethren; my sensuality would always seek self-indulgence; hence I should always need the hardships which a life of voluntary poverty provides.

My visits to the monastery prior to my entrance left a deep impression of the fervor of the community. The singing of the Divine Office in choir, the chief work of the monks, discharged in the name of the entire Church, and indeed for all mankind, was manly, sweet, and true. The brave and celestial melodies of the Gregorian chant accompanied me when I left the monastery; true worship of God whose mighty hand supports all being, but Who receives in return for His great love for men so little love. Ought not the Sacred Heart of Jesus to be consoled? Ought not fellow men whose hidden and unknown longing is for the same God to be assisted to their true end? Those who aim at the ideal of Christianity, the twofold love of God and man, will join with me in thanking the mercy of God which led me to Church and Cloister.

FINDING LIFE AND LIGHT

Rosalind Murray

Rosalind Murray is the daughter of the distinguished British scholar, Professor Gilbert Murray, and Lady Mary Henrietta Howard (eldest daughter of the ninth Earl of Carlisle). At the age of eighteen she enjoyed the unusual distinction of having her first novel, *The Leading Note,* published. Two other books, *Moonseed* (1911) and *Unstable Ways* (1914), followed. In 1926 she published the novel, *The Happy Tree,* and followed it in 1929 with another novel, *Hard Liberty.*

Her father's family was Irish and Catholic; her great-grandfather emigrated from Limerick County after the Napoleonic Wars in which he fought, to escape from the penal laws, under which a Catholic was debarred from promotion in the British Army. This family history made a great impression on Rosalind as a child.

Rosalind Murray was educated chiefly at home and spent much of her childhood at the homes of her maternal grandparents in Yorkshire and Cumberland and in Italy. In

September 1913, she married Arnold Joseph Toynbee, the noted historian. The Toynbees have two sons living, Theodore Philip and Lawrence.

In 1932 Rosalind Murray embraced the Catholic faith. Her Apologia, in the form of a general consideration of the place of the Christian religion in human experience and of the insufficiency of the humanistic alternative, was published in 1939, under the title *The Good Pagan's Failure*.

During World War II she assisted her husband in his wartime organization of the Royal Institute of International Affairs, of which he has been director since 1925. She has recently published *Time and the Timeless*. This was followed by her latest work, *The Forsaken Fountain*, a philosophical treatise in which the author stresses the vital need for a reinterpretation of the truth of metaphysics and of religion, as well as a fresh presentation of the same in terms that will appeal to the average modern man. Because the thinking of Western civilization has so largely concentrated on material progress, the author advocates passivity as a way of knowledge for that "vision in depth" which permits us to see through the stuff of things to the reality behind them. It is a profound and penetrating discussion of the supernatural and stamps the author as a brilliant thinker and a keen metaphysician. Of all her works *The Good Pagan's Failure* is probably the best known in both America and England.

CONVERTS are often asked to tell the story of their conversion: "What first brought the Catholic Church to your notice?" "What decided you to take the final plunge?" And often, in some form or other, the question follows: "What do you really think about it now that you are inside?"

I imagine that for some people the answers to these questions are simple; they can look back to some particular moment, some person or place, perhaps some chance remark, that first awakened their interest, and they can retrace an ordered sequence of inquiries and doubts and hesitations, finally satisfactorily resolved. I can do no such thing. To me, when I look back, the entire journey seems just inevitable and certain, a process of growth and liberation in which I myself am almost passive; far less a change from disbelief to belief than a gradual enlightenment.

If I had to answer these questions shortly, I would say: "I was always conscious of the Church; always so far back as I can remember, wanted to be inside instead of outside; gradually the barriers were removed and I was in. It does not seem to me, as I look back, that I myself took any very positive action, made any very rational decision; I only waited, and did not resist. I always wanted to be a Catholic; why, I could not have explained at all logically, and at a certain point that wanting became so urgent a necessity that it seemed to me it had to happen; it was like a command. I had no doubts; no hesitations at all; none of the intellectual difficulties which torment so many people accustomed to complete freedom of thought. The only thing that now seems strange to me is that I was able to exist so long in that strange indeterminate condition, knowing where I should be, where in the end I must be, yet satisfied, in the meantime, to wait."

So much for the first two questions. Now for the third, "What do I think of it now?"

From the moment of my reception into the Church, I felt complete certainty and peace. What is perhaps stranger, I felt entirely "at home," as though I was at last where I belonged; and I may add that in the seventeen years that have passed since then, this certainty, and this sense of being at home, has never for one moment lessened.

Now I know that as it stands that account of my conversion may not seem very helpful to other people who are approaching by quite different roads. That kind of immediate certainty and conviction, however irresistible it may be to the person concerned, is incommunicable to others; it seems irrational and subjective, perhaps even unbalanced to minds whose mode of working is quite other. The first reaction is very apt to be: "Well, you feel that way and I don't; that's all!"

Of course I recognize this difficulty, but God's ways are necessarily different with different people and there is a lesson to be learned in each, for all. The end to which He draws us is the same, but we who are led into the Church from a far country come from so many and such varied places, from such opposite directions, that the roads we travel are bound to differ, and from this very difference we may learn. When I look back on my own childhood and family background, I still marvel at the way the very conditions which might have seemed the greatest obstacles have proved to be themselves a means of grace. And though my own particular circumstances were in many respects unusual, the principle, I am sure, remains that no conditions of life or upbringing can be too strange or hostile for divine grace to use in its own way; it may be *through* and not *in spite of* the very conditions which seem in human terms most unpropitious that we may find enlightenment to have come.

I will now try to give some account of how this principle has worked out for me. To begin with, I had a complete Godless upbringing; no religious teaching of any sort, but in its place a very intensive form of pagan moralism, highly exacting and idealistic. My father was a liberal humanist; he had rejected all forms of supernatural religion as barbarous and degrading superstition. He believed passionately in human progress, and was concerned to show in his own life that purely human values could command as high, or even higher, devotion and service than any claims of a revealed religion. For him, Greek thought and Greek ideals embodied the highest expression of this enlightened humanism, but he found, in essentials, the same spirit in the humanitarian ideals of English liberalism and was always a wholehearted political Liberal.

The Liberals stood for the progressive reform of social conditions, and in particular for the protection of the oppressed, whether of class or race, in any part of the world. Up to the outbreak of the first World War, they had a long and distinguished record of humanitarian legislation, and in the circles to which we

belong, "Liberal principles" had quite explicitly super-
seded "Christian principles" as the basis of action.

My mother shared my father's views, and behind
them was a bloc of family reinforcement, grandparents,
uncles, and aunts of great energy and dynamism, for
whom this political idealism replaced both loyalty to
any organized church and also personal religious sanction. The family was a phalanx on the warpath. The
moral code this liberalism demanded was exceedingly
exacting; social service and the public good demanded
from these Liberal freethinkers a more wholehearted
and devoted service than most religious bodies dare to
require.

I know of no Christian community which gives so
generously, so unquestioningly, to its church as did
these Liberals to their various causes: prison reform,
factory reform, protection of subject races, of political
refugees, protection for some ill-treated minority in
Europe, and many other causes of the same sort. Instead of our duty to God we were reminded constantly
of our duty to society and this duty became the more
exacting in proportion to any position of privilege. Our
family was in such a position, both socially and intellectually, and the demands of public service on it were
most generously met. Failure in public duty of any
kind, in obligation toward society, would be severely
condemned in such circles as a grave mortal sin by
Christians. Society had in fact replaced God as both
end and sanction of moral action, and in the fervor of
this new religion the old was rigorously excluded. It
was as important to think rightly as to act rightly, to
think according to right Liberal doctrine, and the
orthodoxy was rigid.

I and my brother and sister were not baptized; we
were as rigorously guarded from any direct religious
influence as a child in Soviet Russia today, yet I cannot
remember a time when I was not conscious of this tremendous and forbidden thing.

One of my very earliest memories is of overhearing
our nurse giving instructions to a new nurserymaid:

"And remember, no religion is allowed in this nursery!"

My brother and I were not allowed to attend the "prayers" at our kindergarten class; usually we arrived when they were over, but one morning I remember getting to school too soon and having to wait outside the classroom door till prayers were over. The other children inside were singing a hymn and I overheard the word "Redeemer," and felt it somehow to be a word of power, an exciting word, but one that I was not supposed to hear; I felt exalted and yet guilty. I suppose I was then about four or five years old.

Somehow, though I cannot remember how, I knew that Denis and I had not been "christened," as others were, and felt it terrible and shameful, and hoped that people would not find it out.

With a child's unwavering trust, I never questioned the decision that kept us from this mysterious Tree of Knowledge, yet something seemed to tell my childish mind that it was also in fact the Tree of Life, and I wondered about it and longed for it.

At this first stage, of course, I did not know that there were different kinds of religion, but very early the Catholic Church became a real and definite idea, as different and better than Protestantism, for curiously and paradoxically enough, in spite of this rigorous exclusion of all religion as a living reality, a certain romantic feeling for rejected Catholic loyalties persisted in the family tradition. My father was of Catholic Irish stock, his father having emigrated to Australia as a young man to escape the penal laws then still in force against Catholics in Ireland, and though as a child he seems to have had no instruction, he had himself been baptized in the Catholic Church and retained a sort of religious "patriotism," wholly unrelated to any belief.

We were brought up on stories of persecution, of how our great-grandfather in Ireland had had his horse taken from him by a tramp because it was too valuable for a Catholic to possess, of how he was debarred from high rank in the army, and so on. And the religious loyalty went further; we were not allowed

128

fireworks on Guy Fawkes Day, which English children celebrate with fireworks, because my father said it was in fact an anti-Catholic celebration and he and his brothers were never allowed to keep it.

On my mother's side, too, there were Catholic loyalties, though less immediate and personal, and even the record of two martyrs in the sixteenth and seventeenth centuries. On both sides of the family, in fact, what religion remained at all was Catholic; the various Catholic uncles and cousins appeared from time to time on the horizon and their views were always treated with respect.

This curious situation was in fact less astonishing than it might appear to be at first sight, for religious toleration was a cardinal point in English liberalism, and the Liberals were also the champions of Irish freedom. Yet it seems strange that the vigilance with which we children were guarded from the "undenominational Christianity" of the kindergarten class and the Protestantism of Scotch servants should not in any way have been extended to the possible influence of Catholicism. I can only imagine that to my parents at that time Catholic belief, as they envisaged it, seemed so far removed from modern life, so entirely a romantic relic of the past, that it could not endanger our rationalism, as a more moderate form of religion might.

Of course our uncles and cousins did not speak to us of religion, nor did I ever raise the question with any of them till after I was myself a Catholic too; then, but then only, it became a bond, but the fact of their existence and occasional appearance from either the Antipodes or Rome made a deep impression on my mind.

What they believed, of course, I did not know, but I did know that they still stood for something for which our ancestors had suffered, that they were still inside something that we were outside, possessed something of which we were deprived.

This general impression was made more definite by the arrival, when I was about ten, of an Australian cousin of my own age brought by his father to England

129

to be "educated by the Jesuits." He used to spend his holidays with us, and though again we never talked of religion, he often talked of school and of the Fathers who taught him. When, later, he was at Beaumont College and my brother at Winchester (the oldest and most traditional of English public schools), they used to compare notes, and I remember being struck by the difference in the two boys' relation to their masters; my cousin's was so much closer than my brother's.

True to their principles, my parents were scrupulous in sending Terence to Mass on Sundays; what that really meant I did not know; how should I? But I remember how I envied him!

It never occurred to me to blame my father for having taken Denis and me "out" (that was always the image, being "shut out"). I assumed, I think, that somehow he had had to, but I felt that my cousin Terence was fortunate that his father had not been obliged to do the same to him.

About this same time I remember clearly my first conscious contact with dogmatic belief through a lesson in English history. My brother and I had a Scotch governess of whom we were very fond; she did not, of course, give us religious instruction. Indeed I do not know what her actual beliefs were, but she had the traditional Presbyterian background and in teaching us about the historical Reformation she tried to give us some notion of the difference in religious belief. What I remember so distinctly is her speaking of transubstantiation. I do not imagine for a moment that what she said can have been a correct dogmatic exposition, nor that if it had been I should have understood it, but what emerged was that the Catholics believed that bread and wine were changed into the Body and Blood of Christ, whereas the Protestants knew that of course they were not; and like a flash, it came upon my mind: "But the Catholics were right; it does happen!" and I realized the fact as of immense importance.

I said nothing of course; a child so often says nothing; but the whole scene is as vivid to me today as

130

though it had happened just a few months ago; my brother and I sitting at our two desks and Miss Glaholme sitting opposite us, the shape of the schoolroom window open beside us, and the pattern of peacocks and dovecotes on the wallpaper.

I cannot give any rational explanation of this recognition of truth by a child's mind; I cannot see it as "acceptance of authority," or as "acceptance of the reliability of the witness" in any ordinary sense of the words. For in my case all my known authorities were against it! I did not know and had no means of knowing the Church's claims to teach the truth; I was as ignorant in religious knowledge as any child in a partially Christian country could be, yet I was certain that this thing was true that was presented to me as being untrue. It is for the theologians to explain it; I can only state the fact; I believe that there is in many children an intuitive knowledge of this kind waiting to be awakened and given shape, and I think this is a real ground for hope when we are daunted by the numbers now growing up without religious teaching, just as I was. It is much harder to root out religion than the militant atheists would suppose!

My next conscious contact with religion came about five years later, when I was fifteen. I had been ill and was sent abroad for the winter to Italy. As part of my cultural education I was given *The Little Flowers of St. Francis* to read, and from that I went on to other Franciscan writings. The effect of this Franciscan impact was vital: it opened up an entire new world for me. I got a crucifix and a rosary; I tried in every way I could to become a Christian. I had always prayed in times of stress spasmodically, and with a sense of guilt, feeling that I was doing something forbidden, but now I learned something of real prayer, and felt less guilty; I had the authority of St. Francis for support. But it was still all secret, and had to be. Once I escaped into a church when Mass was going on. It was early morning, hardly light, and I cannot now think how I managed to get there. I only know that I did, and again I had the certainty, "This is real. This is the most important thing in the world!" and also as always, "This is where I belong."

If I had to fix a date for my conversion, as distinct from reception into the Church, I think I should put it during that winter, and should say that St. Francis converted me, but in fact the process had been latent and was to be so still for many years.

I imagine that most American girls would be far more independent at fifteen than I was; although advanced in their political views, my parents were traditional and old-fashioned in their ideas of family obligations and assumed a degree of direction and supervision that was unusual among my own contemporaries and friends. It would have seemed unthinkable to revolt openly against the family beliefs, and when, a few years later, I married, it was into a similar atmosphere.

The glimpse that I had had of a new life and light remained a dream to be ignored or at least put aside, out of the way, but it was not forgotten, it could not be. Experience of life, the problem of evil, kept the religious issue actual, and the problem of my children's education raised it in a concrete objective form. I was determined that they should not be debarred from religion as I myself had been, if I could help it. My husband had refused to have the first two baptized, but when the third was born he agreed that all three should be baptized together, and this was a very great relief to me, though I myself was still outside the pale.

There are, I imagine, phases in all conversions too personal and intimate to be published; I cannot write about the final stages in my own more than to say that at a certain moment the sense I had had so long of having to wait gave way to a conviction that I must wait no longer; yet even then I felt it must depend upon my husband's agreement.

In all these years I had never discussed religion with any Catholic, and though I had read what books I could get hold of, the intellectual circles in which I lived were so entirely cut off from Catholic thought, or indeed any Christian thought at all, that I had had no guidance as to my reading. I asked my husband then if he agreed to my going to see a priest, and suggested one of two whose books I had happened to read. He objected strongly, saying that if once I saw a priest he knew I was "done for," and that it would be "intellectual suicide." It seemed to me that I must do no more, that it could not be God's will for me to persist against my husband's wishes. I must wait longer.

Then, suddenly, quite unexpectedly, he relented; without my saying anything more about it, he came in one day and said he had been wrong, that I should be free to see a priest if I wished to, and that he had in fact arranged an interview for me, through his secretary, who was a Catholic. So once more it was taken out of my hands.

After this it was simple; I had no difficulties or doubts at all. Indeed throughout my instruction it seemed to me that all I was being told, I knew already; that it was what I had really always believed, and just ideas of my own. I did not know that anyone else believed it, still less that this was the official Catholic faith; I understand that this quite often happens, fantastic as it sounds when it is said!

Since then, of course, I have found out how much, how infinitely much, there is to learn. So far from "intellectual suicide," Catholicism has been for me the door to a limitless new world of knowledge; so far from finding my thought stifled or thwarted, it has been stimulated in a quite unprecedented way.

The usual schedule of conversion presents us with a long ordered intellectual process with, at the very end, a "leap to faith"; for me, the order seems to have been reversed; the leap came first, but no sooner was it taken than the need to learn and study followed. "Believe that you may understand" is after all an authenticated order.

I have lived always among intellectuals, with writers and scholars whose contact with the world is largely through books, and it is natural for me to want to read and study, but strong as this intellectual interest is for me, I would not put this aspect of my faith first.

A very usual phase is to find peace in religious faith. That certainly I have found, but that in itself is not enough. If I were to sum up in one word what seems to me the most essential gift which membership in the Church has given to me, I would say, *Life*.

So far from being, as is so often supposed, a restraining and repressive force, the Church for me has been a continual source of life and growth.

And how indeed should it be otherwise, if the Faith that we profess be true?

WHAT I FOUND

Owen Francis Dudley

Owen Francis Dudley has won recognition on both sides of the Atlantic as a penetrating thinker and a novelist of distinction. Born in 1882, he studied for the Anglican ministry at Lichfield Theological College, received the Licentiate of Theology at Durham University, and was ordained in 1911. After only four years in the Anglican ministry he became convinced that the Catholic Church was founded directly and immediately by Christ, and spoke on matters of faith and morals with the authority of her divine Founder.

He was received into the Catholic Church in 1915 and went to Collegio Beda in Rome to study for the priesthood. He was ordained in September 1917 by Cardinal Bourne in Westminster Cathedral, London, and was then appointed chaplain to the British Army. He saw service on the French and Italian fronts and was wounded.

After the war Father Dudley became active in the work of the Catholic Missionary Society and labored indefatigably throughout the British Isles, explaining in town hall, theater, Hyde Park, and mining clubroom the Christian way of life. He describes with keen relish the mining clubroom in which he frequently spoke as "a large hall, open all day, next the church. At night you enter a din of music and a thick mingle of beer and shag. In the center, on a platform, a band crashes out popular songs, the crowded tables all around roaring back a raucous chorus. Great scene!"

To this strenuous work Father Dudley adds "motor-missioning," which he calls "great fun . . . packed with human interest . . . one gets to love the scene each night . . . humanity in the raw . . . hungry, restless, seeking." This active apostolate of lecturing Father Dudley supplemented with the even more far-reaching apostolate of the printed work. He undertook to bring home to his readers the essential teachings of Jesus in popular form in his novels.

His trilogy, *Will Men Be Like Gods?*, *Shadows on the Earth*, and *The Masterful Monk*, treat of humanitarianism, the problem of evil, and the Christian moral code. These novels struck a responsive chord among readers in England and the United States and have been serialized, translated in various languages, and transcribed in Braille.

Encouraged by the reception given to his trilogy, Father Dudley brought out two additional novels, *Pageant of Life* and *The Coming of the Monster*, followed in 1940 by *The Tremaynes and the Masterful Monk*. His most recent book, *Michael*, has received wide acclaim and has further enhanced his reputation as a penetrating thinker and powerful writer.

In 1939 Father Dudley visited the United States while on a lecture tour of thirteen months, which took him to New Zealand, Australia, and the West Indies. During this tour Father Dudley addressed audiences of all types and color from varied pulpits and platforms. In 1933 he was elected superior of the Catholic Missionary Society and gave great impetus to the work of the society in bringing a knowledge of the Catholic faith to vast multitudes in England and Wales. His visit to Australia was instrumental in the launching of a similar movement in that country.

During World War II Father Dudley was busy in ministering to people in the hospital wards of London and in bomb-shattered homes. He wrote during the war: "Our area has suffered terribly. The mission house and rectory have been wrecked by high explosives. All around is a haunted scene of death and desolation. We are all alive and uninjured however—Deo Gratias." Father Dudley has probably as wide a reading audience in America as in Great Britain and his works are going through many editions, thus giving evidence of lasting value.

M Y FIRST introduction to the Catholic Church was being spat in the eye by a Roman Catholic boy at school. He was bigger than I; so I let it pass. But I remembered he was a Roman Catholic.

My next was at a magic-lantern entertainment to which I was taken by my mother. In the course of it there appeared on the screen the picture of a very old man in a large hat and a long white soutane. I must have asked my mother who it was, and been informed briefly that it was the "Pope of Rome." I don't quite know how, but the impression left in my mind was that there was something fishy about the "Pope of Rome."

At school, I learned in "English history" (which I discovered later was not altogether English and not altogether history) that there was something fishy not only about the Pope of Rome, but about the whole of the Pope's Church. I gathered that for a thousand years or more the Pope had held all England in his grip, and not only England but all Europe; also that during that period the "Roman," "Romish," or "Roman Catholic" Church had become more and more corrupt, until finally the original Christianity of Christ had almost disappeared; that idols were worshiped instead of God; that everywhere superstition held sway. No education; no science. Everything and everybody priest-ridden.

I read of how at last the "Glorious Reformation" had come; how the light of the Morning Star had burst upon the darkness; how the Pope's yoke had been flung off, and with it all the trappings and corruptions of popery; of the triumph of the Reformation in England; of the restoration of the primitive doctrines of Christ and the "light of the pure Gospel"; of the progress and prosperity that followed in the reign of "good Queen Bess"; of the freeing of men's minds and the expansion of thought released from the tyranny of Rome.

All this, as an English schoolboy, I drank in.

And I believed it.

Next I did a thing that we all have to do: I grew up. And I grew up without questioning the truth of what I had been taught.

The time came when I decided to become a Church of England clergyman. For this purpose I entered an Anglican theological college. And there I must confess I began to get somewhat muddled; for I could not find out what I should have to teach when I became an Anglican clergyman. Even to my youthful mind it became abundantly clear that my various tutors were contradicting each other on vital matters of Christian doctrine. My own fellow students were perpetually arguing on most fundamental points of religion. I finally emerged from that theological college feeling somewhat like an addled egg, and only dimly realizing that the Church of England had given me no theology. I appreciated later that it had no system of theology to give.

It was during that period at college that I first of all went out to Rome, on a holiday. And while there I managed to see no less a person than the Pope of Rome himself. It was Pope Pius X—being borne into St. Peter's on the *sedia gestatoria*. He passed quite close to where I was standing, and I could see his face very clearly. It was the face of a saint. I could only suppose that somehow he had managed to keep good in spite of being the Pope of Rome. That incident left a deeper impression on my mind than I was aware of at the time.

I kept a diary of all that I saw in Rome, and wrote in it: "I can quite imagine a susceptible young man being carried away by all this, and wanting to become a Roman Catholic." I myself was safe from the lure of popery, of course.

As a full-fledged Anglican clergyman I first of all worked in a country parish. At the end of a year, however, my vicar and I came to the conclusion that it would be wiser to part company; for we were disagreed as to what the Christian religion was.

I then went to a parish in the East End of London,

down among the costers, hop pickers, and dock laborers. I went down there full of zeal, determined to set the Thames on fire. I very soon discovered, though, that the vast mass of East Enders had no interest at all in the religion that I professed. Out of the six thousand or so in the parish not more than one or two hundred even came near the church. Our hoppers' socials in the Parish Hall were well patronized, however. Great nights, and a thrilling din of barrel organ, dancing, and singing. I found the Donkey Row hoppers immensely lovable and affectionate. We had wonderful days with them each September in the hopfields of Kent. It was social work. The mass of them we could not even touch with religion.

I grew somewhat "extreme" in this parish under the influence of my vicar, to whom at first I was too "Protestant." I remember he disliked the hat I arrived in—a round, flat one. The vicarage dog ate the hat, and I bought a more "priestly" one.

For a year or two things went fairly smoothly and I suffered from no qualms about the Anglican religion. How far I sincerely believed that I was a "Catholic" during that period I find it difficult to estimate now. Sufficiently at any rate to argue heatedly with Low Church and "modernist" clergy in defense of my claim. And sufficiently to be thoroughly annoyed with a Roman Catholic lady who, whenever we met, told me she was praying for my conversion to the "True Church," and a Franciscan friar in the hopfields who told me the same. I felt like telling them they could pray until they were black in the face. I remember, too, that whenever I met a Roman Catholic priest I experienced a sense of inferiority and a vague feeling of not quite being the real thing, or at least of there being an indefinable but marked difference between us.

It was when I could no longer avoid certain unpleasant facts with which I was confronted in my work as an Anglican clergyman that the first uneasiness came.

One day I was in the house of a certain dock laborer who lived exactly opposite our church but never darkened its doors. I chose the occasion to ask him why not? His reply flattened me out; it was to the effect that he could see no valid reason for believing what I taught in preference to what the "Low Church bloke dohn the road" taught. I could not give a satisfactory answer to his challenge. I don't suppose he believed in either of us really; but he had placed me in a quandary. We were both Anglican clergymen, and we were both flatly contradicting each other from our respective pulpits.

It set a question simmering in my mind: "Why should *anybody* believe what I taught?" And a further question: "What authority had I for what I was teaching?"

I began, for the first time with real anxiety, to examine the Anglican Church. And with that examination I found I could no longer blind myself to certain patent facts, which hitherto I had brushed aside. The Established Church was a church of contradictions, of parties, each of which had an equal claim to represent it, and all of which were destructive of its general claim to be part of the Church of Christ—directly one affirmed its unity. As far as authority was concerned, it was possible to believe anything or nothing without ecclesiastical interference. You could be an extreme "Anglo-Catholic" and hold all the doctrines of the Catholic Church except the inconvenient ones like papal infallibility; you could be an extreme modernist and deny (while retaining Christian terms) all the doctrines of the Christian religion. No bishop said yes or no imperatively to any party. The bishops were as divided as the parties. For practical purposes, if bishops did interfere, they were ignored, even by their own clergy. If the Holy Ghost, as claimed, was with the Church of England, then logically the Holy Ghost was the author of contradictions; for each party claimed His guidance.

These facts presented me with a quandary which appeared insurmountable, and which remained insurmountable.

I have often been asked, since my conversion, how,

in view of them, Anglican clergy can be sincere in remaining where they are. My reply has been—they *are* sincere. There is a state of mental blindness in which one is incapable of seeing the plain logic of facts. I only know that it was over a year before I acted on those facts myself. And I honestly believe I was sincere during that period. Only those who have been Protestants can appreciate the thick veil of prejudice, fear, and mistrust of "Rome" which hampers every groping toward the truth.

It was about this time that there fell into my hands a book written by a Catholic priest, who himself had once been an Anglican clergyman, who had been faced by the same difficulties, and who had found the solution of them in the Catholic Church. "But the Catholic Church *can't* be the solution," I said. And there rose before my mind a vision of all I had been taught about her from my boyhood upward—her false teaching, her corruptions of the doctrines of Christ. The Catholic Church, though, was the church of the overwhelming majority of Christians, and always had been. If what I had been taught was true, then for nearly two thousand years the great mass of Christians had been deluded and deceived by lies. Could Christ have allowed a hoax, an imposture of that magnitude? In His name? The Catholic Church was either an imposture or——

Or what?

I began to buy Catholic books. To study Catholic doctrines. To read history from the Catholic standpoint.

The day came when I sat looking into the fire asking myself: "Is what the world says of the Catholic Church true? Or what the Catholic Church says of herself? Have I all these years been shaking my fist at a phantom of my own imagining, fed on prejudice and ignorance?"

I compared her unity with the complete lack of it outside. Her authority with the absence of anything approaching real authority in the church of which I was a member and a minister. The unchangeable moral code she proclaimed with the wavering, shilly-shallying moral expediency that Protestantism allowed. She began to look so very much more like the church that God would have made, just as the Established Church began to look so very much more like the church that man would have made.

When I was passing Westminster Cathedral one day I went in and knelt for half an hour before the Blessed Sacrament. I came out terribly shaken—spiritually shaken. It is impossible to describe; but in that short half hour what, until now, I had contemplated as a problem had suddenly assumed an aspect of imperativeness. A problem that had to be solved, not played with. For within those four walls there had loomed up before my spiritual vision an immensity, a vast reality, before which everything else had shrunk away. The church whose clergyman I was seemed to have slipped from under my feet.

I returned to the East End dazed. That night amongst the hoppers I felt like a stranger moving about.

I went about for weeks in a state of uncertainty, undecided in my conscience as to whether I was morally bound to face things out or not—wretched under the suspicion that what "Rome" said might be true—that I was no priest; that my "Mass" was no Mass at all; that I was genuflecting before . . . ? That my "absolutions" were worthless. The more I prayed about it, the more unreal my ministry appeared.

I decided to consult a certain very "extreme" clergyman, whom I believed to be sincere beyond question (as he was), and a man of deep spiritual piety. I had three or four talks with him in all, the general result of which was to leave me more confused intellectually than ever, but spiritually more at peace; though it took me months before I realized that this peace was a false one, and that I had shelved the matter not from its intellectual difficulties, but for worldly reasons. For those talks had opened for me an unpleasant vista of what might happen if I went "over to Rome"—the loss

141

of my position, my salary, friends and all; not only the burning of all my boats but the wounding of my mother and father cruelly. Even more, "Rome" might not accept me for her priesthood; in any case it would be starting all over again, possibly from baptism. If she did not want me for a priest, I should have to . . .

My whole being revolted against the prospect. It was impossible—such a demand. I had been carried away by my emotions. It was a snare of Satan. I should be a traitor to the church of my baptism. God had placed me here in the Church of England. He was blessing my work as its minister. He had given me endless graces.

I buried myself in that work again, and for a time succeeded in forgetting, or at least stifling, the fears that had been my torment—until the haphazard remark of a photographer (registering my features), an agnostic, I believe, opened my eyes to my inability honestly to defend the Established Church's position; it was to the effect that if Christianity were true, obviously the Roman Catholic Church, with her authority, was right. It was the testimony of a man who had no ax to grind. A Jewish dentist made the same remark in effect to me shortly afterward. The man in the street testified the same with his: "If I were religious, I'd be a Roman Catholic."

Whether it was the photographer or not, my fears were released once more from their repression, abruptly and acutely, and this time I resolved that it should be a fight to the finish, either way—that no worldly or material considerations should interfere. The clergyman whom I had consulted had already made one thing clear in my mind—that the issue between Rome and Canterbury, the crux of the whole problem, was the claim of Rome to be the infallible teaching authority appointed by God, and the denial by Canterbury of that claim. The whole question boiled down to the question of infallibility, and on that everything else hung.

I entered upon an intensive study of the point. I read the history of the doctrine, the Fathers and the

Councils of the Church, and what they had to say; examined its rationality. At the end of some months I came to this conclusion—that, as far as Holy Scripture, history, and reason were concerned, the Catholic Church could prove her claim to be God's infallible teacher up to the hilt.

It is difficult after all these years to recapture the exact mode of its appeal to my reason; but it was the appeal that the doctrine of the infallibility of the Church inevitably presents to any man who is prepared to lay aside bias, prejudice, and preconceptions.

I will try to state it in the fewest words possible.

Infallibility is the only guarantee we have that the Christian religion is true. Actually, if I, at this moment, did not believe in an infallible teacher appointed by God, then nothing on earth would induce me to believe in the Christian religion. If, as outside the Catholic Church, Christian doctrines are a matter of private judgment, and therefore the Christian religion a mere matter of human opinion, then there is no obligation upon any living soul to believe in it. Why should I stake my immortal soul upon human opinion? For that is all you have if you refuse the infallible Church.

In itself her claim may be reduced to this: the Catholic Church, when she defines a doctrine of faith or morals, when she tells us what to believe and what to do—in a word, what the Christian religion is—then, and then only, she is prevented by God from making a mistake, from teaching untruth. The Church is God's mouthpiece—His voice. Could God's voice speak untruth? Protestantism, claiming the Holy Ghost and presenting a jumble of contradictions, declares, in effect, that God *does* speak untruth. And only blinded reason prevents its adherents from seeing and admitting that unpalatable fact. Sanity alone should compel every thinking man to halt before the Catholic Church's very claim.

It is commonly assumed that submission to an infallible authority in religion involves slavery, that Catholics cannot think for themselves, that their reason is stifled, that they commit intellectual suicide. "No educated man could accept the medieval dogmas of the Catholic Church." Examined in the light of horse sense and human reason, that shibboleth of the modernist leaders is revealed in all its naked stupidity, as an irrational and unscientific piece of snobbery for gulling the masses and blinding them to the claims of the Catholic Church. In intent, since the dogmas are the same today, it means: "No educated man could submit to what the Catholic Church claims to be infallibly true": or, more simply, "No educated man could submit to infallibility in the matter of religion." For acceptance involves submission to the one Church that claims it.

The obvious reply is: "In the name of all that is sane —why not?" When in every other department of life he is submitting to infallible truth already? Is slavery involved; is reason stifled; is it intellectual suicide to submit to the infallible truth of the law of gravity; do men jump off cliffs on the chance of going up instead of down? To submit, as every scientist does, to the fixed data of science, believing them to be infallibly true; could he be a scientist at all, if he refused to submit? To submit, as every educated man does, by eating, to the infallible truth that the human body needs food? To submit, even if he was not there and never saw it, to the infallible truth of the Great War? To submit, as every mathematician does, to the multiplication table? To the axioms of Euclid? To submit, as every honest businessman does, to the infallible principles of business honesty? As all businessmen do to the infallible requirements for running a business at all? Were a businessman to conduct his business as the modernists conduct their religion, he would close down as the modernists have closed down Christianity for themselves and their adherents.

Examples could be multiplied to show that in every department of life every rational being is already submitting to infallible truth. Is it rational or irrational to proclaim that no educated man could submit in the hundredth case, that of religion, when he submits in the other ninety-nine?

On the face of it the rationality lies with those who submit in the hundredth and most vital case of all. Is it a sign of education to submit to human opinions in preference to the revealed truths of God, who Himself declared that they were to be taught and accepted or refused under pain of eternal damnation? To prefer the negations of modernism to the dogmas of the Church that *must* teach infallibly if she teaches Christianity, i.e., the revealed truths of God? Of the Church that *must* be infallible when she teaches truth, since truth is an infallible thing?

When, as far as reason was concerned, I was satisfied as to the unique claim of Rome, upon which all else depended, I decided to present my case for no longer remaining in the Church of England to one or two prominent scholars among its clergy. I did so. As far as I can recollect, the "refutations" given me made no impression whatever. Though easily my superiors in scholarship, I had sufficient knowledge and logic to perceive that the great chain of scriptural and historical evidence for the Catholic claim remained unbroken by excerpts from St. Augustine, St. Cyprian, and others, conveniently interpreted according to the will of the reader and not to the mind of the author. It is little less than amazing to me now that scholars of repute should endeavor to counter the vast weight of evidence against them with what they themselves must in honesty admit is the less likely interpretation—to fit the rock to the pebble rather than the pebble to the rock.

To my case for leaving a church which was so plainly devoid, in view of its contradictions, of any divine teaching authority, I received no valid answer at all. Every conceivable *argumentum ad hominem* was presented; sentiment, "Roman fever," "intellectual suicide," treachery to the "church of my baptism," "corruptions of Rome," the whole well-worn gamut of objections was paraded. I had read them all, though, already and found them untrue. The great *facts* about

145

the Catholic Church were left standing—unassailable. And those facts demanded submission.

I have been asked again and again, since I became a Catholic, why I left the Church of England, and often the implication behind the question, if not actually expressed, has been that my motive for doing so could not have been based on reason. There is a prevalent idea that converts to Rome are in some mysterious manner "got hold of" or "caught" by "Roman priests." I would like to assure any non-Catholic who may happen to read this that converts are not "got hold of" or "caught." In my own case I had rarely even spoken to a "Roman priest," before, of my own free will and with my reason already convinced, I went to consult one at the London Oratory. It is true that in doing so I was still full of Protestant suspicion and imagined that he would be extremely gratified to "get hold of" a real live Anglican clergyman; I should make a splendid "catch."

The priest in question received me most calmly. He showed no sign of excitement; he did not stand on his head or caper about. He did not even appear to regard me as a particularly good "catch." He answered my questions and invited me to come again, if I cared to, but no more. I left, feeling several sizes smaller.

I learned many things, however, from that interview. It was so entirely different from the interviews with the Anglican scholars. For the priest there was no difficult case to bolster up. Not a single question that I put to him presented "difficulties." There were no awkward corners to get round. I believe his candidness about the human side of the Catholic Church almost startled me. Never once was he on the defense. All that I had been groping toward so painfully and laboriously was so obvious to him as to leave me wondering how it could ever have not been obvious to myself.

I realized, too, from that interview that "going over to Rome" would be very much more than stepping out of a small boat onto an Atlantic liner. It would be no less than coming into the kingdom of God on earth— and the Catholic Church was that kingdom of God. I was not coming in on my own terms, but on hers. I was not conferring a privilege upon her; she was conferring an inestimable privilege upon me. I was not going to make myself a Catholic, the Catholic Church was going to make me one. There would be a formal course of instruction, a real testing of my faith, and finally, a real submission to a living authority—the living authority of God on earth.

I hope I am wrong, but I have sometimes suspected that there are some who have never made their submission to the Catholic Church, and yet who have reached the point at which I stood after seeing that priest; those whose reason has led them to entrance gates of the Kingdom of God, who have seen inscribed above them that word "Submission" in all its naked, uncompromising meaning—and turned away. I wonder if they can ever forget that they once looked into their mother's eyes—and refused.

Reason may submit; the will may refuse.

It is a matter of dispositions and the grace of God, once conviction of the reason has been attained. Actually, it involves an *unconditional* surrender of the will to the will of God—no easy task for the Protestant whose whole outlook in the spiritual direction has been determined by likes and dislikes, who has been accustomed to a religion that costs him little and claims the right of private judgment, who has detested being *told* what to believe and what to do; in a word, who has been habitually indisposed, mentally and spiritually, for anything approaching unconditional submission of the will. I have no intention of hurting feelings, but I am convinced that the supreme difficulty for most Anglicans who would "like to go over to Rome" but do not, is their (unconscious perhaps) inability even to contemplate submission to the one Church that demands it. When the late Archbishop of Canterbury publicly proclaimed that he and the adherents of the Established Church would *never* pass under a doorway upon whose lintel was inscribed the word "Submission" he was precisely expressing the Protestant mind.

147

Mercifully he was unaware that submission to the Catholic Church is submission to God.

I claim no credit, in my own case, for submitting; but rather blame for delaying so long—for the moral cowardice that hesitates to lay the onus of the consequences upon Almighty God, to burn one's boats and take the plunge.

When, by divine grace, I was ready, and had made my decision, there was only one thing to do. I told my vicar, packed my bags, and left the East End. At the London Oratory I placed myself under instruction and, later on, was received.

I would like to mention that my Protestant vicar and a curate who succeeded me in the parish are now also, both of them—priests of the Catholic Church.

"Well—and what have you found?"

I will tell you—and what I was told I should find.

I was told that the Catholic Church always placed the Church before Christ—that Christ was kept in the background. I have found, on the contrary, that she places me in a personal relationship with Christ that can never be attained outside—that Christ is her very being, by Whom and for Whom she exists, and to Whom to unite her children is her one ceaseless care.

I was told that if I became a Catholic my mind would be fettered, my reason stifled; I should no longer be able to think for myself. I have found on the contrary that the Catholic Church places me on a platform of truth from which even a poor mind like mine can rise to fathomless heights. I have found the truth that sets men free.

I was told that in the Catholic Church it was all decay and stagnation. I have found, however, the very life of God himself pulsing through every vein of His Mystical Body. It was like coming out of a small stuffy room with all the windows closed and striding up to the top of some great hill with all the winds of heaven roaring round. I have found life.

Instead of the hard spiritual tyranny of which I was

told, I have found a loving Mother who supplies my every human need. Instead of corruption, sanctity unknown outside.

And sinners, too. For the Church of Christ does not break the bruised reed or quench the smoking flax. Like her Master, she ever seeks and saves that which is lost. She is big enough and loving enough to hold even sinners in the fold; if she did not, she would not be the Church of Christ.

Instead of hatred, I have found compassion for those outside—for the sheep without a shepherd. And I would that I could show them right into the heart of him whom men call the Pope of Rome—the shepherd of the sheep, the Vicar of Christ on earth; for then I would show them no ambitious autocrat striving for worldly power, but a loving father loved by his children as no other man on earth is loved.

And I have found the kingdom of Heaven on earth. The city of God.

That city that "hath no need of the sun, nor of the moon to shine in it; for the glory of God hath enlightened it, and the Lamb is the lamb thereof."

GROWING INTO CATHOLICISM

Hon. Robert F. Wagner

Perhaps no name in America stands as a more fitting symbol for social justice and solicitude for the rights of the laboring classes than that of Senator Robert F. Wagner. For many years he has been the outstanding champion of legislation designed to share the fruits of American industry with all its citizens. Virtually every important piece of national legislation along the lines of social justice, welfare, and security in the last twenty years has either been written by him or been associated with his name.

In recognition of his distinguished services he received the Pope Leo XIII Award from the Sheil School of Social Studies in 1947. The Sheil School was founded by Bishop

Bernard J. Sheil, the senior auxiliary bishop of Chicago, for the promotion of research and study in the social and economic fields. It is unique in that it admits all people who are interested in the lectures to attend without insisting upon academic credits and prerequisites.

Coming to this country from Germany as a poor boy of eight, Robert Wagner graduated from the City College of New York and received his LL.B. from the New York University Law School. He served in the New York Assembly and later in the Senate of that state. He was a justice of the Supreme Court of New York, and since 1927 has been in the United States Senate. He introduced the National Industrial Recovery Act, Social Security Act, National Labor Relations Act, and championed the Pension Law and the United States Housing Act of 1937 and other social and economic legislation.

The solicitude of the Catholic Church for the laboring classes, finding its classic expression in the encyclicals of Leo XIII and of Pius XI, won the admiration of Robert Wagner, whose own soul was aflame with the passion for social justice. Working with Catholics, he became conscious of the influence which religion exercised in their lives. He admired the democracy of the Church, which knows no distinction of class or race and which draws most of its leaders—bishops, cardinals, and pontiffs—from the ranks of the poor and the lowly.

He was received into the Church in January 1946 by Monsignor Robert F. Keegan, who had long been active in the fields of charity and social work in New York City. Senator Wagner is carrying on with tireless energy his efforts in behalf of a living wage, social justice, and the wider diffusion of the wealth of the nation among its people.

LOOKING backward over my seventy years of life I can recall no single event, impression, or idea to which I can point as the first cause or the beginning of my interest in the Catholic religion and the final acceptance of it as my faith. I just grew into being a Catholic. My story is therefore not a very spectacular or dramatic one. It is, indeed, a very simple one.

Yet as I look back it seems almost as though a very careful plan was laid out by God for the purpose of gradually but persistently "edging" me into the Church. My conversion was so gradual, in fact, it was only after experiencing a tremendous feeling of exhilaration and satisfaction such as I had never known following my baptism, that I became truly aware of and fully appreciated the step that I had finally taken. Of course it was with full understanding and consideration that I did decide to take the final step of becoming a Catholic, but when that time came it caused me no great period of pondering or deliberation. There was no other decision possible than to take instructions and enter the Church.

"God-fearing and God-loving" well describes my parents, and my childhood training was strictly in accordance with the Lutheran faith. My mother's father was a preacher and, although he died before I was born, Mother never let me forget him or his biblical admonitions. Probably because my grandfather was a preacher or perhaps because I lived so near the church and could get there first I became the boy who sounded the church bell. Many years later, while a member of the Supreme Court of the state of New York, when I was the honored guest of my birthplace, I again rang the same church bell. I recalled at the time my mother saying: "Nothing you will ever do in life will be more important than ringing the church bell, for you are calling and bringing people to God."

Life in the huge city of New York for an immigrant boy of eight and his family was much different than life in a small town like Nastätten in Germany. There church was the center of town life. On the East Side of New York in those days life was hard and the Church was not the center of activities that it was in Germany. As a result my religion became less formalized and during my college days I attended the Methodist Church, incidentally taking an active part in the Epworth League, a sort of religious discussion group for Methodist youth. In my manhood I adhered to no particular sect, but I attended from time to time a Protestant church conveniently located, or one which had a good preacher.

The house in which I lived as a boy had a number of Catholic families and because my father was the janitor we got to know most of the families quite intimately. I remember my father one night as he lit his perennial corncob, remark to my mother that the Catholics treated us just as well as and sometimes better than our own folks. It was probably the first time I ever gave a thought to Catholicism, or for that matter to a difference in one's religion. It was a fleeting thought, to be sure, but all my life the validity of my father's observation was brought home to me.

I guess my first wish to be a Catholic came from desire to be an altar boy and wear a cassock and surplice like my little Irish pal Timmy. I remember how proud he used to be to wear that shiny cassock. It covered his tattered clothes, and how wonderful he looked to me. I remember also the fact that he sat right up with the priest and was regarded as the equal of the other more fortunate boys whose folks had money. It was the first inkling of what I later came to know as the Church's real democracy.

I many times remarked when discussing the Catholic Church how I always observed that whenever I went into a Catholic Church I would see rich and poor alike sitting next to each other. I never saw a Catholic Church that seemed to be meant just for the rich. It was open to all. Later, too, as I became acquainted and friendly with members of the clergy and the hierarchy, I was impressed with the fact that almost without exception they were from poor families.

As I observed the Church in action through the years I was struck by that same spirit of democracy that was manifest in the complete and total concern of the Church for each individual soul—no matter how poor or rich, or what color or age, or how bad he might be. I always thought it was very significant that not even the Pope could dissolve the marriage of the poorest beggar or the most powerful king.

152

Margaret Marie McTague is, no doubt, the reason I am a Catholic today. She was the typical Irish beauty, a twinkle in her eyes, a ready smile, an equally ready tear. We were married in the rectory. I remember my very close friend and colleague in the New York State Assembly at the time, Al Smith, urging me two nights before: "Why don't you do it right, Bob? Do yourself and Margaret a favor. Become a Catholic before you marry." I often wish that I had, but I guess it wasn't God's way. At any rate I wasn't ready for the Church then. I suppose it is the mystery of God's grace that I had to wait some forty years before I finally became a Catholic.

My wife personified to me what I had noticed and admired in so many of my Catholic friends. She enjoyed life to the fullest and was so terrifically human, yet she was strictly and devoutly religious. When staying out late of a Saturday night, fasting after midnight and getting up early for Mass and Communion seemed so natural and easy for her. Religion was part of her and her personality blended into all that she did. But it seemed natural for a great many others, too, and later on in life when I began to think more deeply about Catholicism it was the naturalness of the Catholic religion that so strongly appealed to me.

The one trivial rift my wife and I had in our married life was the result of my attempt to be humorous one Friday evening. I suggested we go out to Feltman's for a steak dinner, for which they were justifiably famous. Just as she was about to put the first juicy piece into her mouth I reminded her that it was Friday!

Up in Albany while the legislature was in session Al Smith and I roomed together. I always had a very deep and abiding admiration and love for Al. No man ever knew more about government than he, and no man in public or private life was more aware of God's place in his work and in his life. It was as natural for Al to talk about God and God's will as it was for him to talk

153

about a budget for a department or a program for the development of public power, and he talked plenty about both. Some men keep their thoughts about God and His works to themselves and their families, but Al would discuss them with anyone and the subject might crop up in any connection with the most diverse subjects. And no one ever took offense or thought it unusual, because of the open, friendly, and intelligent way he had of discussing things.

Influenced as I was by the mind of Al, I was more influenced by his spirit. I never forgot the first night we roomed together. We got in very late in the morning after a long train ride following a political meeting in Manhattan. We had to be up again in three hours. I already was under the covers when I noticed Al on his knees, rosary in hand.

Al never forgot his God, not for a moment, even when he was in the midst of a campaign for the presidency of the United States. On one occasion during the campaign the schedule of Sunday morning's stops would not have permitted him to assist at Mass. Politically as important as the schedule was, he ordered it changed so that he could make a stopover in a city where he could attend Mass. The humorous part of the story is that the pastor of the church who greeted him after Mass confessed that he had been a Republican all his life, and even the honor of Al's visit to his church would not cause him to change his vote.

It was Kate and Al Smith's sympathetic interest and loyal friendship toward me that constantly kept before my mind the unexpressed prayers that I know were in my wife's heart as she passed on to her Maker about thirty years ago. They knew of her prayers for my conversion and they continued them. I believe it was at the Catholic Charities dinner in memory of Cardinal Hayes that Al Smith said: "Bob, isn't it about time that you did it? My prayers ought to be answered soon." They soon were, but Al had already gone to his reward.

It is during times of sickness and death that the

power and adequacy of our faith become most apparent. It seems to offer one such great consolation. My wife was ill for some time before she died, yet right to the end she managed to get to St. Ignatius Loyola every Sunday morning. The pew where she knelt, incidentally, is still there in her memory, and it always will be. She knew she would not recover, but her faith made her content and she remained happy to the end. Death for Catholics is something holy—it is an expression of God's will. Somehow a Catholic funeral lacked the awful bleakness that I frequently experienced at the funerals of my non-Catholic friends. Yes, you just had to be moved by it all, and I was.

It was my old friend, James A. Foley, who served with Al and me in Albany, from whom I learned most about God and the moral order. Had not Jim chosen the more secluded and scholarly office of surrogate, I often thought he would have become as famous as Al Smith or Franklin Roosevelt—who like me always sought his counsel and advice.

The encyclicals of Pope Leo XIII were first brought to my attention by him. The dignity of work, the worth of the human personality, and the all-importance of family life were the guideposts for his every action. And never did I see a man who could "humanize" and clarify a complicated government problem as he did by bringing in one or more of these principles.

Unlike Al Smith, Jim never would, on his own, bring up the subject of my conversion, although we probably both sensed it as being in the background when we discussed, as we often did, philosophy, religion, or their application. When I finally entered the Church my confidential secretary, Mrs. Marguerite C. Hayes, knowing better than anyone else his tremendous interest in my conversion, made it a point to inform him first. He was on what later proved to be his deathbed. "Never," she later told me, "have I ever seen a man so visibly affected or happy." And only then did he confess that for twenty years he had remembered me in his daily prayers.

It was Maggie, as I affectionately refer to Mrs. Hayes, who most persistently and in a good-natured sort of way "belligerently" carried on a campaign for my conversion. In an effort to arouse her and make her angry I used to find all sorts of fault with the Church and the people in it. When I succeeded in arousing her at infrequent intervals she used to bemoan her wasted novenas. Working close to me, as she has for over twenty-two years, I had the opportunity to observe how, regardless of great sorrow or tragedy, she never lost her good humor or her optimism. "The will of God" has a practical meaning to her. I guess it gradually dawned on me, for after a while I used to hear myself saying, "It's the will of God."

Then there was Bobby, my only child. He was just nine when we were left alone. His mother's last words were about him and his religion. I carried out my pledge to her faithfully and completely, and in doing so I learned more about the Church and saw the good results of his religious training. Every Sunday "Uncle" Michael J. Cosgrove, his godfather, would take him to church and on occasion I used to go along with them.

I remember an early Sunday morning when we were in a little town in Switzerland and I awoke to find Bobby dressing himself and I asked him: "Where are you going?"

"To church," was his reply.

"Do you know where one is?"

"No, but I'll find one," and he did.

There was something about the Catholic faith that gave confidence and inspired determination. Bobby, uninhibited, brought it home to me continuously. I sort of renewed my boyhood and youth with Bobby, and it gave me the advantage of a fresh and intimate view of the Catholic faith and what it stood for.

If I were influenced emotionally toward the Church by my environment, and by my friends and those whom I loved most, I was even more influenced by the intellectual appeal of the Church. The whole of the Church's philosophy seemed to be in good proportion

156

and well integrated. Every piece of its teachings and its doctrines fitted together and reinforced the others. Nothing appeared very extreme. It all seemed to fit in sort of a natural order. I was made particularly aware of this as I became acquainted with the Church's social philosophy—its philosophy as it was applied to the fields in which I could claim some degree of expertness myself.

Reading the encyclicals of Pope Leo XIII on the Condition of the Working Class, we are liable to lose sight of the fact that it was written over a half century ago during the time when Manchester liberalism and unrestricted capitalism in this country held full sway. Concern for the individual workingman and his family was not part of the thinking or concern of those who ruled industry or government. To join, no less than talk of, unions or organizing the working class for the purpose of improving their working conditions was to invite not only social opprobrium but to destroy pretty much one's opportunity for further employment.

Imagine, if you will, how affected I must have been, a young man starting out in political life with a zeal for changing the wretched conditions under which a large majority of the people in those days lived and labored, to find the Pope of Rome saying in much better language and in much more precise terms the things I felt with my whole being.

The whole emphasis of His Holiness was on the welfare of each and every individual. His insistence on the supreme importance of the human personality was something that never left me. It was the motivation and at the same time the objective on which and toward which my legislative and judicial efforts were directed. Every man had a soul—it was as simple as that—and that's why man had a dignity that had to be preserved and enhanced. Man imprinted his personality on that on which he labored, and to his work was lent his dignity and his personality. Work was therefore something honorable and the expression of God in man.

157

It followed that man should not be oppressed or controlled by his work, but be lifted up and enabled to control his own destiny through it. Man by his work should be able to bring up a family in a fashion worthy of his human nature. The "living wage" was not merely a social ideal. It was the concrete and material economic expression of the philosophy of man and his nature. With man's work should go some control and responsibility, and thus it was that Pope Leo recognized the need for workingmen's organizations through which men could effectively exercise control and responsibility in an era of mass production and industrialism.

While Pope Leo's encyclical attacked "socialism" and "liberalism" as false and misleading doctrines, the emphasis of Pope Leo's teaching and the major part of the encyclical was devoted to a positive and constructive program. Like everything else in the Church, the solution offered was the kind that would appear just and common-sense-like to the average man of good will. It was sort of a "middle way." For those in control it was "far to the left." Certainly the social doctrines of the Church, becoming a part of me, as they did, greatly influenced my final acceptance of all the teachings of the Church.

I have often been attacked as a socialist and even as a communist for my authorship or espousal of the National Labor Relations Act, the Social Security Act, the Fair Labor Standards Act, the Full Employment Act, and more recently for sponsoring Health Insurance. Yet it was with reference to just these programs of action that Pope Pius XI, following in the path laid down by his holy predecessor, Pope Leo XIII, could be quoted most solidly and specifically as supporting.

I had the privilege of an audience with Pius XI and I felt that I caught the spirit of the man, and his words to me always meant a great deal more, perhaps, than to others less fortunate than I. Great minds and men of eminent stature in the life of our nation like Bishop Francis J. Haas, Monsignor John A. Ryan, Monsignor

John P. Boland, Monsignor John O'Grady, Monsignor Robert F. Keegan, were some of the men who defended me and encouraged me in my legislative efforts. I remember Cardinal Hayes patting his hand on mine one day after a vicious attack on my "radicalism" had been launched in a prominent editorial, saying, "Senator, don't give up. You are doing God's work." Certainly I would be less than human if all this didn't leave its mark.

In the United States Senate it happened that those with whom I had the opportunity of working most closely were also Catholics. It was as a freshman senator that Tom Walsh of Montana took me in hand. He gave me a good lesson in practical Christian statesmanship in his able and fearless conduct of the Teapot Dome investigation. My close friend and colleague, Senator Jim Mead, the rich but humble and progressive Jim Murray, hard-working and effective Dennis Chavez, brilliant Joe O'Mahoney, and more recently forward-looking members of the Senate like Howard McGrath, Frank Myers, and Brian McMahon—we all worked together for the same progressive social program, as if in confirmation of my past observation and ideas.

But I doubt whether I would be a Catholic today except for my long-time friend, Monsignor Robert F. Keegan. It was he who could always explain to those outside the Church things difficult to understand. It was he who pulled all the threads together for me. It was he who by the grace of God visited me in my hospital room at the very moment I was thinking of my wife's prayers, of Al Smith's urgings, my son's patient prodding, and of my own deep-seated inclination. His face gave me the answer, and I asked him if I could become a Catholic.

On the morning of January 24, 1946, it was Monsignor Keegan who baptized me. I always thought no one else could so impressively or with greater dignity perform the beautiful rituals of the Church. I paid particular attention to this when he performed the nuptials of young Bob and christened his first child.

Shortly after my baptism the door of my hospital room opened and there stood Archbishop Francis J. Spellman and Bishop J. Francis A. McIntyre. Although the archbishop was in the midst of his preparations preceding his trip to Rome, where he was to be made a cardinal, he took occasion to drop in on me to wish me well and to ask me if I would wait until he returned from Rome so that he could confirm me. On May 19 I was permitted the rare privilege and honor of being confirmed by the new cardinal in his private chapel.

In the course of my instruction under the brilliant young canonist, Father James P. Kelly, he asked me what the hardest thing about being a Catholic appeared to be. I told him: "Not understanding why everyone else isn't a Catholic." Once you have come to the Faith, it is difficult to understand how one could be content without it, especially if you come very much in contact with it. It is as though a maze of thousands of different lines in utter confusion without end suddenly shaped themselves into a beautiful, harmonious, and thrilling picture.

FROM MARX TO CHRIST

Douglas Hyde

In the tumble-down editorial offices of the London *Daily Worker* in Gray's Inn Road, Douglas Hyde, news editor for five years and a Communist for twenty years, put the first edition to bed on the night of March 14, 1948, walked into the office of the editor, William Rust, and announced that he was quitting. "Are you feeling quite well?" Rust asked anxiously. Hyde assured him that he had never felt better in his life.

On March 19 Hyde's reasons for resigning hit the front pages of British newspapers (but not that of the *Worker*, which buried the story in five factual paragraphs at the bottom of page 3). In a written statement Hyde announced that he had renounced Communism and, with his wife and children, was joining the Catholic Church.

Hyde had been increasingly disturbed by Soviet Russia's foreign policy and by events in eastern Europe. He became convinced that Communist opposition to the Marshall Plan could bring nothing but misery to the common people of Britain, that the movement was destroying those very freedoms and decencies for which it claimed to be fighting. He felt that many Communist Party members were likewise deeply disturbed and that the time was ripe for large-scale resignations. "Many young people who joined during the war years," he said, "won't take so long as I did to make up their minds."

At home Hyde said that he had no money or job and wondered whether to give away his six hundred Communist books or burn them. He revealed that he had led a Jekyll-and-Hyde existence since the previous October when he and his wife decided to enter the Catholic Church. He and his wife and their two children were received into the Church by Father Joseph Corr of Wimbledon.

Born in 1908 of Methodist parents, Douglas Hyde aspired as a youngster to be a missionary in India. But at the age of seventeen he joined the Communist Party in Britain and, along with his wife, became a zealous disciple of Karl Marx.

During his five years as news editor of the London *Daily Worker* he turned out many articles which stamped him as a writer of force, with a sprightly and engaging style. He acknowledges his debt to the works of Chesterton and Belloc in giving him an insight into the richness of Catholic culture, and now he gives promise of developing into an able and brilliant writer, walking in the great traditions of his fellow converts, Evelyn Waugh, Bruce Marshall, and Graham Greene.

POLITICAL disillusionment and sanctifying grace have combined to change me from an almost life-long Communist to a Catholic. For twenty years I had been an active member of the Communist Party, from the time I was just under eighteen years of age, in fact. For eight years I had been an executive of the British Communist Party's only daily paper, the *Daily Worker;* for the last five I had been its news editor.

I started out at the age of seventeen to study theology (I was to be a Methodist missionary in India), but before the year was out I had joined my first Communist organization. Now I am back full circle again, but this time as a Catholic.

But you can't spend all those years working, thinking, living as a Communist and come back just as you set out. I have left behind me a trail of good, promising people I got to sign up as Party members in the past; they include people who today are writers, local councilors, prospective parliamentary candidates, in their turn influencing others as I had influenced them. I have brought with me to Catholicism a knowledge of the British trade-union and labor movement and of Communism such as only the news editor of a Communist daily could get, a habit of thinking quickly as the world situation twists and turns—and a knowledge that I have a great deal of evil to undo before I can hope to get rid of my guilty conscience.

There were plenty of things in the Communist Party of 1928 to appeal to a thoughtful youth possessed of his full share of idealism. I was interested in India—the Indian nationalist movement was capturing the imagination of quite a lot of people on both sides of the Atlantic—and the Communist Party in Great Britain was fighting for the Indian people's independence.

I wanted to identify myself with the poor, the downtrodden, the victimized and persecuted. The Communist Party appeared to me to fight for all these. Like most youths, I wanted to break free from convention— and the Communist Party was certainly unconventional. I wanted a new world, and the Communists had one to offer. I was attracted by these people who, in a world which appeared to be drifting along, knew exactly where they were going and how they were going to get there.

It was exciting to learn that the Russian Revolution, about which as a tiny child I had heard horrific stories, was, despite what the spoon-fed public believed, the great hope of the world. It was exciting, too, learning that all the old habits of thought must be thrown over-board; that the old preoccupation with right and wrong was simply cant; that only what served the class struggle really mattered and by this all things could be judged.

There was a brand-new, complete, and, it appeared, wholly satisfying philosophy of life to be acquired; abstruse economic theories to be studied, and action, positive action, action without ceasing, on behalf of the cause.

Some or all of those things which attracted me attract the average Communist Party member too. They are by no means entirely bad in themselves, and those who join the Party are, many of them, good types brought in on the appeal of qualities equally good.

The sin of the Fascists was that they organized the lowest and the worst on the behalf of a bad cause. The sin of the Communists, however, is a greater one; they take some of the most active and intelligent of the working class, the most promising of the intelligentsia, and pervert them; they take the best qualities which are in all too small a supply today and distort them, using them for ends which are evil. Communists, I believe, are definitely convertible. The trouble begins when Catholics assume that Communism is likewise convertible.

All over Europe today Catholics are discovering, too late, that the Communism which they swore had so much that was good in it and which they attempted to work with is now engulfing them. And where Communism is victorious there can be nothing for Catholicism but persecution with final extinction as its aim.

If Communism in its aims is evil, why then do men of good faith remain so long in the Party? In order to answer this from my own experience let me return to my story.

The early thirties were an exciting time for any Communist. Although never unemployed for long myself, most of my activities in that period were on behalf of the unemployed who congregated daily at the labor ex-

163

changes, seeking the jobs that never came. Always there was too much to do. Demonstrations for bread, work, or relief. Baton charges by the police, broken heads, arrests. The arrests meant new demonstrations on behalf of the "class war prisoners"—and a new round of court cases, imprisonment, and demonstrations began all over again.

We talked of the deepening crisis of capitalism, and one of our leading theoreticians wrote a book called *This Final Crisis*. Out of all the misery and degradation which accompanied the economic slump, we believed, would come increased political understanding on the part of the workers, leading to support for revolutionary policies and—who knew?—before long the revolution. The revolution became an end in itself. About what followed after, each had his own ideas. We used catchwords and slogans—justice, liberty, the future classless society, the emancipation of mankind, and the ending of the exploitation of man by man.

But what we meant by them was known only to each of us individually. Each poured his own content into the mold. For me, socialist Britain was going to be much more the socialism of William Morris, the artist-craftsman-revolutionary, than of Marx. None of us, I believe, really thought that it would be simply modeled on Russian lines.

There were idealists who, lacking any Marxist theory, had only to visit the Soviet Union to be disillusioned. Most Communists, however, understood the undesirable features of the Russian system and forgave, remembering that czarist Russia was one hundred years behind the West in culture and totally without democratic traditions. When Communism came to the West it would be enriched by Western traditions and culture, it would become less soulless, more colorful.

Then the threat of war set the whole of industry once more in motion, and the Communist Party established itself in the factories. "Every factory a fortress" was the slogan and, if the economic crisis had

164

receded, a new and more serious one appeared to be descending upon capitalism.

In the days before the tactic of the popular front we had talked frankly of the possibilities which accompanied imperialist war. "Workers will turn war into civil war" was the catchword which summed it up. And so, without having to state it in public now, we knew that once again the overthrow of the capitalist state might possibly present itself, and with this in mind the Party organized in the factories and, later, in the armed forces.

The U.S.S.R.'s corrupt deal with Nazi Germany seemed only a clever piece of military and political expediency (although it lost the Party some of its intellectuals at the time), and since expediency or inexpediency, and not right or wrong, is the Marxist test, there was nothing surprising in this. To support the war we had formerly opposed was natural enough when Russia was attacked. It might mean the postponement of a showdown farther West, but now it was a question of defending the one strong point in the hands of the international revolutionary working class. And if Russia won, then new opportunities might arise.

So every Communist assisted Russia in every possible way. In industry it meant harder work, increased production; in the forces, impatience to go into action in Europe; at home, a great agitation for the opening of a second front. That is the way Communists as a body must always be expected to behave where Russian interests are involved.

Under the circumstances, Soviet spy rings are almost an extravagance, for every Communist feels a greater loyalty to Russia as the focal point of the revolution than to anything else and will quite naturally act on Russia's behalf no matter what his work or what his responsibilities.

Just when my own doubts and disillusionment began it is somewhat difficult to say. As a writer I got involved five years ago in a libel action with the *Weekly*

165

Review, a Catholic paper, and, in preparation for what was expected to be an important political case, studied its files back over a period of months and scanned each issue as it came out, determined to know my opponent's case as fully as possible.

But that Catholic paper in time taught me quite a lot. My cultural interests had always been with the Middle Ages: in poetry, Chaucer and Langland, in architecture, Norman and Gothic; in music, plainsong and Gregorian chants. The *Weekly Review* brought home to me the fact that the Middle Ages were those when men still loved God and that that was the reason for the great outpouring of the human soul of that period; that their culture was a Catholic culture and that the Catholic Church today was the sole custodian of that grand and ancient culture.

For a leading Communist writer to start thinking that way was absolute heresy, and I had to put my medievalism into a separate, watertight compartment of my mind in sheer self-defense. The position was reached in time where I had to admit to myself that I was looking forward to the morning when the messenger boy put the latest issue of that little Catholic paper on my desk.

Maybe a psychologist would readily understand why, in the following period, I worked harder than ever for the Party I had served so long. But the fact is that the seed was sown. From the *Weekly Review* I went back quite naturally to G. K. Chesterton and Hilaire Belloc and reread them in a new light. I discovered Eric Gill, whose sculpture I knew, as a writer, too, and the things for which these men stood were attractive.

When the Red Army went marching through eastern Europe into Germany, the countless dead they left behind inspired me—but the living who reached Berlin troubled me a lot. It was true that in the main they came from the less industrialized and therefore more backward parts of Russia, true, too, that many of the stories filtering back to Britain were obviously exaggerated. But those Red Army men, raping and looting like any other victorious army, took a lot of explaining away. The only way to deal with such stories in the *Daily Worker* was frankly to admit the backwardness of the areas from which the Red Army was drawn, but this, however, blew sky-high a lot of our prewar propaganda—despite all the allowances we had made for Russia's political shortcomings.

With the ending of the war my doubts grew. Russia's policy of intransigence at U.N., and at one conference after another, seemed at first to be but an expression of the usual hard bargaining one expects after wars, but soon it was clear that it was being driven to a point where, instead of uniting the human race, Communism was dividing it both horizontally and vertically.

Events in eastern Europe were extremely disturbing too. Having said for over a quarter of a century that Communism cannot be exported, it must be homegrown, Russia began busily to export it in a big way to the countries where the Red Army or the N.K.V.D. still had the last word.

There were less than three hundred Communist Party members in Rumania, I knew, when the first postwar government was formed. Overnight, as in the other countries in eastern Europe, it was permitted to grow into a mass party organizing every sort of ex-Fascist, yes man, adventurer, careerist, and logroller—strange material from which to build a new society, indeed.

Our reporters went from the *Daily Worker* to the various Russian-dominated countries and in due course reported back to the paper's executives on what they had seen. Their reports appeared to thrill my colleagues—they became increasingly shattering to me. I had started saying for the first time for many years, "This thing is morally indefensible. That is utterly wrong." Quite clearly I was losing my grip as a Marxist.

I thanked heaven I was not the foreign editor, responsible for "selling" eastern Europe and Soviet foreign policy to the British public. As it was, as news editor

167

I was responsible for organizing the coverage of home events.

We were still seeking a way out of Britain's postwar economic problems, still driving hard for increased production, which had been the Party line since Russia was brought into the war. I was responsible for the paper's production drive and proud of the job I was doing. Only that made my position on the paper at all tenable.

Then the Cominform was set up, and after some time the new line came through to the British Party leaders. We were to oppose the Marshall Plan and drop our support for increased production. Literally overnight the job we were doing was dropped; a new, exactly opposite campaign was started in its place. I knew then that it was only a matter of time before I made the final break.

Meanwhile I had become increasingly confirmed in my support for Catholic teaching. From being attracted by a rich Catholic culture I was now ranging over all aspects of Catholic thought.

Then came the night when I admitted to myself that I believed in everything connected with Catholicism—except the first necessary premise, belief in God, which Communism had long since destroyed in me. I decided that only an act of faith could take me past that point. You cannot read or think yourself into such belief. Call it actual grace, call it what you will, it worked.

We had our two children baptized in the local Catholic church in January while I was still an executive on the Communist daily paper. We started instruction at the same time—with one eye over our shoulders in case members of the Communist local should see us visiting the priest.

Leaving the movement in which I had spent my adult life to date meant a big break—with friends and with a cause which was once my life. The death of Jan Masaryk made that break, I felt, urgent and necessary.

There was a qualitative difference between Czechoslovakia and the rest of eastern Europe. The Czechs had enjoyed a high level of culture and a democratic system. There was no excuse for any form of police state in Czechoslovakia. Yet it came, despite the Czech Communist leaders' own attempts to find a new way which took account of their people's traditions. It came because any more democratic form of Communism would be a reproach to Rumania, Bulgaria, and the rest, so the Czech leaders were made to toe the line. Czechoslovakia was forced into the same Moscow-manufactured mold as the rest—a foretaste of what will happen in any other Western country which "goes Communist."

In the last resort I believe it is now a question of Christianity or Communism. They cannot coexist. Either we sink to the immoral depths or we rediscover that faith and culture and those spiritual values which once bound diverse nations together into a single whole called Christendom.

But the conquest of Communism will have to be achieved by positive Catholic action, not simply by negative anti-Communism, and least of all by the atom bomb, for Bolshevism thrives on misery and devastation.

WHAT I GAINED

Willis D. Nutting

Holding two degrees from Oxford University and a Ph.D. from the University of Iowa, Professor Willis D. Nutting has won recognition both as a historian and a clear and penetrating thinker. He stems from a long line of teachers and ministers; his father was a distinguished scientist and the head of the Department of Zoology at the University of Iowa. Graduating from the University of Iowa, Willis Nutting won a Rhodes Scholarship to Oxford. Living at Keble College, he came in contact with many of the leaders of the Anglo-Catholic movement and decided to study for the Anglican ministry.

After his ordination at Oxford he was assigned to the British West Indies. Returning to the United States, he was assigned to a parish in Colorado. While serving in Colorado he found himself at variance with his bishop as well as with the official formulations of Anglicanism as expressed in the prayer book and canons. He began to feel that his religion was just private judgment with some historical and ceremonial trimmings. Accordingly he entered upon exhaustive study of the Catholic faith, finding helpful guidance in Newman's *Essay on the Development of Doctrine.*

Becoming convinced of the divine character of the Catholic religion, Willis Nutting formally severed his connection with Anglicanism and entered the Church in 1930. Following this he spent a year on a ranch in California and then returned to enter the graduate school of the University of Iowa, majoring in philosophy from 1931 to 1933. In June of the later year he received his Ph.D. From 1933 to 1936 he taught at St. Theresa's College in Winona, Minnesota.

In 1934 he married Eileen Barry, a Catholic. In 1936 Dr. Nutting joined the faculty of the University of Notre Dame, where he has since been teaching in the Department of History. He is the author of *How Firm a Foundation?,* a scholarly work which examines the bases of modern philosophy and traces particularly the influence of Cartesianism upon philosophic thought. This was followed by *Reclamation of Independence,* which develops the theme of man's return to the land where he can best control his economic needs and thus achieve independence.

Professor Nutting has two great interests, namely, the liturgical movement and the rural life. He is deeply interested in all aspects of the Church's liturgy and seeks to apply it in every way possible to enhance the beauty and the dignity of worship and of man's devotional life.

An ardent advocate of back-to-the-land movement, Professor Nutting practices what he preaches: he has established a home in the country near Notre Dame where he and his wife and three children cultivate a thriving garden that supplies them with all their vegetables. Supplementing the garden have been four goats which supplied all the milk for the family, until very recently when the goats were replaced by a cow. In addition to his teaching duties at Notre Dame, Professor Nutting lectures on the rural-life movement and is a contributor to historical journals and scholarly periodicals.

I T IS remarkably difficult, after eighteen years, to reconstruct the steps by which the Faith was approached. It is not at all easy to put oneself back into the states of mind that prevailed in the different stages of the process. It is possible that the possession of the Faith so colors everything that one imagines the past to be quite different from what it actually was. This is all by way of saying that I do not trust myself any too well to give a true report. However, I will try to make it as objective as possible. But objectivity, in such a subjective matter as conversion, cannot obviate the use of the first person singular to an extent far beyond the bounds of good taste. For which I ask pardon in advance.

In their journey toward the Church no two people start from the same place. No two have the same heritage or the same environmental situation. There are a great many who move along paths of complete secularism until in a blinding flash the whole brilliance of the Catholic faith comes upon them. With such this present story has little in common but the ending. My own background was distinctly religious, my ancestors on both sides having been teachers and ministers. My father upheld Presbyterian orthodoxy at a state university which was already being called irreligious by the small denominational colleges. My parents were praying and hymn-singing people of the sober and dignified variety. It is a wonder to me now that they, being sincerely religious, took almost no interest in my own religious education or practice. I went to the Presbyterian Sunday school, which was taught by very good people. We got some ideas of morality and decency, but almost nothing of God. As long as my mother put me to bed I said my prayers. When she stopped coming upstairs with me I stopped praying, and as far as I can remember no questions were ever asked.

I suppose the beginning of my conversion can be

171

put when I was fourteen, when I began again to pray, this time on my own initiative, quite unbeknownst to anybody, and completely unrelated to what I was doing and learning in the Sunday school at the time. My praying was a thing completely apart from the rest of my life and, as far as I can see, had little effect on what I thought or did. But I remember that I spent considerable time at it. One of the things I prayed for was to know God better. But this petition was not the result of a burning desire to know God. I was definitely not interested. My asking to know God must have been a mere formality, put in because I had perhaps heard it in some prayer that stuck in my mind.

The things which I asked for so ardently I have no recollection of receiving. Indeed, I have forgotten what most of them were. But the thing that I asked for only with my lips, with no heart in it, has been progressively given to me even though I didn't want it consciously. What has happened to me since seems to have been the answer to this very unfervent prayer, and it proves, to my satisfaction at least, that God gives abundantly beyond what we ask or even can imagine.

When I review the steps in my approach to the Church, I seem to have played rather a small part in the process. I am not aware of there having been any longing for something that I did not have, any discontent with the condition I happened to be in, or any anguish or soul searching at all. When I first entered the Church my friends would always ask me two things: "Did you find what you were looking for?" and "Are you happy?" And I could answer truthfully that I was not looking for anything, and that I was happy, but that such a statement did not mean much, because I was happy before.

When I was eighteen my father conducted an expedition from the University of Iowa to the West Indies, and I was allowed to go along. There, in the British islands, I came in contact with the Anglican Church. At first I was not much impressed. When we were stationed on the island of Antigua, however, we were visited by several of the clergy and entertained by them. The dean of the cathedral, Rev. Henry Shepherd, invited me to his place for a week end, and out of courtesy I went to church. It was here, all unexpectedly, that I had my first "religious experience." The service was vespers or "evensong." The church was filled with black people singing the Psalms. The whole atmosphere was quite alien to me. I was an outsider. Then all at once I was not an outsider. I belonged. I had a firm conviction that I was at home and that my future would be with these people.

That is all there was to it, but that moment was the turning point of my life. My interests, my motives, my ambitions, and my activities have dated from that time.

Things began to happen immediately, and with plenty of fireworks. My announcement that I was going to enter the Episcopal Church was received by my parents first with unbelief and then with very real grief, and my father was not a man to suffer in silence. On the voyage home, and indeed through all the remaining years of my father's life, there was constant battle on the subject of religion. And with the uncharity of youth I took delight in emphasizing the points of difference between us and in showing my contempt for my parents' religion, a contempt which I by no means feel now. As a result of this conflict I never had a man-to-man friendship with my father.

I entered with vigor the life of the Episcopal Church in Iowa City. I was a sophomore in college and became an ardent propagandist for the claims of Anglicanism, making myself a nuisance to my fellow students, I have no doubt. I neglected my courses to read in the library all the books I could lay hands on that dealt with my new enthusiasm. I am sure that is the best way to learn —privately, in defiance of prescribed courses of study, and in opposition to what teachers are trying to cram down your throat.

In these early Anglican days I received for the first time the idea that the Church is an integral part of the Christian religion, and that the Church is something more than a voluntary collection of like-minded people. The person more responsible than anyone else for showing me this was the rector of my home parish, Rev. Paul Boynton James. He was a man out of place —an Anglo-Catholic in an extremely Low Church parish. But he had a way with students, and there were six of us who decided to prepare for the ministry.

As I look back on that period now, I can see that we were pretty "half-baked" in our enthusiasms, pretty obnoxious in our self-assertion, and extremely intolerant. But we had a superabundance of zeal and went fiercely to work opening up abandoned little wooden churches in the small towns of eastern Iowa and holding services before the three and a half people that we could persuade to come—and paying out of our own pockets our railroad fare, our meals, and even the cost of coal for the churches in winter. The results were small, but that was unimportant. We had all the *esprit de corps* of young Athanasiuses against the world. Never have I worked so hard.

It was during this period that for the first time in my life I was brought face to face with the fact of the Roman Catholic Church. A person can't think about the visible Church of Christ without becoming aware that there exists a very large organization that claims exclusively to be that Church. I had my attack of "Roman fever" along with the others, but it did not last long, and did not return. It is not easy for me to understand now why it was that with my very vivid conception of the Church extending back through history and over the world in space, I managed to be so assured that the Anglican communion was that Church. But at the time I was very little troubled.

I could read Cardinal Gibbons' *Faith of our Fathers* and apply all that he said concerning the glories of the Church to the rather small body of Christians who were in communion with me. The reason for this was perhaps that I had already had the experience of "at-homeness" in the Anglican Church before the conception of the Church Universal dawned upon me.

174

Anglicanism was already in possession of my loyalty and affection, and what new ideas came around were gathered into that net of sentiment.

But there were some arguments, besides, that seemed good at the time. The Roman Church appeared to us in the Middle West as a foreign institution, and one completely out of touch with contemporary American life. The Episcopal Church, on the other hand, was the historic religion of the English-speaking people, who were of course the dominant race in the world. It was our part, in the divine economy, to convert to this Church the very uninterested contemporary American public. If we could succeed in doing this the great numbers of the Roman Church would not look so impressive. When we argued with Roman Catholic students at the university we did not think that we came off badly. Our great concern, however, was with American Protestantism. This we attacked in the persons of the few who would uphold it and we had the triumph of bringing in a few—very few.

After two years as a combatant for Anglicanism at the University of Iowa, I had the good fortune to win the Rhodes Scholarship, and thus could spend the next three years in England. My experience of my communion on its home grounds was in every way heartening—great numbers of people thinking as I did, Anglo-Catholics of the second and third generation, institutional parishes, elaborate ceremonial, religious communities with a very real spiritual life. And still, with all this solidity, there was the exciting air of a nation to be won. There were low churchmen and modernists as numerous and as active as we were, and in the perfect freedom of Oxford every cause could prosper only on its merits. We thought we were prospering. The report was that the priests at Pusey House received at least one convert every day of term time.

Then there were the colorful personalities of the movement to supply objects of hero worship to young men. Father Waggett of the Cowley Fathers, who had been a biologist and had been instrumental in the conversion of Romanes, I could regard as a personal friend, especially interesting because he knew the English scientists whom I had heard my father speak about all my life. Roscow Shedden, Bishop of Nassau (and yachtsman), would drop in to my college (Keble) once in a while and impress us. Bishop Gore, the theologian, gave a course of lectures at St. Barnabas'. Heroic missionaries came and went—from India, from Australia, from the "Universities' mission to Central Africa," the greatest of these being Frank Weston, Bishop of Zanzibar and recognized leader of the Anglo-Catholics. The Anglo-Catholic Congress of 1923 was the high-water mark of the manifestation of the strength of the movement. Many thousands of us met in the Albert Hall to pray, to sing, to listen to addresses—and to send a message to the Pope, while outside in the rain several bedraggled individuals of Low Church persuasion picketed the meeting with signs declaring, "These men are leading you straight to Rome!"

One could not have all these experiences without receiving a certain satisfying feeling of catholicity in Anglicanism. We did not seem to be a provincial outfit. We were world-wide. This comforting sense of universality was strengthened in me by a five months' visit to Greece to study the religious life of the Orthodox Church. Although the goal of intercommunion which we so much desired had not yet been attained, my impression was that it would come soon. The Greek clergy were more than kind to me and were eager to learn something about Anglicanism. They seemed to take my religion at my own rating of it and to regard me as a brother. (I was in Anglican deacon's orders at the time). Indeed the exiled Patriarch Meletios offered me the job of teaching Anglican church history and theology at the University of Athens, an offer which sounded enticing until he went on to say that of course the American Episcopal Church would have to furnish my salary. I came away from Greece with the conviction that a union of the churches was just around the corner. The Anglican Communion was shortly to receive the seal of approval from the venerable Church of the East!

The training that we got at Oxford—not formally, but by association, reading, and conversation—was nothing to be held in contempt. There was a keen interest in ascetic and mystical theology. The teaching given in retreats at the Cowley Fathers' house was of very fine quality. The Oxford University Church Union conducted village missions which were thoroughly serious affairs. We carried a cross through the streets and spoke whenever we came upon a group of people. We prayed in the churches. The "we" sometimes meant twenty or thirty people. It was from the men connected with that movement that I learned what intercessory prayer really was, and how very strong that brotherhood is which is formed by men praying together.

All these things I mention simply to show that what I was receiving at Oxford was something calculated to give me an abundance of contentment with my own religious position and a complete disinclination to seek further for my spiritual home. There is an opinion prevalent among Catholics that "Anglo-Catholics" in general are on the brink of coming into the Church but that they just can't take the final step. "What is keeping them back?" is the favorite question. But this question, I am sure, indicates a complete lack of appreciation of the position of most of these people. I have met a few who had perpetual "Roman fever," and who were always asking themselves and others, "Should I or shouldn't I?" But my friends and I, and assuredly the majority of Anglo-Catholics then and I suppose now, were not only confident of our own cause, but aggressively proud of it. For such people there is not needed the removal of an impediment but a complete alteration of point of view, a real renewing of the mind. And this is the work of the Holy Spirit.

After having been ordained in Oxford I went again to the British West Indies to take the place of Dean Shepherd, who was badly in need of a vacation. This work was to be only temporary, but exposure in a tropical hurricane made it even shorter than it was supposed to be, and I had to return to the States somewhat the worse for wear. My brief sojourn in the islands, however, pushed yet higher my contentment with Anglicanism. The West Indian clergy were in general not very "High" Church. (Indeed some of them thought me quite popish.) But I have never seen such devotion and such sacrifice. They were extremely poor, and their people were poor, and perhaps because of this poverty there was a very beautiful pastoral relationship between them, a relationship which it was my privilege to enter for a very little time. Here were no heroics, no excitement, no colorfulness, but just love between pastor and people. It is the one portion of my Anglican ministry that I can look back on with approval. It lasted only six weeks.

Back in the States my poor health made it advisable to by-pass my own diocese of Iowa and take a position in Colorado, and there I remained until I gave up my ministry.

The circle of Anglo-Catholics centering around St. Andrew's Church, Denver, was very small, but it had a double dose of aggressiveness. We held celebrations and get-togethers at the drop of the hat, and liked nothing better than to prod the rest of the clergy, including the bishops, by flaunting a succession of "Romish" practices calculated to scandalize the weaker brethren. The place in the mountains where I was stationed was the location also of a summer conference to which people of the Anglican persuasion came from all over the country. It was definitely a show place, and we were one of the exhibits. We were experimenting with the religious life. The situation was another Oxford as far as interest, not to say excitement, was concerned.

During this time I naturally came somewhat into contact with the Roman Church. There was no parish near where I was, and once in a while I had to fetch a priest up to care for a dying Catholic. I had a Catholic neighbor who delighted me by handing me copies of popular Catholic periodicals. I say "delighted," because when I read them I was more than ever convinced of Anglican superiority. Occasionally I attended a Catholic service—a funeral now and then, or a ceremony at a college. My impression was that we did these things better, with more reverence, with more understanding, and also with more elaborateness. I definitely did not like the Catholic clergy. They spoke so different a language that there was scarcely any meeting of minds possible, and their attitude toward us seemed completely patronizing. I say all this to indicate that the Catholic Church had little sentimental attraction to me at that time. The one thing that I did admire was the thorough goodness of some of their laity, and their loyalty in the face of what I considered shabby treatment of them by their clergy. I could wish that I had laymen as loyal.

In the late summer of 1929, after I had been more than five years in the ministry, a series of events took place which again altered the course of my life. Four boys who had been attending a nearby seminary were kicked out. They had violated some minor rules, but they were in my judgment the best boys in the place. I invited them to come and study with us in the mountains. After considerable conciliatory work on the part of a mediator, the bishop was appeased and permitted them to stay with us.

In drawing up a course of study for these boys I had to ask myself the fundamental question: "To what are you going to try to direct their loyalty? You believe that authority is an integral part of the Christian religion. You believe that the one visible Church is the seat on earth of that authority. What clear-cut teaching are you going to give these boys about the visible Church and the ways in which its authority is expressed?"

Since it would be rather strange to present to the boys a system which I myself did not follow, I naturally asked myself what I was loyal to, and what authority I submitted to, and what my definition of the visible

Church was. A small amount of meditation on these questions led me to some startling realizations. I was certainly not loyal to my bishop. I had rather prided myself on disregarding him. I was not at all loyal to the official formulations of Anglicanism as expressed in the prayer book and canons. Along with other Anglo-Catholics I had long ago rejected them in spirit. But neither was there any objective thing even in Anglo-Catholicism to which I was loyal—no body of doctrine and no discipline to which I submitted wholeheartedly. I did not agree with the religious opinions and practices of any of my colleagues. The people trained in my parish could find no place else in the world where they would get the same teaching or worship in the same way.

All this meant that I had made myself the judge in all things. It was *my* idea of Christianity to which I was loyal, and this idea corresponded to no reality. It was to *my* ideas and mine only that I was ready to submit myself. In every case I would accept no judge of my beliefs and actions but myself.

What did I mean when I said that the Church taught thus and so? I simply meant that that was what *I* believed. "*L'Eglise, c'est moi*" might have been my motto during the preceding six years. My religion was just private judgment with some historical and ceremonial trimmings!

What did I mean when I said I believed in One Holy Catholic and Apostolic Church? If the Church must be visibly one, then either the Anglican Church must be the One Church or I was not in the One Church. But if I were content with an invisible unity (whatever that may mean), then how did my position differ from the Protestant conception of the "Church Invisible"? The idea that there is a unity among various conflicting religious bodies simply because they all possess the historic episcopate and valid sacraments now began to seem preposterous. Almost all the early heretical bodies possessed bishops and valid sacraments, and yet I had always regarded Arianism as outside the unity of the

Church. If an Arian with his bishops and sacraments was outside the Church, how could an Anglican, even if he had this same equipment, consider himself inside?

As I turned these questions over in my mind it became evident that there was no rationally and historically justifiable conception of the visible Church which could include the religious body that I belonged to. Either the gates of hell had prevailed against the Church, or there was the True Church somewhere and I was not in it. Either way things were disconcerting for me and for my project of training those boys committed to my care.

Now all this realization did not come because I had any new information at my disposal. All the facts that I now made use of were familiar to me. But the obligation to establish my students on a firm religious foundation had forced me to consider these facts from a new point of view. The sum total of circumstances which made Anglicanism fascinating to me now had to be looked upon in another light.

It was of course obvious to me that I could not deliberately teach my boys the flagrant individualism which I now realized I had been practicing. And it was equally obvious that since I now knew it for what it was I could not keep on practicing it. There was a complete contradiction between it and the idea of an authoritative Church. But if I gave up my individualism and submitted to the existing Anglican authorities and formularies, I would be condemned to live in a religious system with which I had no kinship, no understanding, and no liking.

Thus the realization came rather rapidly that the Anglican Church could no longer be my home. This was the most difficult readjustment of thought that I had been called upon to make, for all my religious experiences, all my speculations, all my plans and dreams of the future had all been based upon my "at-homeness" in the place where I was. And I had not the least bit of attachment to any other religious system. The bottom dropped out of my world and left me with

181

a complete spiritual numbness. I could not stay where I was, and there was no place to go. My past life, in which I had seen so clearly the guiding hand of God, now seemed absolutely meaningless.

The Anglican Church having turned out to be but an overnight hostel, I had now to set about finding a real home. It was natural that the Roman Church should come under consideration again, for one cannot be looking for the One Holy Catholic Apostolic Church without seriously reviewing Rome's claims to be that Church. So I went over again the old ground that I thought I had covered years before, but this time without the emotional confidence in Anglicanism, indeed with a definite lack of confidence in it.

The standard type of Catholic apologetic left me completely cold. The *a priori* approach was so contrary to my own mental procedure that there was little in common between me and the apologists. But there were some writings that helped. Leo XIII's pronouncement on Anglican orders seemed to me, once I had ceased to regard Anglicanism with loyalty, to be eminently sensible. Newman's *Essay on the Development of Doctrine* perhaps helped me the most, by showing that it is the Roman Church that possesses a continuity with apostolic times through a legitimate development of theology and practice, and that such a continuity is real, whereas the attempt to return to "the primitive Church" was a break in continuity.

One thing that had bothered me in what I knew of Roman Catholicism as revealed in the Catholic press was a unanimity which I could only explain as the result of a cramping of the intellect. I had the idea that Catholics thought alike on everything, that there was no controversy, no criticism of leaders, no admission of mistakes, and a fierce resentment of any criticism. The Catholic press held this up as a proof that Catholics had the Truth. It seemed to me to be rather a proof of intellectual apathy.

Fortunately I was soon led to realize that the picture of monotonous uniformity within the Church was not quite correct. I happened just at this time to be introduced to the writings of Baron von Hügel. His case fascinated me, not because I was particularly attracted by what he wrote but because a man so "out of line" still seemed to feel quite at home in the Roman Church. I also heard some pretty thorough criticisms of the clergy by people who appeared to be loyal Catholics, and this gave me considerable encouragement. As I look back on it now, it seems to me that those facts about the Church which apologists try to cover up were the things that helped me most. The anomalies, the disagreements, the dissensions—all these things which I found out about only accidentally helped put the Church in a favorable light. Perhaps it was because they indicated a certain rich diversity in Catholicism which I had not expected. It showed that the Church was a family rather than an army, a society rather than a well-running machine.

The whole process of my transfer of loyalty from Anglo-Catholicism to the Roman Catholic Church took less than a year. I had resigned my ministry at Easter time and returned to my home in Iowa City. I was received into the Church in July 1930.

What has been the gain?

In surface satisfactions, which surely are an unworthy standard of measurement for anything so important as religion, my life has not been too different from what it was before. Peace of mind, freedom from perplexity, etc., come and go as always. It took me some time to feel at home in my new home, and to become accustomed to the fact that most of my brethren had inherited a culture much less traditionally "American" than mine. There was much perplexity as to what God's will for me was. There was much pondering over the "why" of my being led into the backwater of Anglicanism. This has not all been cleared up yet.

I cannot say that Catholicism has the answer to all problems. Each generation faces new ones, both intellectual and moral, and has to find answers that are at least fairly satisfactory. But the Catholic faith does give a person orientation. It enables him to weigh his problems and to judge the relative importance of each of them. It gives the principles upon which right and just solutions can be attempted. And it gives the zeal to seek for solutions and at the same time a willingness to accept the fact that some questions cannot be answered in this present life.

If I were to name the greatest gain that comes from entering into the Church from outside, I would say that it is *depth*. In the old days, exciting and earnest as they were, we were running around on the surface of life. There was a lack of gravity, and our earnestness was so much spent for things which I now know to be small change. We would fight and bleed and die for the right to use incense or to be called "Father." We are still earnest, now in my new home; but we are now interested in social justice, the kind of society suited to man, the deepening of family life, the nature of liberal education, the function of the laity in the worship of God. This is not small change.

With this depth comes a broader charity and an understanding of those who differ from us. How I regret now my contempt for the religion of my parents and my assertiveness which hurt them so much! Being confident in the knowledge of God given me by the Faith, I am no longer "touchy" about my religion. The Ark of the Lord will remain firm without my having to steady it. I know it is not going to fall, and I do not have to jump in to counterattack everyone who disagrees.

With this depth also comes freedom. The Faith is so much more than any professor of it that one is liberated from the domination of colorful personalities; one worries no more about public opinion; and one no longer feels obligated to join the scramble for worldly success.

But most important, there is a depth of understanding of the meaning of the worship of God, and a depth of participation in that worship which could not exist elsewhere. And with this deeper participation in the worship of God comes also a deeper knowledge of God. Thus I am confident that the prayer to know God, begun perfunctorily thirty-four years ago, is being answered more and more fully in every Mass I take part in.

FINDING A WAY OF LIFE

George B. Harrison

Outstanding among the English scholars of Canada is George Bagshawe Harrison, professor of English and head of the department at Queen's University, Kingston, Ontario. A graduate of Cambridge University, he received his Ph.D. from the University of London and has won international recognition for his research in English literature of the Elizabethan period, to which he devoted sixteen laborious years. He has been a lecturer at the University of London and at the Sorbonne in Paris.

An authority on Shakespeare and on John Bunyan, Professor Harrison has written extensively on them and on the England of their day. His original research into the records of the sixteenth century enabled him to shed many an interesting light upon the characters and customs of that era. His life has not been lived, however, within an ivory tower; he has participated in two world wars and knows the meaning of suffering and the loss of ones near and dear.

Born in 1894, George Harrison was educated at Brighton College and at Queens' College, Cambridge. In the first World War he served in the Queen's Regiment from 1914 to 1919 in India and Mesopotamia. In 1919 he went back to Cambridge and studied English literature, specializing in the Elizabethan period. He was for many years reader in English literature in the University of London.

In the second World War he returned to the Army and served in the R.A.S.C. and the Intelligence Corps. In 1943 he was released from the Army to go to Canada to take up the position of head of the Department of English at Queen's University.

His best-known works are the four volumes of *Elizabethan* and *Jacobean Journals* in which he traces from day to day those events, great and small, which excited Shakespeare and his contemporaries. He is author of *Shakespeare at Work, The Life and Death of Robert Devereux, Earl of Essex, Elizabethan Plays and Players,* and editor of *The Bodley Head Quartos,* and *Penguin Shakespeare.* Other famous books by Mr. Harrison are: *Shakespeare's Fellows, Shakespeare: The Man and His Stage* (with E. A. G. Lamborn), *John Bunyan: A Study in Personality, An Elizabethan Journal, The Pilgrim's Progress and Mr. Badman, The Lancaster Witches: 1612,* and *The Letters of Queen Elizabeth.*

He has recently published a college Shakespeare which is being used in many of the colleges and universities of the United States and Canada. He has accepted an invitation to teach at the University of Michigan, where he will begin his duties in September 1949.

Professor Harrison narrates the story of a pilgrimage that stretches from the countries of the Old World to the New, over a road with many windings, but a road that led at last to the long-sought goal. Replete with evidence of a cultured and disciplined mind bent on finding the fullness of truth, this narrative discloses the inner drama of the human soul seeking union with its Maker.

A PROFESSOR of English literature has two main duties: to know something of the nature of words, and to interpret their use by the masters of writing. The more he studies literature, the more acutely he realizes that words are the most elusive of all symbols, and how rarely even the simplest statement conveys the same meaning to two different hearers. Yet it is by words that human beings express their needs, laws, transactions, intentions, thoughts, emotions, longings, hopes, and creeds. Indeed plain statement is so inadequate for anything beyond the simplest of notions that the masters of expression must try to convey their intenser feelings in poetry. Poetry is the record of individual experience, and its study is to quite a considerable extent concerned with emotional and religious experiences of every kind. To expound the creeds of others, the interpreter must first attempt to realize his own.

My religious education began early. As soon as I could be trusted to behave myself in public, I was encased in a starched sailor suit and escorted by my parents to Christ Church, Brighton, where we sat through a service of the Broad to Low pattern which was normal in the Anglican Church in the 1900s—morning prayer with choir (litany extra once a month), three hymns, and twenty- to forty-minute sermon. This was followed by a walk on the Hove Lawns to view the church parade as prelude to an enormous and delectable Sunday dinner. I was made to say my simple prayers morning and evening, and encouraged to read the Bible by myself, which sometimes acutely embarrassed my mother when I sought her light on some of those words and incidents in the Old Testament which puzzle the innocent mind. There was little attempt to inculcate any formal doctrine beyond a general feeling that God was a kind of super-Father and that Jesus, though—in the words of the hymn—a "friend for little children," always sided with the grownups in a family crisis.

Our family, however, from time to time was favored with a visit from the Rev. James Neil, who might have stepped straight from the pages of the Old Testament. He had a Hebraic nose and a long white curly beard, and an air of vigorous authority. James Neil was nominally a minister of the Church of England, though he had developed a kind of evangelicalism all his own, based on his reading of the Hebrew prophets. In early manhood he spent some years in Palestine as chaplain to the Bishop of Jerusalem and thereafter made it his mission to write and lecture on the customs of Bible lands. He was a considerable Hebrew scholar, a magnificent lecturer, and a combative talker. He was probably the greatest religious influence in the lives of my parents, and on his occasional visits to our house he certainly instilled in me an antiquarian interest in the Bible. I have the warmest memories of this kindly, aggressive old man.

187

At the age of thirteen I was sent to Brighton College, one of the smaller English public schools; and thereafter began my day's work with a short service in the school chapel wherein I learned by heart many of the Psalms and the more popular hymns. I certainly enjoyed the school chapel, especially in my last three years at school when I had come under the influence of one of my friends who was a zealous Anglo-Catholic. Indeed I was beginning to feel that my career would lie in the Church of England.

In 1913 I went up to Queens' College, Cambridge, which at that time was almost a theological seminary, for of the fifty-five men of my year, about half were intended for the ministry. I had not finally decided what I should do when I left for Cambridge, but I entered myself as an "ordinand." Ordinands could study in any field they wished—mine was at first classics —but we were expected to attend some theological lectures. I therefore sat under Professor Henry Swete, a dear saintly old man, who lectured in a gentle voice on the Apostles' Creed to a large audience of lively and sometimes rowdy undergraduates who stamped their feet whenever he made a debating point in favor of High or Low Church.

I experimented a good deal in religion in my first year at Cambridge, for I was still uncertain. The more earnest evangelicals repelled me, for I had a distaste for amateur prayer leaders, but so also did the extreme Anglo-Catholics (known as "spikes"). Aesthetically I was attracted by the High Church ritual but I found it difficult to accept the doctrine of the Real Presence because, however earnestly I followed the devout preparations recommended in the manual, I could never achieve any feeling of reality behind the vestments, lights, incense, or music.

My career at Cambridge came to an abrupt end when the first World War broke out in the summer of 1914. In September I was commissioned to an infantry regiment and at the end of October we were on our way to the East. For the next year I lived in the strange new environment (now defunct) of Kipling's British India.

I saw much outwardly of the great Indian religions, a little of Anglican missions, and too much of the formality of church parade. Yet I remained a regular weekly communicant, although the chaplains in India were seldom chosen for their gifts of spirituality. Most of them tried with poor success to keep a balance between social heartiness and conventional respectability. There were a few exceptions to the general dreariness and conventionality of official religion: a lovely little Anglo-Catholic church at Naini Tal and a chaplain of exceptional sincerity at Meerut.

After a year my regiment was sent to Mesopotamia and I remained in that country until the end of the war. For the first nine months I was encamped at Nazarieh on the Euphrates within sight of the great ziggurat of Ur of the Chaldees, Abraham's home. Here the enthusiasms of the Rev. James Neil recurred to me, for the Arabs were still living the biblical life, and we British were the invaders, much like the Assyrians and Babylonians who descended into Palestine in the days of the kings of Israel and Judah. King David, I guessed, must have been just such a man as the local Sheikh Khaiyoum, who caused us much trouble and many casualties, or like Ibn Saud, who even then was regarded as a likely menace from the desert. I saw also the Tower of Babel, Nebuchadnezzar's palace at Babylon, and Ezra's tomb by the Tigris; but on the whole after four hot summers by the Euphrates there was not much romance left for me in the historical books of the Old Testament.

Nevertheless when I was at last demobilized and came back to England I inclined to my original idea of ordination, but was still undecided because I felt that my religion had little depth and lacked real conviction. I had met many men and women in the past five years and on the whole the professedly religious were so much less attractive than the frank pagans. Moreover of the various army padres, from the hearty regular who preached on "Adam and his mem-sahib" to the bewildered little curate who had been forced into the army by his bishop and hated the whole business, few seemed to have any real conviction that religion meant much more than church parade and handing out cigarettes in the Y.M.C.A. There were few Catholic chaplains, but when they came to say Mass our handful of Catholics went in a body.

I returned to England in 1919 and married the sister of my Anglo-Catholic friend. Then I went back to Cambridge to finish the course for my degree. In the first days of our married life my wife and I were regular communicants, but it very soon became clear to me that the Catholic Church was right in forbidding her priests to marry. It was obviously beyond human capability for any man happily married as I was, and especially after I became a father, to give to the Church his whole or even his first care. I therefore gave up the idea of ordination.

After taking my degree I taught for two years at a small public school[1] in the country. Our religious decline began from this time. Services in this school chapel were formal and uninspired, and in the village church inconceivably tedious, and it was not long before we ceased to go to church beyond the quota expected of all masters. From this school we migrated to Cheltenham, where I taught in the Training College, an evangelical foundation controlled by a principal who had some local reputation as a popular preacher but who carefully avoided doctrinal and controversial topics.

I was becoming acutely critical of the Established Religion in these years, for its foundations seemed so unsure. As the Church of England by Law Established, it had considerable privileges in the state and rich endowments but it exercised no discipline over its lay members and very little over its clergy. A vicar or

[1]The English public school is entirely different from the public school in the United States and is similar to the private academy preparing students for college in this country.

rector, once appointed to a living, was irremovable unless for notorious evil living or flagrant neglect, and a congregation was stagnant or sturdy solely because of the personality of its parson. There was no universally recognized doctrine; at one church the ritual and dogma were hardly distinguishable from Roman Catholic; at another the clergyman denounced his High Church brethren as "Romanizers" and administered evening communion as a memorial service and no more. All owed a nominal obedience to the same bishop, who was appointed by the Prime Minister of the day, usually because he was a safe man, with guaranteed social graces and a degree from the University of Oxford. The clergy could and frequently did defy their bishop, and disputes between a rector and his congregation on matters of church practice were often settled in the civil law court. As for doctrine and church organization, the final arbiter was the British Parliament, which included Baptists, Methodists, Unitarians, Quakers, Jews, pagans, and atheists. Indeed in the 1920s a revised Book of Common Prayer was submitted for the approval of the House of Commons—and rejected by that miscellaneous assembly.

Our growing criticism of the Church of England was considerably increased by its treatment of my father-in-law. Rather late in life he had left a business career to be ordained, but without first taking a degree at a university. He was thus at a disadvantage compared with his colleagues and especially as he was a shy quiet man, inexpert in catching the eye of his bishop. After a few years he was appointed curate in charge of a village church in Lincolnshire because the official rector had been declared bankrupt and suspended from the living. Thereafter for twenty-three years my father-in-law was forgotten in a great rectory on an income which seldom reached three hundred pounds a year, ministering to an unappreciative village congregation until—while his wife lay dying of cancer—he was informed that he must vacate immediately as the original rector had paid off his debts and was returning. The rector was quite within his legal rights, and the bishop was powerless to interfere.

So long as we were at the Training College I was expected for example's sake to attend chapel, but when I was appointed to the University of London even this form of compulsion ceased. From time to time we would make honest attempts to resume churchgoing but always with the same conviction—that the services of the Church of England were for us a tedious and meaningless ceremony; and in time I came to regard the Church as a great ship whose engines had stopped long ago but was still carried along by the sheer momentum of custom and social prestige, rapidly dwindling.

By my late thirties I developed a vaguely Epicurean philosophy. It was certainly inconceivable that the universe should have come into being by blind chance or that so intricate a mechanism as the human body could have evolved itself, but the Mind that had conceived it was so immense and complex that it could not be comprehended within any human headpiece, not even when worn by Eddington, Jeans, Joad, or one of the Huxley family. This Supreme Being was a sort of super-Scientist, endlessly and unemotionally experimenting. Man was one of his experiments, a quarrelsome, lecherous little creature but fascinating. The Being was not particularly interested in the individual man who was born and perished on the same terms as any other animal. Nevertheless there were rules for existence which applied to man, and human happiness lay in conforming to the pattern of the universe. This pattern was revealed by the various scientists—physicists, biologists, physicians, psychologists, and the rest.

My faith in my scientific colleagues was in time shaken as I observed that in spite of their expert knowledge they knew less rather than more of the graces of life; and as for the "leaders of modern thought," most of them conspicuously failed in the practice of their own theories. In the 1920s much was heard of the various guides to happiness put out by Bertrand and Dora

Russell, who helped to popularize the notion that happiness consists in freedom from all restraint and that since the act of sex is the greatest of human pleasures, men and women, married or single, should be entirely free to sleep wherever they choose. After a few years it appeared that even the Russell paradise had been invaded by a serpent.

Nor was I much impressed by the theory of education that a child should be brought up to express itself without discipline or control; for he will ultimately have to live in a hard world and he may as well get used to that fact from the first. The children of my acquaintances who were allowed full, free, self-expression were peevish, neurotic, offensive unhappy brats while—in spite of the psychiatrists—the conspicuously happy and healthy children were usually well disciplined and obedient to their parents. It is perhaps unfair to generalize, but about 1933 I had some firsthand experience of the modern psychiatrist at work.

For some years my wife had been plagued with migraine headaches; the medical specialists failed to find cure or remedy; perhaps the trouble was psychological; and if so, an examination of our marriage by a psychiatrist might reveal the hidden cause. Accordingly in separate sessions we stirred up the dregs of our minds for the inspection of this expert. He suggested to me that the best way of strengthening our marriage was for me to throw off all my restraints and have a love affair, preferably with one of my female colleagues. As none of the academic women in the University of London aroused in me any libido for that kind of self-expression, I never tried the experiment. Meanwhile the migraine continued; and shortly afterward my psychiatrist's wife left him.

Nevertheless in these years I was becoming more and more aware of the Catholic Church. I wrote or edited several books for the tercentenary of the birth of John Bunyan and so came to have a fair insight into the nature and grim tenets of Puritanism. They did at least establish several positions in my mind. The first was that the Puritans, far from being the champions of true liberty, were in fact the most oppressive of all; they clamored for liberty of conscience not because they believed in the individual's right to worship as he pleased but in order to force their own doctrines on others. *Everyman* and *The Pilgrim's Progress* were two notable specimens of Catholic and Puritan doctrine. The Catholic Everyman, for all his weaknesses, gets to heaven because he has Good Deeds to plead for him; in *Pilgrim's Progress,* poor Ignorant is popped into hell even after he has crossed the river and reached the gates of the Holy City because, no matter how many good deeds to his credit account he was predestinately damned. Furthermore, if one took up the argument on the Puritan level and accepted the Bible literally as the sole, final, and indisputable authority for all beliefs, no amount of Protestant casuistry could explain away the text, "Thou art Peter and upon this Rock I will build my Church," or deny that the Church of Rome was that church, and a more impressive edifice than any built by Luther, Calvin, or even Henry VIII.

Nevertheless, though I hated his creed, I had a vast respect for John Bunyan as a man; and his analyses of human conduct and motives were often profound. His description of the "nine steps that lead down to apostasy" was uncomfortably like my own progress, though I preferred the label "nine steps away from childhood's superstitions."

In another direction I was at the same time much impressed by a very different historical figure—Thomas More. Several of my colleagues in the University of London were devoted to the study of his works, especially R. W. Chambers—a man much loved by his friends—who wrote the definitive life of More. Indeed I was surprised that after he had made this contribution to the beatification of More and Fisher, Chambers remained an Anglican. More was the kind of saint that everyone can understand—a successful man of the world, an adored father, a scholar, a lawyer, perfectly honest, unostentatiously devout, an entrancing wit, very good company for all occasions, and yet on a matter of ultimate principle utterly rigid. Whether one agreed with his religion or not, he was right on the political issue involved in the decision of Henry VIII to make himself head of the Church of England; for Henry (who professed himself a Catholic to the end) by rejecting the supremacy of the Pope cut off his country from the family of civilized European nations. After studying the life of More I felt that the English Reformation, viewed solely as a political event, was an incomparable blunder. I do not know what miracles were attributed to St. Thomas More in the process of his canonization, but I know of one in which he had no small share. And as for St. John Fisher, he was for a while president of my college at Cambridge, so that all Queens' men regard themselves as faintly perfumed with the odor of his sanctity.

My work on the *Elizabethan Journals,* which covered a period of about sixteen years of my life, took me into all kinds of records of the sixteenth century. My hope and intention in compiling those volumes were to present a truthful picture of an age as contemporaries saw it. I had no theories to establish and I tried to be as impartial as was humanly possible, I therefore gathered material from every kind of source including many Catholic publications and records, and I read dozens of sermons and much propaganda from all parties. The Elizabethan government, I felt, had very good reasons for protecting itself against the politically-minded Catholics on the Continent but it was quite clear that the Jesuit missionaries who came over to England in the 1580s and 1590s were solely concerned with propagating their faith. Whatever might be said against Father Parsons and his dubious friends, such Jesuits as Edmund Campion and Robert Southwell were willing and even eager martyrs. A man who cheerfully sought and faced the rack and the beastly death of a traitor in Elizabethan times had an extraordinary certainty in something which I could imagine but did not share.

The ultimate choice of a philosophy or religion thus lay between the Catholic faith, which demanded acceptance of dogmas that seemed quite irrational, and an agnosticism which recognized that the knowable was very limited, but that the scientist was likely to be better informed than the theologian. At this stage agnosticism seemed to be the only possible creed for an honest man; and if so, then it was one's duty to abide by that belief and not to allow emotion to smother reason. This was, I believe, the general attitude of my academic colleagues; in England most men in the intellectual professions are freethinkers who seldom attend church services except for a christening, a first marriage, or a funeral.

At the same time I was convinced that the saints and mystics had indeed experienced visions, ecstasies, and an intuitive conviction of the fact of God which were entirely real to them. It was no valid criticism to say that these experiences were illusions, for no man is capable of judging an experience which he has not himself felt. Nor was it a good argument to deny the actuality of a religious or emotional experience because it cannot be recorded by any physical device. This was brought home to me in my study of Elizabethan witchcraft. I could only accept the position that I was not the kind of person to whom such experiences came, and that I was capable only of judging matters within my own limited range; beyond that one could not go.

But if an Epicurean agnosticism was my philosophy, I unconsciously practiced the very common religion of child worship. By this time we had four children and our hopes for the future lay with and in them. So that they might be brought up in a healthy environment we moved into the country, bought a lovely old house with five acres of ground, and for nearly ten years we lived as a family till the early months of 1939, when my eldest son went out to Rhodesia and my daughter left home to begin her career. We then abandoned our country home and came to live in outer London. Soon afterward the second World War broke out. Academic life ceased in London and I was left with an unwanted and miserable year of "leisure" until someone cared to employ me on "work of national importance." After Dunkirk the army was much more cordial to the veterans of the first war and in October 1940 I became a supply officer in the Royal Army Service Corps in the north of Scotland. Thence by various degrees I transferred into the security side of Intelligence and was posted to the headquarters of the expeditionary force which was kept ready poised in northern Ireland. In our large and very mixed mess one again noticed the difference between the Catholic and Anglican padres. The Catholic was a wise, witty old Irish priest who had won the Military Cross on Dunkirk beaches.

Our family was now scattered and separated. My eldest son was in an officers' training unit in India, and it seemed that the pattern of his life was very closely following mine. We had always been very good friends. He was now a man and the prospect of meeting him again on new and equal terms was exciting. In July 1942 he died.

The philosophy of Epicurus breaks down at such a time and one is left with the bleak consolations of *Lear*—

>   Men must endure
> Their going hence, even as their coming hither:
> Ripeness is all.

And in the first bitterness one echoes—

> As flies to wanton boys, are we to the gods,
> They kill us for their sport.

However, we still had three children; our sorrow was common; and there was so much to keep our minds busy in the war that one hoped that in time the wound would film over.

From Ireland I was transferred to the War Office in London, where my immediate chief was a devout Catholic. He had that air of serenity and inner strength which causes so many Catholics to view the rest of

197

mankind with a kind of good-tempered sympathetic tolerance—and which is so baffling and irritating to Protestants.

In 1943 I was released from the army to take up the position of head of the Department of English at Queen's University in Canada, and in the late summer my wife and I reached Kingston, Ontario. Here we had to adjust ourselves to a new mental atmosphere. The university was originally a Presbyterian foundation, and most of my new colleagues were members of the United Church of Canada. There is also a small Anglican cathedral which a few of those who have come out from the Old Country attend; but the Anglican Church in Canada is one of the smaller sects. Our greatest surprise was to find that living in Canada, far from being more modern than in England, is in fact about forty years behind. We felt that we had stepped back into our childhood as we encountered in so many houses the stuffy Victorian furniture, the petty social ceremony, the mental outlook on social problems, and the regular Sunday churchgoing of my colleagues. Yet the academic tradition of the place was very free and tolerant. No one attempted to attach us to any church; indeed in three and a half years no minister of religion of any denomination ever came near us.

Once again in an unobtrusive way one became aware of the Catholic Church. In those parts of England where we had lived it is rare to find a Catholic church in a village. In Ontario about a fourth of the population is Catholic. In Kingston the Catholics have from the first been predominant, and the cathedral is a fine large building, now a hundred years old, and so cleverly sited that it is the most conspicuous landmark for miles around. Moreover from time to time my colleagues would mutter at the encroachments of popery; and of course there is always French Canada!

Meanwhile in these war years we suffered a continual frustration. Our children, now grown up, were either in the services or in other ways controlled. We could neither reach them, nor they us; and the two goldfish which swam round and round our small aquarium seemed fit symbols of ourselves. The war ended at last but for us the controls continued, though Canadian parents regained their sons in a few months. Our youngest meanwhile was sent to the Near East to waste his young manhood in such futile occupations as guarding German prisoners in a desert camp in Egypt.

We spent part of the summer of 1946 by one of the Ontario lakes and again encountered the Catholic serenity in the mother of seven lively children from whom we had hired our cottage. There was nothing tangible or definable but we realized acutely that this family had something which we had not, and I experienced once more that mild envy of Catholics which often came over me—a wish that I had been born a Catholic, for I certainly could never become one.

Meanwhile there was some hope that we might at last see our children again. Our daughter was allowed to join us, and our youngest son was expecting release from the army within a year. Early in January 1947 he was sent up to Palestine; two days later he was accidentally killed on guard.

This second blow hurt far more than the first, and for weeks we moved about in a state of physical numbness and mental pain which was too bitter to share or even to mention. Our friends and colleagues showed us every kind of delicate sympathy, yet of the many letters which we received one only seemed to suggest any sense in this cruel accident; it was from our Catholic friend of the summer.

About ten weeks later, during which the bitterness decreased hardly at all, we were moved to face our troubles. Our vague philosophy was useless in times of devastation, and a religion of child worship demands that the parents shall die first. Others found an answer and consolation in religion. But the Anglican Church held nothing for us and still less the other Protestant sects.

The Catholic Church?

In spite of the malice and abuse of her enemies the Roman Catholic Church went serenely on her way, never changing her doctrine to meet the bidding of a dictator or the latest theory of a scientist, speaking always with an air of supreme authority, receiving the absolute loyalty of her children. Moreover alone amongst the Christian churches, the Church of Rome was yearly growing stronger, even in England. Yet it seemed at first sight most unlikely that we could ever assent to Catholic doctrine, and if we took this step we should be binding ourselves irrevocably to all the practices of the Catholic Church and to accept her discipline. The discipline indeed was one of the strongest attractions. Other churches on a Sunday said, "All are welcome." The Catholic Church said to her own children, "YOU WILL COME."

This discussion took place late one night in Holy Week, and we ended by resolving that after Easter we would carry the matter further, at least to the extent of some firsthand enlightenment about the Catholic faith. From that moment the urge became stronger and more insistent every day. It was a force external, uncontrollable, and quite different from anything that either of us had ever before experienced. Psychiatrists doubtless have a name for it; Catholics call it an act of grace.

I was thus forced to reconsider my whole position, and my line of reasoning—so far as I can now set it down in order—ran thus. The individual can only perceive the minutest fragment of truth, and even that fragment he cannot express in words because words are so woefully inadequate for any precise definition. The doctrine of transubstantiation, for instance, is for a Catholic an adequate explanation of an incomprehensible mystery; but he must first apprehend and experience the mystery before he can understand the explanation. On the other hand only a fool would counter the doctrine by demanding a chemical analysis of the Consecrated Host. If only one could get through and behind the words to the inexpressible meaning, one might at least comprehend the mysteries of the Christian religion. The real difficulty in accepting Catholic doctrine was not so much the ideas, once one could grasp them, but the meaning of the words, for Catholics who have been born in the Faith are used from the first to seeing the natural everywhere suffused with the supernatural. There is thus in Catholic dogma a certain stark directness of phraseology which is quite meaningless to those who have no sense of the supernatural, and who indeed usually regard "supernatural" as another name for "superstition."

At this point certain analogies suggested themselves which were—to me—helpful, particularly a story which I sometimes use in my lectures. Some years ago a traveler on returning from a remote region wrote a letter to the London *Times* wherein he commented that a certain mountain was flat-topped, like a lump of sugar. The next day an old explorer retorted that the traveler had evidently never seen the mountain because, far from being flat-topped, it was conspicuously cone-shaped. A few days later a yet more experienced traveler capped the controversy by noting that from the north the mountain appeared flat-topped, but from the east it appeared cone-shaped. Truth is like that. If one shifted one's point of view, the whole pattern was changed, but the central mass of truth remained.

The fundamental problem was this. The Catholic Church claimed its authority from its history and supernatural origin. If one accepted the historical claim, then everything followed. If one did not accept the historical claim, then how to account for the Catholic Church? The historical evidence for the life, death, and resurrection of Jesus Christ is better authenticated than the historical evidence for the life and death of Julius Caesar. We accept without any question the story of Julius Caesar because dictators are common and they are usually assassinated. The evidence for the resurrection of Jesus Christ is rejected solely because other dead men have not risen from the dead—but this Man, as it happened, was unique. However strange, at first sight, some of the Catholic doctrines might seem, yet throughout the centuries many men of supreme intellect had accepted them as obvious truth, and many more of the best minds of our own times have come to accept them, or in plainer words have become converts to Rome. Could it indeed be that St. Thomas Aquinas knew more about God, the pattern of the universe, and the nature of man than the late Dr. Sigmund Freud?

Belief in any doctrine or theory which cannot be proved by exact physical demonstration must be a combination of intuition that it is so and of intellectual conviction that it must be so. Until intuition and conviction merge there can be no belief, but intellectual conviction can come second, and indeed even in scientific discoveries the intuition often comes before the discovery of the supporting facts. Moreover many of the "facts of science" are unproved guesses liable to be upset and discarded when some new fact comes to light. Astronomers, for instance, who think in terms of millions of "light-years" are dealing rather with matters of faith than conceivable fact.

Faith is not just an endless gullibility or a desire to be duped. It is the power to believe the unprovable; it is something that is given to a man—or withheld. And here again I found certain very simple analogies helpful. A man who wears glasses which are out of focus sees everything distorted and suffers from a perpetual headache; give him glasses in focus, he sees clearly and loses his headache. Faith is like that. Or again, one may hear a plane flying at a great height. One scans the sky and sees nothing. Suddenly the plane is perceived and thereafter every movement is clear. Faith is like that.

Faith cannot be forced, nor can it be found solely by argument or reasoning. So long as there is a gap between intellectual conviction and inward intuition there is no faith. Faith comes at that moment when the two merge into one. After that the whole pattern becomes clear and the difficulties disappear. For those who were born with the Faith there is no difficulty in reconciling conviction and intuition; they have always seen the mountain from the east.

Then there were the difficulties in accepting certain particular claims of the Catholic Church, such as the infallibility of the Pope. This difficulty soon disappeared. The Pope claimed infallibility in matters of faith and morals binding Catholics; but it is implicit in any supreme authority, be he king, dictator, judge, captain of a ship, commander of an army, or even a college president, that he has the final and indisputable decision in any matter that concerns his command. As for confession and absolution—one of the sorest points with Protestants—if one accepts the Gospels, Christ's words are clear and unequivocal: "Whose soever sins ye remit, they are remitted unto them; and whose soever sins ye retain, they are retained." With nineteen centuries of experience and training behind him, it might be assumed that the priest would know his business and perhaps be better informed than some modern experts in human behavior who shift their ground every ten years.

Once one could accept the central position—that the Church as a corporate body, divinely and supernaturally founded, fortified by centuries of accumulated wisdom and experience, was more capable of interpreting the supernatural and of defining a dogma than any individual, no matter how gifted—then all the difficulties would disappear; but the act of submitting private judgment would be hard, for academics are by training and profession thickly coated with intellectual arrogance.

As we knew no Catholic priest and had heard much of the kindness of the Archbishop of Kingston, we asked for an interview and laid our problems before him. I expected eager encouragement. He said, "This step will greatly injure you in your profession; you must not be in any hurry." So he gave us some books, Monsignor Ronald Knox's *The Belief of Catholics* among them, and told us to come back again if we were still interested. A fortnight later we began our instruction. By this time we were convinced that we wanted the Catholic faith; our main desire was to learn what the Church demanded of us.

There were several surprises. It is popularly supposed by Protestants that the Roman Church uses all the wiles of the traveling salesman to ensnare the guileless. Actually at no time was any effort made to persuade us. The doctrines of the Church were explained step by step without paraphrase or compromise, and at each stage we were asked if we wished to go on. But we were astounded to find how grossly and ignorantly those doctrines are misrepresented and misunderstood by those who have never troubled to discover what they are.

Another surprise was to find that each Sunday the cathedral (which holds about fifteen hundred) was filled for at least three of the four Masses, and the worshipers, as one looked at them critically, bore none of the blank, dull, sinister, or furtive looks of persons suffering from superstition, poverty, disease, ignorance, imbecility, or priestcraft, which are supposed to be the accompaniments of popery. On the contrary, though very mixed, the congregation seemed to enjoy being there, and many of them we already knew from daily business in the banks, offices, and shops. And there were swarms of children.

Our instruction completed, we were received into the Church and confirmed by the archbishop on June 14, 1947. I had never expected that I should receive a direct religious experience of any kind. When it came it was so deep and intense that for a long time I was afraid that there would be a corresponding reaction. More than a year has passed, and with each week new cupboards are opened, new experiences gained, roots reach down deeper.

There may be some who hesitate to accept the Faith because they are afraid of the hostility of their friends. Our experience has been almost wholly happy. One of my colleagues was heard to express surprise that "a man of his education could swallow all that superstition." Two or three have since regarded us with that look of pained regret that is directed at one who commits a social lapse at a dinner party; but for the most part we have been moved rather by the tolerant understanding of our friends than by their criticisms. We do, however, have the good fortune to live in an unusually generous-hearted community. By Catholics we have been received everywhere with natural kindness, neither regarded as interesting prodigals nor resented as late-comers demanding our penny for a very short day's work.

The profession of faith demanded of a convert is devastatingly comprehensive and admits no reservations; but once a man has let go with both hands and wholly entrusted himself to the Church, she abundantly fulfills all her promises But one cannot understand Catholicism until one has become a Catholic. The Catholic faith is not a matter of subscribing to certain dogmas or of performing certain ritual actions. It is a way of life; once experienced, it is infinitely and increasingly satisfying. Our one regret is that it took us nearly thirty years to find our way through the door.

ONLY ONE THING TO DO

Sheila Kaye-Smith

One of the most prolific of all the novelists of England at the present day is Sheila Kaye-Smith. She has published thirty-one books, chiefly novels, and a number of them have become best sellers in both Great Britain and America. From her earliest years she was determined to be an author and spun tales about the children on Sussex farms where she and her sister spent the holidays. While still at school she wrote several novels of 22,000 words, each of which constituted a splendid apprenticeship for the novels she was later to publish.

The daughter of a hard-working surgeon and of a mother of French and Scottish ancestry, Sheila Kaye-Smith was born in 1887 in Hastings, England. Along with her parents and sister, Sheila was accustomed to spend her holidays in Scotland and in Devonshire, and these scenes stirred her imagination and constitute the background of some of her later novels.

A deeply religious child, Sheila had a genuine devotion to Christ and strangely enough thought of the Pope as the head of the Church, though her parents were Low Church Anglicans. Her first published novel was *The Tramping Methodist*, the story of an itinerant preacher against the background of the countryside she loved best. Her second novel, *Starbrace*, a story of highwaymen and their desperate deeds, was written entirely from imagination. Both novels were well received despite the fact that the author was not yet twenty-one and had little experience of the great outside world.

Her first encounter with Catholicism was an evening at Alice Meynell's home, where she was deeply impressed with the artistic cultured atmosphere. Upon the publication of her third novel, *Spell-land*, she received an advance payment from the publisher and journeyed to Paris. From the suggestion of W. L. George, a French novelist, grew her fourth novel, *Sussex Gorse*, marking a departure from her previous books. This novel features the story of a man who sacrifices himself to the land he cultivates and achieves an enormous success.

Other novels, such as *Joanna Godden, The End of the House of Alard, The George and the Crown, Saints in Sussex, Joanna Godden Married, Iron and Smoke, The Village Doctor*, and *Shepherds in Sackcloth*, followed at intervals ranging from a year to eighteen months. Her literary fame was now well established and publishers were eagerly seeking the products of her gifted and versatile pen.

In 1924 she married an Anglo-Catholic clergyman, Rev. T. Penrose Fry, who had a curacy in South Kensington. When tired of the constant disputes of Anglo-Catholics with the Church of England, which were prevailing in that locality, they turned to the Church of Rome, where such factional strife was unknown. In 1928 they decided to go to Italy and while there came to perceive more clearly than ever before the provincial and merely national character of Anglicanism.

Returning to England, her husband resigned and they both received religious instruction for six months from Father Charles C. Martindale, S.J., a noted Oxford scholar, and were received into the Church in 1929.

They settled at Little Doucegrove, a farm they bought in Sussex. As they were nine miles from a Catholic church they arranged for a visiting priest to say Mass on Sunday for the scattered Catholics of the district and, for the first time since the Reformation, Mass was publicly celebrated there in 1930. Soon a small church was built in a neighboring field and Sheila Kaye-Smith found herself doing more parochial work than she had done as a parson's wife: caring for the sanctuary, answering the prayers of the Mass, teaching the children, rounding up the backsliders, and visiting the sick.

Her first novel after conversion was *Susan Spray,* and this was followed by *Mirror of the Month,* a book of meditative essays on the religious significance of each month. Her first really Catholic novel was *Superstition Corner,* a historical work which further enhanced her literary fame. *Gallybird, Rose Deeprose, The Valiant Woman, Ember Lane, The Secret Son,* and *Tambourine, Trumpet and Drum* (1943), a war novel, attested to her versatility, her wide range of interest, and her skillful delineation of character. Her religious autobiography, *Three Ways Home,* is characterized by great sincerity, simplicity, and power. In a recent lecture in London she told the audience that not less significant and meaningful than her conversion is the fact that she has never experienced a moment's regret during the twenty years which have intervened since her entrance into the Church.

I N WRITING about my conversion I must avoid the pitfall of being wise many years after the event, for I am aware of a temptation to credit myself with thoughts and feelings which really came later. I am a Catholic now for many reasons which, though they may have been dormant, did not actively influence me at the time I first became one. I should like to think that I joined the Church because I saw the choice offered me between two civilizations—the civilization of Catholic Christianity, with its entirely spiritual values, and the material civilization of the world-state which may at some future date rise out of the fused ideals of Moscow and Hollywood. But I cannot delude myself that I realized this alternative till I had read Mr. Aldous Huxley's *Brave New World*. Then I saw where I stood and was thankful; but I cannot claim the vision for my own.

I am, of course, in a different position from many converts in that for some years before my reception into the Church I believed and practiced much of its teaching. I called and thought myself a Catholic for twelve years before I actually became one. I did not have to face the difficulties that commonly beset converts from a definitely Protestant form of religion or from no religion at all. I believed in transubstantiation, in purgatory, in the sacrifice of the Mass; I prayed for the dead, I invoked the saints, I went to confession. Though I now see that I did not quite believe and do those things as I believe and do them now, I was very differently situated from those who have to learn about them for the first time. In many ways my position was easier, but in others it was more difficult, in that the issues for me were not straightforward, but confusing and uncertain.

I should think many non-Catholic readers will exclaim: "If I could believe in transubstantiation and all the rest, I shouldn't waste twelve years in the Church of England. I should go the whole way." I hope they would. I wish I had. Thirty years ago I looked at Catholicism and turned away from it because it repelled me, whereas the religion of the Anglican High Churches did not, but attracted me with its color and warmth and sense of personal romance. Catholicism still repelled me, even when the other had lost its attraction, and continued to repel me in a decreasing measure until I was actually inside the Church.

But I cannot regard those twelve years of Anglo-Catholicism as wasted, though I am sorry I made the choice I did. As an Anglo-Catholic I learned much of the faith and practice of the Universal Church. I was "under instruction," as it were, though for about two dozen times as long as most catechumens.

I preached as well as practiced my religion: I wrote and spoke, attended congresses, visited the principal High Churches. But I often felt doubts of my position. These were sometimes explicit—I once consulted my Anglican confessor, and he set them at rest, because—I realize now and half suspected then—that was what I really wanted. More often my doubts were implicit: I can see now, looking back on those days, that some of my most decided gestures on behalf of Anglo-Catholicism were due to a secret uneasiness, the need to justify myself.

For instance, a few years after I joined the High Church movement (not in the first flush of my enthusiasm, when I wrote such novels as *Tamarisk Town* and *Joanna Godden,* but later, when my zeal was losing some of its warmth), I wrote a novel dealing with Anglo-Catholicism in a country village—*The End of the House of Alard.* This was, I realized even at the time, an attempt at self-explanation—to myself as well as to others. I also colored the picture attractively for my own sake—I painted Anglo-Catholicism as I hoped and dreamed but only half believed it to be. I had certainly never known a parish like Vinehall or a parson like Father Luce. I created them as part of a wish fulfillment, and idealized that which I could not quite face as I saw it.

I should never want to write such a book about Catholicism, and those Catholics who have sometimes said they would like a Catholic novel from me will, I fear, be disappointed—that is to say if they mean a novel of the same type as *Alard.* I no longer feel the need to justify myself—to myself or to anyone else. I have been given a faith which is objective, and I am delivered from that uneasiness which accompanies most subjective ventures, and which urges the venturer to give them substance and objectivity by whatever means he may have in his power.

But in spite of these occult uncertainties it is quite

possible that I should never have become a Catholic if it had not been for my marriage. This may seem strange to those Catholics who, I know, almost gave up praying for my conversion when they heard I had married a Church of England parson. But the fact remains that my marriage did more than anything else to shake me out of my place in the High Church movement. It worked in three ways. In the first place it broke up certain friendships which might have kept me where I was. In the second it brought me into close association with a mind which had never fallen to the glamor of Anglo-Catholicism in the same sense as I had. My husband, though believing all that the High Church party stood for, was inclined to be critical of some of its actions and personalities. He had not the same enthusiasm for it as a cause, and his Quaker ancestry had made him less sensational and more evangelical in his methods. I came to see a good many threadbare patches through his eyes.

The third effect of my marriage was perhaps the most far-reaching. It showed me the Church of England from within. I was now, so to speak, thrust into its inner circles, to watch its methods, hear its rumors, and realize some of its inhibitions. I could no longer, as I had done hitherto, take refuge in one "extreme" corner and ignore the rest. The ostrich had to take her head out of the sand, to find—as one might have expected—a desert.

Though brought up in the Established Church, I had never really taken kindly to it or believed in its official position, and I should probably have had nothing to do with it after I was grown up but for my conviction that Anglo-Catholicism would soon transform it—had in fact already done so. As a parson's wife I saw how far this was from being the case. In certain ways the High Church party had undoubtedly tidied up the Church of England, but on a closer view it all seemed superficial and external, with no real change of heart. Moreover, for one parson who came to believe in the Immaculate Conception there would be two who came to disbelieve in the Virgin Birth: modernism was having just such a powerful sweep as Anglo-Catholicism, and a far less critical reception.

As a parson's wife I saw how limited and unrepresentative was the appeal of official Anglicanism, and I also became convinced that Anglo-Catholicism was just as incapable of appealing to the nation as a whole. I could not help realizing that it attracted only certain types of mind. Here I must be careful, and not attribute to myself more than I realized at the time. Now I see Anglo-Catholicism as the religion of the over-sublimated, of natures that can feel, temporally, at least, at home in the subjective. Hence its appeal to women, and the rather hectic atmosphere of some of its religious externals. "Churchgoing without the Church" was a phrase which came into my mind, and made me wonder: were all these women demanding all these services of their overworked clergy—one clergyman I knew had to celebrate twice daily during holiday time for a mere handful—because their churchgoing was a substitute for a missed reality? The psychologist as well as the Catholic priest would answer yes, though they might differ in their interpretations of reality.

Then another chance phrase came along. I was discussing with a friend the Woman crowned with the stars in the Apocalypse and seeing the figure as Our Lady rather than as the Church. My friend—a non-Catholic—replied: "But Our Lady is the Church."

It will be difficult for Catholics to realize that these words gave me an entirely new conception. Till then I had never thought of the Church as a living thing. I had regarded it as a vast organization, and I had accepted the "branch theory," as commonly taught by Anglo-Catholics, according to which there are three branches of the one society—the Anglican, the Eastern, and the Roman. But once one conceives the Church as a living personality, it is impossible to see it divided and yet remaining alive. "The hand cannot say to the foot: 'I have no need of thee.'" My branch theory

211

would not work once I saw the Church no longer as a mere organization but as the living Body of Christ.

These reflections brought me to the conviction that I was in schism, and there seemed only one thing to do—to return to the unity from which I was cut off. I found a certain number of Anglo-Catholics shared my conviction, but it did not affect them in the same way. The only question for them was the validity of their orders, and they were convinced that the Catholic Church was wrong on that point, while accepting her teaching on every other, even on the infallibility of the Pope. I was told that I was a member of the One True Church, no matter what the One True Church said to the contrary, that I had a right to all she offered, from indulgences down to the dispensations of her prelates as to fasting and abstinence. So why should I change? If I waited, reunion would come. Rome would become less intransigent and welcome back into her fold those sheep who had hitherto managed to enjoy its privileges while remaining outside. I could not believe it.

Finding myself in every point of belief a Roman Catholic, and intellectually convinced of schism, there was only one thing for me to do. For many reasons I now wanted to do it, but for many others I did not. At first I had been repelled by the austerity of the Catholic Church, and though after twelve years of Anglo-Catholicism, I no longer felt the same aversion, I still expected to find dryness, coldness, a certain unscrupulousness and unspirituality. Of course, I did not find them, but the fact that I expected to find them caused my heart to lag some weeks behind my mind. For a long time I was unable to feel much happiness in what I was doing. But I remembered the story of Coventry Patmore, who almost up to the last was unable to bring himself to accept emotionally the Catholicism which his mind had long received. I knew that there were psychological reasons for this difficulty, due to the mind's undertow, the pull of hidden currents under the turning tide. It was only a question of waiting for the heart's release, for the day which came surely, when I could say: "I rejoiced at the things that were said to me: We shall go into the house of the Lord."[1]

UNDER THE FIG TREE

Clare Boothe Luce

Clare Boothe Luce was born in New York, the daughter of William Boothe and Ann (Snyder) Boothe. She attended St. Mary's School in Garden City, Long Island, and Miss Mason's School in Tarrytown, New York, from which she was graduated at the age of fifteen, summa cum laude.

She was formerly married to George Tuttle Brokaw (deceased) and they had one daughter, Ann Clare (deceased). In November 1935 she married her present husband, Henry Robinson Luce, editor.

Mrs. Luce has attained distinction in a notable variety of pursuits: as journalist, gifted columnist, feature writer, war correspondent, editor of women's magazines, playwright, public orator, and political figure.

Her career in journalism began in 1929 on the Nast Publications. She became managing editor of *Vanity Fair* in 1933. She resigned in 1934 to conduct a newspaper column and to do free-lance writing. As a reporter for *Life,* she went to Europe in 1939; to the Philippines in 1941; and to Africa, India, Burma, and China in 1942. In 1948 she covered both the Republican and Democratic conventions as a columnist for a nationwide syndicate.

From 1933 to the present she has distinguished herself as an author, lecturer, playwright, and screen writer. Most notable of her writings were two books—*Stuffed Shirts* (1933) and *Europe in the Spring* (1940); and three plays —*The Women* (1936), *Kiss the Boys Goodbye* (1938), and *Margin for Error* (1939). All of these plays had long runs on Broadway and were later produced as motion pictures.

Mrs. Luce became active in Republican politics during the 1940 presidential campaign. She served two terms as representative from the Fourth District of Connecticut. As a member of the Seventy-eighth Congress and the Seventy-

[1]Psalms 121:1

213

ninth Congress, Mrs. Luce has established a reputation as a liberal Republican, introducing or defending many bills and resolutions specializing in anti-discrimination, protecting the interests of minority groups and labor. She was considered one of the best-informed representatives on foreign affairs, particularly in the Orient. While in Congress, as a member of the House Military Affairs Committee, she visited the Mediterranean and European war fronts. In 1947, Mrs. Luce retired from political office.

Mrs. Luce was received into the Roman Catholic Church in February 1946. In 1947 she wrote the story of her conversion—*The Real Reason*—as a series of articles in *McCall's Magazine*. She has given much of her time since 1946 to writing and lecturing on religion and social questions before Catholic and non-denominational groups. In addition to numerous articles, she has written two screen plays of religious character. In 1948 she made a cross-country lecture tour, speaking on "Christianity in the Atomic Age."

A CONVERSION—by which I mean the awareness of having given a complete intellectual assent to Catholic truth—may happen in many ways. It may strike with dramatic suddenness and blinding impact, as it did St. Paul on the road to Damascus. Or it may, almost imperceptibly over a long period, prick at conscience and pull on reason, as it did in the case of Cardinal Newman. The convert may be engaged, like St. Augustine, in what seems a successful fight against the Faith, at the very hour when it comes to vanquish him and throw him down in a humiliating defeat. Faith may come only after he has tirelessly sought it everywhere under false aspects, and, in despair of finding it, hurls one last anguished cry of helplessness into the void—and is answered. Or it may come to him sweetly and reasonably, without crisis, as it did to G. K. Chesterton. But whether the light of faith dawns as slowly and coolly as a December day, or whether it bounds into sight like July's majestic morning sun, every convert agrees on this: his conversion was the end of a process that had his whole life for its beginning. In retrospect, he sees all the days of his non-Catholic years as a preparation for the divine act of grace which called his soul from darkness into light.

This perception comes only some time after his conversion. In the springtime of his assent the convert is largely absorbed in the miracle of love that seems to be happening to him, and in giving praise to its Author.

> For giving me desire,
> An eager thirst, a burning ardent fire
>   A virgin infant flame,
> A love with which into the world I came,
>   An inward hidden heavenly love,
> Which in my soul doth work and move,
>   And ever ever me inflame
> With restless longing, heavenly avarice
>   That never could be satisfied,
> That did incessantly a paradise
> Unknown suggest, and something undescribed
>   Discern, and bear me to it; be
>   Thy name for ever praised by me.

He feels his soul turn—or rather, *will* to turn—from the love of self to the love of God, and he is possessed by a sense of passionate obligation to do His will, through His Church, in perfect and loving submission. He yearns to be, not only better, but transfigured. ". . . a man cannot see the kingdom of God without being born anew."

He is so breathless in his eagerness to *go* to God that he forgets, momentarily, what has really happened: God has come down to him.

"Nobody can come to me without being attracted towards me by the Father who sent me, so that I can raise him up at the last day."

But as he grows in the Faith, and as the Faith grows in him, he sees ever more clearly that no matter how dramatic the event that marked his conversion, it was, in reality, the climax to a thousand other secret acts of grace, equally dramatic, and the *convergence* of all his conscious or subconscious memories of them. He examines now the law of his heart with "the eye of the soul" and finds that One Word was written there at its first beat.

His whole life is revealed to him as a unique and tremendous drama—the drama of his own salvation. It is full of hairbreadth escapes from perdition, climaxed by this happy last-minute rescue by divine love.

The convert always sees himself as having narrowly missed damnation—so narrowly, in fact, that he is never altogether convinced that he has. "Too late, oh Ancient beauty, have I loved thee!" wept St. Augustine after his own conversion.

The memories of every encounter with creatures and circumstance—books he read or refused to read, conversations left unfinished, chance meetings, pleasures, temptations, follies, boredoms, hobbies, enthusiasms—all are reviewed and revised in his new knowledge that they were all in reality instruments of God's grace. God had not let a day go by without sending someone or something to seek entry for Him. Everything that ever happened to him had a supernatural as well as a natural meaning. "All that is in heaven is also on earth," wrote Plotinus. Every thought the convert ever had, every word uttered, every judgment, decision, choice made, great or trivial, had eternal as well as temporal significance. Every act of his life was a divine pun of the order Portia makes to the vengeful Shylock:

> Not on thy sole, but on thy soul,
> thou makest thy knife keen . . .

Now all the past, sweet or bitter, harsh or gentle, brilliant or shabby, is seen to be the harrowing and seeding time of God, the preparation of his soul for this blossoming of faith.

If happiness was the background of conversion, as it sometimes is—especially with the young and the innocent—that happiness in retrospect seems a wonderfully mysterious and lovely act of grace. These might be called the Palm Sunday converts. They sing their hosannas *before* His triumphal entry. The blithe and innocent converts recall the words of a fourteenth-century English mystic writing about some young cloistered nuns: "The true anchoresses are birds of heaven that fly aloft and sit on the green boughs singing merrily. A bird sometimes alights on earth to seek food, but never feels secure there, and often turns herself about." The happy convert feels that his former happiness was a song sung in the instinctive certainty that his soul's joyous flight to God was imminent.

> Soyons comme l'oiseau, perché pour un instant
> Sur des rameaux trop frêles;
> Qui sent ployer la branche, et qui chante pourtant,
> Sachant qu'il a des ailes.

The bird does not depend on the branch, even though it sits there to sing its song, but on its wings. . . .

Most converts are Good Friday converts. They have entered His kingdom through the gates of pain. After their conversion they view their old misfortunes and afflictions, the hardships and handicaps, in an entirely new light. They seem no longer the vicious visitations of a blind fate. The bludgeonings of chance that once left the convert's head bloody—and generally bowed—are God's harrowing, the plowing up of his hard heart, lest it become like the heart of Baudelaire's Climene, a

> Coeur racorni, fumé comme un jambon,
> Recuit à la flamme éternelle.

Grief was his favorite messenger. The bitterness and anger, the tumultuous passion with which he greeted this dark guest hid its blessed nature. Pride, anger, lust, despair always bring about this occultation, this concealment of life's supernatural content.

Above all, the convert rejoices in past defeats, even dishonor, as blessed initiations into the glories of Christ's fellowship. "For gold and silver are tried in the fire, but acceptable men in the furnace of humiliation."

But if his old life was a great drama of his soul's

encounters with the Divine Protagonist, it was also a mystery story. Why, wonders the convert, was *he* picked, among so many millions, as the object of God's love? And why, when He chose, did He pick *that* moment? "How dost thou know me? Nathanael asked; and Jesus answered him, I saw thee when thou wast under the fig-tree, before Philip called thee."

Before Philip called him to come and see the Master, he had been chosen. *What*, wonders Nathanael, was he doing or thinking or saying under that fig tree that made it the crucial moment in God's eyes? This is the mystery the convert will not solve this side of heaven. But he never tires of meditating on it.

> And having tasted it I speak of it,
> And praise Him thinking how I trembled then
> When His touch strengthened me, as now I sit
> In wonder, reaching out beyond my ken,
> Reaching to turn the day back, and my pen
> Urging to tell a tale which told would seem
> The witless phantasy of them that dream.[1]

The convert is a great reminiscer, a tireless autobiographer of his travels from darkness into light. And this for two reasons.

First, as he reviews his past *sub specie eternitatis* it is given to him to live his whole life over again, and under infinitely happier circumstances. "And you must not fall in with the manners of this world; there must be an inward change, a remaking of your minds. . . ." His futile past has been redeemed *in* and transformed by the present. "Strange, futile, piteous thing" though he was at every instant of his life, he was also a most wonderful and important thing—the object of the tireless solicitations of love.

He never grows weary of reflecting on the variety, the "passing strangeness," of the ways in which God, in Francis Thompson's tremendous word, *hounded* him, and brought him to bay. Now he sees a thousand ways by which *he* might have speeded up the hour of

[1]Robert Bridges, *Joy*.

his conversion, but none by which God might have been expected to do so. Daily he is overcome with contrition for his long recalcitrance, and with gratitude for God's infinite persistence and ingenuity in pursuit.

> Praise to the holiest in the height
> And in the depths be praise:
> In all His words most wonderful;
> Most sure in all His ways.

Second, he feels required to tell all who will listen that they, too, are being constantly pursued. "Make one another free of what is yours ungrudgingly, sharing with all whatever gift each of you has received, as befits the stewards of a God so rich in graces."

Unhappily, even the most articulate convert encounters many difficulties in writing or talking effectively about his conversion. The greatest today comes from the fact that the average non-Catholic, eager though he is to know "what *made* you do it?" doesn't understand what is meant in the first instance by grace—no less its *manifold* character. And as grace, abundant, ubiquitous, and ineffable, *is* precisely what made him do it, he is placed under an almost insurmountable handicap if grace is a concept without meaning to his hearers.

It does not always follow that the true explanation of a matter will be either understood or accepted.

Let us imagine you, the reader, as having a lively interest in the tremendous discoveries of modern physics. And you are given the opportunity of interviewing Professor Einstein. Realizing, as you do, the impact of the Theory of Relativity on all modern science and philosophy, you ask Mr. Einstein what *brought* him to Relativity, or to use the jargon of our times, what "sold" him on it? And he answers in the best way he knows by scribbling on a bit of paper:

$$M = \frac{MO}{\sqrt{1 - \dfrac{V_2}{C_2}}}$$

He then adds: "As for example, the mass of a stick or the tick of a clock varies when the stick or the clock is moved through space with the speed near to that of light—186,324 miles per second . . ."

It is questionable whether you would understand this, even though it were the truest—indeed the only true—explanation for his conversion to the Theory of Relativity. Would you then refuse to accept it? The chances are you *would* accept it—on faith. How else?

The modern mind, asserting as it does the primacy of the scientific method in forming opinions in all matters, thinks of itself as pooh-poohing *all* attitudes of "faith." And yet it is constantly prone to accept entirely on faith the most unintelligible scientific propositions. If Mr. Einstein's explanations of Relativity were treated in the same manner as the convert's explanation of grace so often is, it would be dismissed as "superstitious symbolism," or "meaningless jargon." And yet the gift of faith, through God's grace, while more difficult to *understand,* is *not* so difficult a proposition to *prove* as the formula for Relativity. Thank God it is not! It is said that only six men in the world truly understand Einsteinian physics. But millions upon millions have possessed the gift of faith: they have experienced grace and proved it, for themselves. They speak of what they know when they cry:

Take heed of the marvelous manner of grace in thy soul.
It speedily springs unto God as a spark from the coal.

Moreover, in order to prove Relativity, that is to say, experience it, Einstein had to posit it: he had to *imagine* Relativity *before* he could find the formula. But God's grace is not a hypothesis or a theory. It is a condition and a fact. If we fail to put the matter into wholly convincing language, the fault lies with our human limitations which are most cramping when we seek to convey our intimations of the Infinite. "For God is more truly thought than expressed—and He exists more truly than he is thought."

Anyone who has experienced God's most amazing

act of divine grace, a conversion, knows that the convert is discovered by grace, and not grace by the convert. Indeed, almost until the moment when it apprehends him, he generally fails to perceive that the thing with which he has been at all times forced to deal in his life was grace. The moment he *seems* to be adducing or positing it, that is to say, imagining it, as an explanation of any of the circumstances of his life, his conversion has already begun.

> Is my gloom, after all,
> Shade of His hand, outstretched caressingly?

Then what does the convert do, who is eager to explain his conversion when he finds he cannot make his listener understand the nature of grace, no less its manifold character? How would he explain the means by which water becomes ice to a man who had never lived in a climate where the temperature fell below eighty? Or, to an intelligent group of Tibetans who had never seen or before heard of an airplane, the means by which an airplane takes off and is driven on and up, if he could not use the word *propeller*, or any synonyms or analogies for it? And how, the convert wonders, can he explain how he was lifted from the natural plane of experience to the supernatural when he cannot find the words or analogies to make grace intelligible? "Nobody reaches God's presence until he has learned to believe that God exists, and that he rewards those who try to find Him."

Well, he must face the facts of his own experience: the only way that those who honestly do not know what is meant by the grace of God will ever come to know is—by God's grace!

There remains only one course for the convert to pursue: To shift his emphasis from the supernatural *cause* to the natural *effects* of grace in his own life. He performs a sort of literary *kenosis*—a self-emptying of the divine content in his story. And under this self-imposed limitation he is misunderstood and suffers accordingly. He is generally willing to be misunder-

221

stood, just so long as he is listened to. For he dares to hope that the attention being given to what he writes or says, even though it is not being understood, is a grace given to his hearers. *Fides ex auditu.* If a man brings no more than his ears to the convert's story, he has made one beginning toward his own conversion.

Not realizing that the convert, unable to discuss the primary and essential cause of his conversion, is driven by necessity to discussing its effects, there are many who feel that convert literature is too personal, too revealing. At the same time, so wondrous a thing is grace, even those who would not accept it as a cause suspect in the story of the convert who omits it some significant omission, some important concealment. Impatiently they plead with the convert for the "real" reason.

But even in reporting the effects of grace the convert encounters difficulties. Which of the many effects shall be set forth as the most compelling, and in what order? Painfully and clearly aware of the effects of grace in the very *hour* of conversion, he is not always so clear about its antecedent acts. ". . . when thou wast under the fig-tree, *before* Philip called thee." Our Blessed Lord told Nathanael far more clearly than He tells most converts the actual moment of His calling. The "labyrinthe ways" by which God pursues the convert are easier traveled than retraveled. All roads lead to Rome, but when are we on the road, and when on one of its many detours?

The convert would need the help of a theologian, a philosopher, a historian, and a psychologist—most especially a poet—to pluck from his own life exactly those scenes and events which really were the most fraught with significance. "How dost thou know me?" he cannot answer to his own satisfaction. Then how shall he inform another?

Often, the most cogent circumstances affecting his conversion remain in his subconscious. He knows the reasons in part—but he does not know them as they are known to God.

Again, there may be some experience which he believes to have a bearing on his conversion but withholds, however willing or able he is to tell all relevant facts. He may do so for a variety of reasons: the fact may not be *his* story to tell; or it may be too intimate a revelation; or it may seem too hazy, inconsequential, or lacking in apologetic value. Does it mean little, or nothing, or much? he asks himself, and because he cannot answer, omits it from his recital.

Let me give one example from my own experience of the honest difficulty in revealing all that seems important to a conversion.

It is an experience which occurred when I was perhaps sixteen or seventeen years old. I no longer remember where it took place, except that it was a summer day on an American beach. I seem to remember that it was early morning, and that I must have been standing on the sand for some time alone, for even now I distinctly remember that this experience was preceded by a sensation of utter aloneness. Not loneliness, but a sort of intense solitariness.

I remember that it was a cool, clean, fresh, calm, blue, radiant day, and that I stood by the shore, my feet not in the waves. And now—as then—I find it difficult to explain what did happen. I expect that the easiest thing is to say that suddenly SOMETHING WAS. My whole soul was cleft clean by it, as a silk veil slit by a shining sword. And I *knew*. I do not know now what I knew. I remember, I didn't know even then. That is, I didn't *know* with any "faculty." It was not in my mind or heart or blood stream. But whatever it was I knew, it was something that made ENORMOUS SENSE. And it was final. And yet that word could not be used, for it meant *end*, and there was no end to *this* finality. Then joy abounded in all of me. Or rather, I abounded in joy. I seemed to have no nature, and yet my whole nature was adrift in this immense joy, as a speck of dust is seen to dance in a great golden shaft of sunlight.

I don't know how long this experience lasted. It

223

was, I should think, closer to a second than to an hour
—though it might have been either. The memory of it
possessed me for several months afterward. At first I
marveled at it. Then I reveled in it. Then it began to
obsess me and I tried to put it in some category of
previous experience. I remember, I concluded that on
that certain day the beauty of nature must have con-
corded with some unexpected flush of tremendous
physical well-being. . . . Gradually I forgot it.

The memory of it never returned to me until one
day several years after my conversion, during the first
minute of the liturgy of the Mass, where the server
says: *"Ad Deum qui laetificat juventutem meam . . ."*

My childhood had been an unusually unhappy and
bitter one. I had brooded about it increasingly as I
grew older. Indeed until the very day of my conversion, it was a source of deep melancholy and resentment.

"Unless the cup is clean, whatever you pour into it
turns sour," said Plato. A conversion cleans the heart
of much of its bitterness. Afterward I seldom remembered my marred childhood, except at one strange
moment: at the very beginning of the Mass, during
the prayers at the foot of the altar. The priest says:
"I will go in unto the altar of God." And generally a
small altar boy responds in a clear, shy, thin, little
voice: "Unto God who giveth joy to my youth." This
phrase, unhappily, always awakened faint echoes of
bitter youth, and I would think: *Why* didn't God give
joy to *my* youth! Why was joy withheld from *my* in-
nocence?

One day, long months after I had been a convert,
as these words were said, the bitterness did not come.
Instead there suddenly flooded into my mind the experience of which I speak, and my heart was gently
suffused with an afterglow of that incredible joy.

Then I knew that this strange occurrence had had
an enormous part in my conversion, although I had
seemed to forget it completely. Long ago, in its tremendous purity and simplicity, and now, in its far fainter

evocation, I knew it had been, somehow, the most real experience of my whole life.

But how exactly did this affect my conversion? Why had I forgotten it? Why had I remembered it? God only knows! And what use is it to recount it to anyone interested in "Why I Became a Catholic"?

I mention it here partly to elucidate the real difficulty of "telling all," and partly lest anyone think the convert is not aware of the mysterious movements of his own soul, and that much of a conversion may take place on subconscious levels.

Uncertain of being sure that he *is* picking or choosing wisely among his own best "secondary reasons" for his conversion, the convert does the next best thing: he presents the reasons he thinks his audience will be most drawn by. "I will praise God with the best member I have." St. Thomas Aquinas points out that everyone is moved, impressed, convinced, converted by that which appeals most to his own nature. *Quidquid recipitur ad modum recipientis recipitur.*

A friend of mine, who is an artist, remembers first being drawn to Catholicism in a concentration-camp prison, when he began to draw pictures of the Crucifixion on the walls of his cell. Another friend, whose father was a famous writer of humorous stories, was greatly influenced at the beginning of her conversion by what she considered the hilarious conduct of St. Joseph of Cupertino, who could not control his ecstatic fits of levitation. Another, a professor of history who is also a musician, was struck by the compelling role of the Church in history, and the splendid liturgical music of the Church.

The convert telling his story will generally emphasize those aspects which he believes will have weight with some group that he thinks he ought to reach—usually those with his own social or intellectual background.

And in tempering his apologetics to the shorn lamb, he has the example of St. Paul:

"With the Jews I lived like a Jew, to win the Jews; with those who keep the law, as one who keeps the law (though the law had no claim on me), to win those who kept the law; with those who are free of the law, like one free of the law (not that I recognized no Divine law, but it was the law of Christ that bound me), to win those who were free of the law. With the scrupulous, I behaved myself like one who is scrupulous, to win the scrupulous. I have been everything by turns to everybody, to bring everybody salvation. All that I do, I do for the sake of the gospel promises, to win myself a share in them."

But however much the backgrounds of converts differ, or how dissimilar the actual events that bring them to God, most convert literature stresses a central theme: that of pain. Mental, emotional, physical, and spiritual suffering play the greater part in the best of these stories.

There are few men and women who reach maturity who have not, in their lives, lived intimately with grief. Convert pages are often blotted with tears, not because sorrow is peculiar to converts, but because the exiled children of Eden inhabit the valley of sighs and mourning.

Sooner or later, the dreaded unwelcome message of pain is printed on every threshold where mortals dwell, sings Schiller sadly.

> Die unerwünschte
> Schmerzliche Botschaft
> Früher oder später
> Bestellt es an jeder
> Schwelle, wo ein Lebendiger wohnt.

But the poet also knows the power of pain to purchase heaven:

> Millions, bravely sorrows bearing,
> Suffer for a better time!
> See, above the starry clime
> God a great reward preparing!

Grief has a great purgative value, since God cannot fill the soul until it is emptied of trivial concerns. And a great grief is a tremendous bonfire in which all the trash of life is consumed.

It may turn a man from God, or it may turn him to God. But it never leaves him unchanged. Pain and sorrow, anguish and woe throw the soul into a state of crisis. The Chinese word for crisis is composed of two characters, that for danger, and that for opportunity.

A man is never so near being wrong as when he is nearest being right. Lucifer, closest to God, fell. Magdalene, *de profundis*, rose. We are never so free to choose God's love as when in our extremity we seem to have the most "reasons" to hate Him.

"Though he slay me, yet will I love him," is the greatest love line any mortal ever uttered, until Jesus said, "Father, forgive them . . ." Grief gives man the opportunity to make Job's gift to God: the gift of his trust in ultimate goodness, when he seems most to be the victim of evil.

"Souls," writes Raoul Plus, "are won by words, won by example, but above all, they are won by sacrifice." "When I am weak, then I am strong," wrote St. Paul. Conversions often have the look of agony, precisely because when a man goes into Gethsemani against his will, he often finds there the God who chose to enter of His own free will—and for his sake.

The word was created in the joy of the Father. It was converted by the sorrow of the Son.

In the final analysis, conversion stories are convincing in proportion as the author reveals himself an *alter Christus*—one who has been or is willing to be crucified. When Our Lord told Peter that henceforth he would be a great fisher of men, the promise was based on a tragic condition: that the Peter who had thrice betrayed Him, and had thrice been forgiven, would then pick up the Cross of martyrdom.

Appreciation of the purgative and redemptive role played by pain, and gratitude for God's use of this keenest of all instruments of grace, is what gives most convert stories that "masochistic" flavor which makes them so unpalatable and even revolting to many modern minds. (It makes them particularly fascinating to some psychologists, who would not seem to be altogether guiltless of sadistic tendencies: they savor the pains of the convert so much more than his joys.)

The average non-Catholic mind today views pain, rather than sin, as the prime evil in life. The man who rejoices in his suffering—even in retrospect—seems somewhat perverted. Those who hear the convert's story, unconvinced, can seldom quite forgive him for his refusal to damn pain as the cardinal evil, even though sorrow and misery and frustration and confusion predominate in their own lives.

"Suffering," said Leon Bloy, "does not last, but *having suffered* lasts forever." But as they bear their own unresolved sorrows in their hearts with difficulty, in spite of themselves they envy the culminating experience of his conversion: great happiness. "They that sow in tears shall reap in joy." Paul Claudel, in the familiar vein of converts, wrote to Jacques Rivière, "Whatever you may think, you will never approach happiness without approaching its source, which is God and Christ." The Dutch convert, A. J. D. Van Oosten, wrote a book called *The Joys of the Convert*. Ernest Pischari, the grandson of Renan, wrote when he knew he was going into the Church, "I knew where I was going. I was going towards the abode of peace, I was going to joy. I wept with love, happiness and gratitude." All converts agree that to draw near to God is to draw near to the source of all happiness.

For the rest, the role of a Catholic convert apologist is not a happy one: he suffers because of a triple folly—his own, for having taken so long to see the truth; the folly of his friends who are being equally stubborn; and the folly they impute to his belated wisdom. And while many of the convert-writer's friends can forgive him "for being such an ass," they cannot forgive him for "telling the whole world about it."

Perhaps the convert who writes about his conversion *is* an ass: Balaam's ass. And Balaam *is* the prototype of all clever, even brilliant friends who "ride" him about his conversion.

Balaam, you remember, was a man with a great reputation in his day for being very wise—a reputation so great that the King of Moab sent for him in the dire political extremity that afflicted his throne. But God said unto Balaam: ". . . Thou shalt not go with them, nor shalt thou curse the people: because it is blessed." (God was always a great defender of the common man, as anyone who reads the Bible will discover.) But Balaam, who was receiving very cogent arguments from Moab (in the form of promotion and pay) would not hear Him. So Balaam saddled his ass and went to meet the King of Moab. And the Lord sent an angel who stood with a drawn sword across his path. And Balaam, though a man of very high intelligence, certainly a philosopher, no doubt familiar with all the soundest scientific and philosophical ideas of his own day, did not see the angel of the Lord. But the little ass saw him! And the ass turned aside and went into the field, although Balaam beat her and she fell under him. And Balaam smote her with his staff, and allowed that if only he had a sword he would kill her. And the Lord opened the mouth of the little ass, and she said to Balaam the wise, and Balaam the angry: "What have I done upon thee that thou has smitten me? Am I not thine ass upon which thou hast ridden? Was I ever wont to do so to thee?"

Is the convert Balaam's ass? Possibly. But why should the wise friends of the converts whose nostrums and panaceas, credos and philosophies they have supported so long, and so dumbly, smite them so sore when they will no longer go forward because they dare not?

And let the wise men remember the rest of this extraordinary story: In the end it was the vision of the

dumb little ass that finally saved Balaam, for as the
angel told Balaam when his eyes were opened: "Unless she had turned, surely now also I had slain
thee. . . ."

TORCHES TO LIGHT OUR WAY

John A. O'Brien

THE TRAVELERS along the road to Damascus
have told the story of their pilgrimage. At the
end of their trail they found God. Minds which
were searching for truth found it; hearts which were
restless found peace; souls which were groping in the
darkness found the light. The stories of these pilgrims
are the torches which light our way.

Their experiences provide a much-needed antidote
for the uncertainties, bewilderments, and confusions
which constitute the spiritual distemper of our day.
That debilitating anemia is traceable to man's uncertainty concerning the three supreme realities of the
spiritual life: God, Jesus Christ, and the Church which
He founded. There are the transcendent realities which
alone give meaning, purpose, and direction to human
existence. Without them, man is like a ship without a
rudder, tossed about by every wind that blows. Uncertainty about these truths paralyzes the nerves of
action and fills man with a vast nostalgia that nothing
in all the material universe can relieve.

Let us consider the first of these transcendent realities: God. Few deny His existence and virtually all pay
Him lip service; but a careful scrutiny of the language
of many in referring to Him discloses that He has become for them not much more than a name, a meaningless collocation of words, an oblong blur in the sky. He
is sometimes used as a synonym for nature or the
cosmos or a metaphysical abstraction stripped of all
personality; He has become a shell from which the

inner kernel of reality has vanished. It is this gnawing uncertainty concerning a personal God, a heavenly Father, which perhaps more than any other factor has desiccated and withered the spiritual life of millions today and fills them with a cosmic ennui, a *Weltschmerz*, and a haunting loneliness.

Christopher Morley portrays this prevalent mood in *Where the Blue Begins*, wherein the central figure, Gissing, is tirelessly searching through the mire and maze of human affairs for God. "The very solitude that Gissing craved and revelled in," says Morley, "was, by a sublime paradox, haunted by a mysterious loneliness. He felt sometimes as though his heart had been broken off from some great whole, to which it yearned to be reunited. He felt like a bone that had been buried, which God would some day dig up. . . . People who have had an arm or leg amputated, Gissing reflected, say that they can still feel pains in the absent member. Well, there's an analogy in that. Modern skepticism has amputated God from the heart; but there is still a twinge where the arteries were sewn up." How apt a symbol of the malady and mood of this generation.

God is not a mere dream: He is not a hypothesis or the projection of our hopes and dreams upon the frail canvas of illusion. He is the meaning of the universe and the hope of humanity. He gives a cosmic undergirding to the ideals of truth, justice, and righteousness which point like slanting arrows of light to the Source from which they emanate.

"To know God," said Dante, "is to learn how to make our lives eternal." Long before Dante, St. John proclaimed this important truth, almost lost in the contemporary fog: "This is eternal life: That they may know thee, the only true God, and Jesus Christ whom thou hast sent."

A deity without personality, and hence without consciousness, is no more capable of awakening the sense of religion in the heart of man than is the all-pervading air or the universal force of gravitation. Hence all attempts to substitute the cosmos or nature—even when written with capitals—for a personal deity are so many arrows aimed at the heart of religion. Man can admire the autumnal coloring of a tree, the fragrance of a rose, the beauty of a sunset. He can no more talk to them, however, than he can to a stick or a stone. Personality, consciousness, intelligence, the power to hear and the power to answer, constitute then the core of the concept of a deity required for religious purposes.

Religion is thus seen to be essentially a personal relationship. It is the relation of the creature to his Creator, of the subject to his Sovereign, of man to his God. In that relationship man turns with outstretched arms, seeking to clasp the hand reached down from on high. He opens his lips to a listening ear: He pours out the love of his heart to a heart which reciprocates with an overwhelming love. Religion is not a one-directional line: It is not talking to a deaf mute. Reciprocation is of its very essence: God both listens and replies. Says James Russell Lowell:

> God is not dumb, that he should speak no more;
> If thou hast wanderings in the wilderness
> And find'st not Sinai, 'tis thy soul is poor.[1]

Those who train their ears to catch the answering echoes from the mind and the heart of God hear a message which carries courage and inspiration; they feel a love which fills them with a rapture transcending all the pleasures of earth and sense. It is this union of the soul with God in perfect love which constitutes the end of all religious striving, a union approximated in this life by high moral perfection and achieved in the next life by the soul, which experiences a joy that no tongue can describe. "Eye hath not seen," says the Apostle Paul, "nor ear heard, neither hath it entered into the heart of man, what things God hath prepared for them that love him."[2]

The second factor responsible for the withering of the spiritual life of millions is vagueness about the

[1] *Bibliolatres.*
[2] I Corinthians 2:9.

nature of Jesus Christ. If He be a mere man, a sort of Jewish Confucius, then the uniqueness of His personality vanishes and He differs not in kind but only in degree from Moses, Plato, Socrates, Solomon, and a host of other ethical teachers. The bottom drops out of Christianity as a religion *sui generis;* it becomes but another cult.

If, on the contrary, Jesus Christ is divine, then He is entitled to our homage, loyalty, love, and obedience. He speaks to us with the authority of God himself. The counsels, commandments, and teachings which He gives us are those of God. The revelation which He bequeaths to all mankind becomes a divine revelation of timeless and unchanging truth. The Church which He founds and clothes with His power and authority becomes an institution that can no more mislead her members than God Himself could mislead them. Upon the divinity of Christ, then, hinge consequences which shoot through the whole of the spiritual and religious life of man.

The third factor responsible for much of the prevailing uncertainty concerning the content of divine revelation and the consequent religious confusion and bewilderment is the widespread ignorance concerning the institution which for more than nineteen centuries has proclaimed the teachings of her Founder, Jesus Christ. Divine in her origin and in her teachings, she is human in her officials and in her membership. That historical Church is the extension of the Incarnation and the perpetuation of the voice of Christ to men.

Just as the Apostles, though men subject to infirmity, were empowered by Christ to teach in His name, so the Church, though consisting of frail and mortal men, was authorized to carry His teachings to all mankind and was promised His abiding protection and assistance in the execution of that mission. Peter, through human weakness, denied His Lord; yet he never deceived his hearers as to the truths which Christ commissioned him to teach. So, too, his successors, the pontiffs of the Christian Church, though human and subject to similar personal lapses, have never failed to proclaim the divinely revealed truths entrusted to them by Christ.

The reader finds a vivid and significant light thrown upon these three central realities—God, Jesus Christ, and the Church founded by Christ—in the experiences of the fifteen travelers recorded in this volume. With a view to lending a helping hand to other wayfarers, the contributors share their experiences. From different bypaths and over varied terrain they come to the main highway leading to Damascus. A careful reading of their stories discloses, however, that, regardless of such differences of approach, belief in a personal God and a recognition of the Godhead of Jesus were usually the signs pointing to the wisdom of examining the Mother Church of Christendom, studying her marks, scrutinizing her credentials . . . and ultimately crossing her threshold and coming to her altar.

The links in their line of reasoning are exceedingly simple and clear: God is our heavenly Father interested in the welfare of His children. Accordingly, He sent His only begotten Son, Jesus Christ, to be our Redeemer and to reveal to us the truths of eternal life. To transmit those truths to all mankind in all ages, Christ founded a Church and clothed it with the power and authority necessary to fulfill its world-wide mission. In following the guidance of that Church, they are manifesting their faith in the fidelity of Christ to His promise: "And behold! I am with you all days even to the consummation of the world."

There, in a nutshell is the line of reasoning running through the stories of these contributors. And incidentally it is the line of reasoning which prompts more than 400,000,000 members to give their spiritual allegiance to that Church and to enjoy at the same time the implicit confidence that Christ will not let them down.

There is another important point which these stories bring out: the appeal of the Catholic religion is primarily and chiefly to the intellect and only secondarily and slightly to the feelings and emotions. In some cases the latter may not be involved at all. This was true in

Arnold Lunn's case. "The cold clear light of reason," he observed, "is all the guidance a man needs to find his way to the Church." So, too, it was with Gilbert K. Chesterton, who afterward confessed: "I had no more thought of becoming a Catholic than of becoming a cannibal." Similar is the experience of Evelyn Waugh. After satisfying himself concerning the philosophical and historical credentials of the Church, he reports: "And so on firm intellectual conviction but with little emotion I was admitted into the Church."

Between the conversion resulting from the perfervid appeal of the revivalist who arouses his hearers to a pitch of emotional excitement in which they shout, sing, and sway in near frenzy and the conversion resulting from a calm intellectual study of the credentials of the Catholic religion, there is little in common except the name. Starting with the premise that man is a rational creature and should be guided by reason, the Church proposes no doctrine for his acceptance for which she does not offer ample, rational grounds and objective evidence. This is true all the way from the first truth with which she begins, namely, the existence of God, to the forgiveness of sins in the sacrament of confession.

No institution in the world lays such mighty and everlasting stress upon reason as the Catholic Church. While she recognizes that the emotions have a legitimate place in the religious life, she maintains that they must always be guided and controlled by the intellect. She distrusts blind emotionalism and considers it an unsuitable foundation for a stable and enduring faith. Embraced with fervor today, it is discarded with equal precipitancy tomorrow. Not so, however, a faith based on reason. It will endure as long as the intellect sits in the driver's seat and the individual remains sane.

The writer walked one evening into a Mohammedan mosque just off the street called Straight in ancient Damascus. Here one could see the howling and the whirling dervishes as they worked themselves up into frenzy: it was a capital illustration of the surrender of reason to the emotions. The substitution of emotion for reason has had a long and ill-starred record in the history of religious cults and denominations.

While conversion in the Catholic religion comes as a consequence of an intellectual investigation, aided by God's grace, it is not necessarily a dry and cold affair. It may often be accompanied with strong emotions of joy and gratitude. Indeed it would seem only natural for the discovery of truth to awaken sentiments of exultation, rejoicing, reassurance, confidence, and a deepening of love for God and man. Such emotional elements are probably present in the overwhelming majority of converts; but they are concomitants and by-products of the intellect's discovery of truth—the results of the conversion and not its cause.

The intellectual and emotional patterns of people are so infinitely varied that the experiences of individuals upon embracing the Catholic faith are likely to differ enormously. With some, the recognition of Christ as "the way, the truth, and the life" made unmistakably clear by His Church—the essence of conversion in the Catholic religion—may come quickly or after a long and painstaking investigation. With some it may be quiet and tranquil, while with others it may tear and rend the soul.

In the conversion of Augustine, the emotions leaped with the reason in the whole-souled embrace of Christ and His way of life. A profoundly intellectual soul, Augustine likewise possessed an emotional nature capable of the strongest passions. There is something peculiarly gratifying and exultant to the reader to see both these endowments leaping to twine twin arms around the divine Redeemer as one's Lord and Master.

They resemble Peter and John racing to the sepulchre of Christ, consumed with eagerness to see their risen Lord. Though John outstripped Peter, with gracious deference to his superior he waited till the panting Peter arrived that he might enter first: so too when the emotions outrun the intellect, it will be well to restrain them till reason catches up so it may enter first. In fact, bishops and priests not infrequently feel compelled to put the brakes upon individuals whose enthusiasm and ardor for the new kingdom they have glimpsed prompt them to seek admittance before all the evidence is in. "Later perhaps," smiles the kindly priest, "but not now . . . for you are not ready yet." Herein is a fitting recognition of the primacy of the intellect in the life of man.

Since conversion comes at the end of a careful process of study and investigation, patience and perseverance are of the utmost importance. One cannot reasonably expect to learn a new language or master an art or science in a few sessions: neither can one expect to secure a co-ordinated knowledge of the teachings and practices of the Christian faith in a few hurried meetings. The clear realization that one is seeking to obtain a priceless treasure will fortify and hearten him for the long hours of patient study and reading which precede admittance into the fold.

This symposium brings out the shift in authority which has occurred in the field of religion. Christianity was universally recognized for fifteen centuries as a religion with authority to speak to the individual concerning the destiny of the human soul and the means of attaining it. That authority was conferred upon the Church by Christ. The establishment of the principle of private interpretation at the Reformation shifted it to the Bible with unexpected results: soon hundreds of conflicting interpretations were given to scriptural passages by individuals who regarded themselves as courts of first and last appeal. Hundreds of warring sects arose, with the result that authority outside the historic Christian Church has virtually disappeared.

Chaos and anarchy are widespread. Indifferentism, springing from a feeling of inability to find religious truth in the midst of such anarchy, confusion, and differences, is biting into the fabric of their faith and producing an ever-growing army of churchless people who are religious only in name. The consequences of such disintegration of religious faith are distressing to all Christians. They show in a vivid and striking manner that religious faith, to say nothing of religious unity, cannot long endure when the only remaining vestige of authority reposes in the subjective feelings, fancies, and caprices of each individual.

The craving for unity, for consistency, for certainty, so evident in these chapters, can be satisfied only where the principle of authority, established by Christ, stands like a Rock of Gibraltar against the shifting winds of private fancy. The Catholic Church has preserved her unity of belief and practice through nineteen hundred years because she has never surrendered the authority conferred upon her by her divine Founder to teach His doctrines unerringly to all mankind. In embracing that faith, one does not surrender his reason: he simply emancipates it from the possibility of error by bringing it under the sweet yoke of Christ, who is Truth Incarnate.

He believes on the best authority conceivable: the authority of God, who has revealed it. This act of faith comes only after the individual has come to perceive that a revelation of truth has been made by Christ to man; that Christ is divine; and that He has endowed His Church with the power and authority to transmit that deposit of divine truth to all generations. Faith then means putting one's hand in the hand of God with the certainty that God will not mislead him. Hence no conviction could be deeper, firmer, or more unshakable than that achieved by supernatural faith.

We say supernatural because in making such an act the mind is illumined and the will is moved by the grace of God. "For by grace," declares St. Paul, "you are saved through faith, and that not of yourselves, for it is the gift of God."[3] That helping hand of God is not withheld, we believe, from one who humbly asks for it. It is the same Apostle to the Gentiles who has given the most penetrating and profound definition of faith.

[3]Ephesians 2:8.

"Faith," he says, "is the substance of things to be hoped for, the evidence of things that appear not."[4]

Once the inquirer has come to the clear realization that he has the authority of God revealing for the embracing of His teachings, all vacillation and hesitancy vanish before the *overwhelming* certainty that a divine authority imposes upon the intellect and will. "He is as certain," points out Cardinal Newman, "that the doctrine is true, as that God is true; he is certain, because God is true—because God has spoken."

Viewed from the outside, the figures in the stained-glass windows of a church may appear blurred, meaningless, and even grotesque. Viewed from within, the grotesquerie disappears and the meaning and beauty of the figures become immediately apparent: so too the teachings of Christ, when viewed from the inside, from the vantage ground of faith, take on vastly increased clearness, beauty, co-ordination, and cogency.

"As in some rich design," points out Professor M. A. D'Arcy of Oxford, "whether of a Cathedral or poem or tapestry, the significance of the parts shines out for the first time when the mind of the onlooker coincides with that of the builder or worker, so the evidence for the truth of the Catholic Church gathers itself up into an irresistible converging mass of evidence. But—and this brings out the point of the word "overwhelming"—the truth thus revealed is a way of life, not a theorem, a way of life which stretches out to limitless spaces, full of promise but also full, as divine truth must be, of mystery; and it imposes itself upon the convert as a duty, as something final and imperative. There is no option possible; the yoke must be worn and the old life with its inner reserve of human planning and self-assurance must be surrendered."[5]

The increase in clarity of perception, in cogency of understanding, and in depth of vision, gained by viewing the doctrines from the vantage point of faith, was

[4]Hebrews 11:1.

[5]*Conversion to the Catholic Church*, Burns, Oates & Washbourne, London, p. xxi.

recognized and aptly expressed by Evelyn Waugh. To the friends outside the fold who consult him, he says: "Come inside. You cannot know what the Church is like from outside. However learned you are in theology, nothing you know amounts to anything in comparison with the knowledge of the simplest actual member of the Communion of Saints."

Once the individual has made an act of faith, he leaves the quagmires of vacillation and the valleys of doubt and climbs the sunlit mountain peak. God's vast universe stretches out before him; but it is no longer a *terra incognita*. He is equipped with a map and a compass; and he can chart his course with new assurance and certainty. Faith is invigorating. Streams of divine grace flood his soul and make him kith and kin with the Apostles as they went forth from the upper chamber on that first Pentecost to carry the teachings of Christ to all the nations and to change the face of the world.

"Faith," observes Dr. Charles H. Parkhurst, "is a kind of winged intellect. The great workmen of history have been men who believed like giants." It dedicates the individual to the noblest and highest life and to an all-embracing love. "Faith," says William Ellery Channing, "is love taking the form of aspiration." It is the answer to man's cry for help to vanquish the anxieties and fears which obsess him. St. Paul speaks of it as a shield whereby one is able to extinguish all the fiery darts of the most wicked one. Says Thomas S. Jones, Jr.:

Faith is the cliff on which the weak wave breaks
    The tree around whose might frail tendrils twine,
    In cloudy skies it sets a starry sign,
And in the sorrowing soul an altar makes.

When the inquirer has come to perceive that back of the truths proposed for his belief is the authority of God revealing, the time has come for prayer and action. There is no point in further vacillation: continued indulgence therein begets an abulia that paralyzes the will and robs it of the capacity for determined action.

Into every life there come great moments when decisions must be made and courses charted; otherwise the opportunity may be lost perhaps forever. In *Julius Caesar*, Shakespeare gives a memorable voicing of this important truth:

> There is a tide in the affairs of men,
> Which, taken at the flood, leads on to fortune;
> Omitted, all the voyage of their life
> Is bound in shallows and in miseries.[6]

One must not expect an angel to tap him on the shoulder and say, "Now is the time to act." In the divine economy, reason is enlightened to formulate the decision and the will is empowered to implement it: there is an awareness that God is calling us to a high destiny and we must not falter. "Every individual has a destiny," points out Professor M. A. D'Arcy, "and at moments of vivid experience, in childhood, in adolescence, and at maturity, each of us has a sense that the stars in their courses and the whole suspended universe are ready to fight against us or to offer us their service; each of us is the expected one, the unique child of destiny. The moment passes and we pass down into the valley and become a number in a multitude, and our lives are passed in the mists of prejudice, local and national customs and habits and narrow calculations. But there is an everlasting city on the hill, where destinies meet and a Word has made his tabernacle."[7] The travelers in this symposium tell how they made their way there, slowly, painfully, or with swift feet, and have found there "the substance of things hoped for."

Running through all the stories is the note of humility: surprise is expressed that they were found worthy. This is the authentic and unfailing mark of the true convert, dumfounded at the thought that God should deem such unpromising material suitable for so high a destiny.

"The Church should feel honored," said an acquaint-

[6] Act IV, Scene 3.
[7] Op. cit., p. xxiii.

ance to Orestes Brownson shortly after his conversion, "that so eminent a philosopher and writer should join its ranks."

"On the contrary," replied Brownson, "I've brought the glorious Church of Christ nothing but my sins."

We selected the contributors to this volume chiefly because they are authors of note and as such are especially adept in describing the inner stirrings of the soul and the line of reasoning which they followed; they thus enable us to share with them their own significant and moving experiences.

It is scarcely necessary to point out, however, that the souls of the lowliest waif and the humblest pauper are infinitely precious and dear to Almighty God: His hand is outstretched as tenderly to them as to a king. The limelight of this world's fame is no antecedent condition to the tapping of the wellsprings of God's grace and love.

The reader will derive profit largely in proportion to the open-mindedness which he brings to the repeated reading of this volume: it will richly repay reading several times a year. If in advance he closes his mind to the possibility that these pilgrims have found their way to the City on the hill, he will naturally derive little assistance in charting his own path. If, however, he will follow with open mind and open heart the journeying of these earnest men and women, he will not fail to note the various bypaths that lead to the road to Damascus where God's light and grace work their age-old yet ever new transformation in the heart and soul of man. Such help can rightly be expected; for Christ said to His followers: "You are the light of the world. . . . So let your light shine before men."[8] The torches of these earnest pilgrims will light the way for others to the City set upon the hill where waiting for them is the Divine Master, who said: "I am the light of the world; he that followeth me, walketh not in darkness, but shall have the light of life."[9]

[8]Matthew 5:14–16.

[9]John 8:12.

Not less essential in finding God than an open mind, however, are a pure heart and a clean conscience. A hunger for God, a thirst for righteousness, a sensitivity to the moral law and a willingness to walk in the paths of humility, mercy, purity, and love are requisites for the vision of God. An evil life, full of meanness, pettiness, and hate, is an insurmountable barrier to God: one must be willing to burn the bridges to that life before he can think of entering the kingdom of God.

"Grant me the grace of purity," cried Augustine. Then as he thought of the sensual pleasures whose renunciation this would entail, he would add "but not yet." That "yet" was a long time in coming; but not till it came did he come to the vision of God. Pregnant with spiritual significance and psychological reality are the words of Christ: "Blessed are the pure of heart; for they shall see God."

More important than intellectual subtlety and endless dialectics in seeing God is a clean heart. When Ignatius, the Bishop of Antioch, was being led to martyrdom, a Roman soldier asked him leeringly: "Who is this Christian God of yours?" Gazing into his sensual, brutal face, Ignatius replied: "You shall know Him when you are worthy of Him." An open mind, a conscience sensitive to the echoing of the moral law, and a heart full of love for God and man will lead the earnest searcher along the road to Damascus and unto the vision of God.

The Mother Church of historic Christianity possesses those paradoxical qualities which Chesterton was quick to perceive and quick to admire. She is the greatest conservative force in the world, yet the most adventurous; she possesses the mellow wisdom of two thousand years and the eager enthusiasm of youth; she discarded the heresies of fifteen centuries ago which have become the novelties of today; she does not embrace every new scientific theory that is marshaled into the public square with the blare of trumpets and the beating of drums because she does not wish to be a widow the day after tomorrow.

She smiles at the deadly seriousness of the nationalists sitting in the saddle of all the countries today and seeking to remake the world. She smiles because she has seen the idol of nationalism, along with many others, rise and fall. When Edith Cavell, one of the noblest martyrs of our modern religion of nationalism, was about to face the firing squad of earnest German soldiers, intent upon the service of the fatherland, she cried out: "I see now that patriotism is not enough." The cry stirred the people of England as though it were a great and a startling discovery. To the Church, however, it was as ancient as the second of the two great commandments: "Thou shalt love thy neighbor as thyself."

The loyalties of patriotism are secondary in time and in logic to the law of universal morality, to the two great commandments of love, which contain the whole law and the prophets. To the nationalist who champions the totalitarian authority of the state, the authority to speak in matters of religion as in affairs of politics, she answers with the pulverizing plainness of the Book of Job: "Where were you when the foundations of the world were laid?" Contrasting her antiquity with the recency of any of the nations of Europe, the Church might well inquire of them: "Where were you when the foundations of the Church were laid?"

"It is absurd to forget," observes Chesterton, "that the Church itself received the first loyalties of men who had not yet even conceived the notion of founding such a national and separate state; that the Faith really was not only the faith of our fathers, but the faith of our fathers before they had even named our fatherland."

The truth of the Catholic Church, points out Chesterton, is like a magnet with powers of attraction and of repulsion. The repulsion arises from the vague fear that one may be caught in a baited trap; but the bait is simply the truth. "The moment men cease to pull against the Catholic Church," he says, "they feel a tug toward it. The moment they cease to shout it down they begin to listen to it with pleasure. The moment they try to be fair to it they begin to be fond of it. But when that affection has passed a certain point it begins to take on the tragic and menacing grandeur of a great love affair."

There is something majestic in the manner in which the Church has withstood all the heresies of the centuries and all the vagaries of human thought and speculation. The procession of paganism, bibliolatry, absolute imperialism, monarchies, democracies, representative or alleged, down to dictatorships, the fashion of the hour, pass before her in a long parade. From her throne on the stairs of the centuries she watches them come and go. She can live under any form of government because her concern is with the souls of men and her kingdom is of the spirit.

"There is no end," says Chesterton, "to the dissolution of ideas, the destruction of all tests of truth, that has become possible since men abandoned the attempt to keep a central and civilized Truth, to contain all truths and trace out and refute all errors. Since then, each group has taken one truth at a time and spent the time in turning it into a falsehood. We have had nothing but movements; or in other words, monomanias. But the Church is not a movement but a meeting-place; the trysting-place of all the truths in the world. . . . The Church is a house with a hundred gates and no two men enter at exactly the same angle."

How aptly does the story of the pilgrimages of these fifteen travelers illustrate the truth of Chesterton's words; for no two of them entered at exactly the same angle. The story of their spiritual Odysseys is an intensely human document; it is not propaganda. None of the writers digress from their story to engage in hortatory appeals to others to follow in their footsteps: neither shall we.

No religious institution in the world shows greater restraint in the presentation of its credentials than the Catholic Church. Realizing that faith implies the free internal assent of the mind and will, the Church avoids any measures which might smack of pressure, even

245

the pressure of adroit or high-powered salesmanship. Truth, the Church believes, is its own advocate and its own salesman; to be accepted, it needs but to be stated simply and clearly.

The restraint of the Church is sometimes construed as lack of interest and solicitude for those groping their way; some of these fifteen pilgrims express surprise that priests to whom they applied for instruction and admittance not infrequently advised them to proceed slowly, carefully, and tempered their precipitate enthusiasm with words of caution and restraint. Between insistent salesmanship and utter indifference verging upon unfriendliness there is a golden mean—a reasonable interest tempered both with friendliness and restraint in acquainting others, especially those with no definite church affiliations, with the teachings, credentials, philosophy, and devotional life of the Catholic faith.

We follow that golden mean; we make no fervid appeal to the reader to rush to the nearest Catholic Church to have his name added to the parish roster; indeed we know full well that no priest would accede to such a request. We content ourselves simply with saying that if, after listening to the stories of these pilgrims, a person wishes to learn more about the Catholic faith, he will be given every reasonable assistance and guidance. He can secure such information by consulting any Catholic priest or layman, and by reading any authoritative exposition of the Catholic faith.

You will find a Catholic priest or a layman friendly and willing to help you; but he will not exercise the slightest pressure upon you nor even invite you to join. The initiative must come from you . . . in answer to your prayer, "Lord! That I might see." If no priest is available in your community, you may secure gratis a course of instruction by mail by sending a postcard to the Confraternity Home Study Service, 4422 Lindell Boulevard, St. Louis 8, Missouri.

SUGGESTIONS FOR FURTHER READING

The following annotated list of books is suggested for those who may wish to secure an accurate understanding of Catholic faith and practice:

Catholic Background and Philosophy

THE SPIRIT OF CATHOLICISM, Karl Adam, The Macmillan Co., New York.

> A scholarly and well-reasoned interpretation of the spirit of the Catholic religion by a professor at the University of Tuebingin; it will be read more profitably by those who bring a somewhat scholarly background to the task.

TRUTHS MEN LIVE BY, John A. O'Brien, The Macmillan Co., New York.

> A popular but scholarly presentation of the fundamental truths underlying the Christian faith in the light of the findings of modern science and philosophy. A college background, while not essential, will enable the reader to understand and appreciate it better.

THEOLOGY AND SANITY, Frank J. Sheed, Sheed & Ward, New York.

> A well-reasoned presentation of theological dogmas suitable especially for university-trained readers.

Catholic Belief

THE FAITH OF MILLIONS, John A. O'Brien, Our Sunday Visitor, Huntington, Indiana.

> A popular exposition of the credentials, teachings, practices, and devotional life of the Catholic religion; it is widely used for inquiry classes since it covers all the important points of faith and practice.

THE BELIEF OF CATHOLICS, Ronald Knox, Sheed & Ward, New York.

> An exposition of the main dogmas of the Catholic religion by a convert from Anglicanism, who is now a Catholic priest.

THE FAITH OF OUR FATHERS, Cardinal Gibbons, P. J. Kenedy and Sons, New York.

> A popular and friendly exposition of Catholic faith and practices; written fifty years ago, it was one of the best sellers of its day and is still useful.

FATHER SMITH INSTRUCTS JACKSON, Noll and Fallon, Our Sunday Visitor, Huntington, Indiana.

> A very simple exposition of the Catholic religion in conversational form; it is within the ken of all readers and is widely used.

THE QUESTION BOX, Bertrand L. Conway, Paulist Press, New York.

> A well-indexed presentation of practically all the common questions concerning the Catholic religion with clear, cogent answers; it has long been a classic in this field.

THE EXTERNALS OF THE CATHOLIC CHURCH, John F. Sullivan, P. J. Kenedy and Sons, New York.

> A helpful presentation of the sacramentals and of the utensils used in Catholic worship and in the devotional life of the Church.

REBUILDING A LOST FAITH, John L. Stoddard, P. J. Kenedy and Sons, New York.

> An appealing exposition of the rational grounds for the fundamental doctrines of the Catholic faith; it mirrors the author's own experiences and is written in an interesting manner.

Biblical and Devotional

THE NEW TESTAMENT, Revised Edition, St. Anthony Guild Press, Paterson, New Jersey.

> A splendid edition which uses modern English, and through the use of topical headings and paragraphs makes the inspired word of God more readable; can be secured in the ordinary edition as well as in a student's edition which is in a smaller format.

THE FOLLOWING OF CHRIST, Thomas à Kempis, P. J. Kenedy and Sons, New York.

> A splendid presentation of the chief moral teachings and the counsels of perfection of the Christian faith; it is a classic, unsurpassed for spiritual reading by all Christians.

Where I Found Christ

THOMAS Merton, Dorothy Day, Avery Dulles, Jocelyn Toynbee, Daniel Sargent, Raïssa Maritain, and eight other noted men and women of today tell how they found Christ—in the Catholic Church.

Their stories "are told with reverence, humility, and a sincere desire to help others. They are neither propaganda nor chapters of a sales talk. The writers have no axes to grind, no bread to butter, no premium to collect. They narrate their stories . . . with the sole thought that their disclosures may point out to other groping souls the paths that lead to Christ and to His Church . . . a channel . . . to souls grown weary searching for the truth."

Each of these dramatic, inspiring stories is preceded by a helpful biographical sketch of the author. Father O'Brien contributes a helpful introduction and conclusion.

Catholic Transcript: "This book will open the eyes and stir the soul of many a wanderer in the twilight beyond the walls of the household of the Faith."